L Born to Love

Gay-Lesbian Identity, Relationships, and Marriage • Homosexuality, the Bible, and the Battle for Chaste Love

Born to Love

Gay-Lesbian Identity, Relationships, and Marriage • Homosexuality, the Bible, and the Battle for Chaste Love

John R. Waiss

Foreword by:
Father Benedict J. Groeschel, C.F.R.

Outskirts Press, Inc.
Denver, Colorado

Foreword

When Father Waiss asked me to write an introduction to this book, I was well aware that he chose me because I have had considerable experience over the years with Courage, a movement for people with same-sex attractions who work to lead chaste and holy lives in compliance with the teachings of the Catholic Church. Along with Father John Harvey, O.S.F.S., the founder of Courage, I have written previously on this challenging subject.

I was delighted with Father Waiss's book. The dialogue format he uses is effective. He confronts difficult issues forthrightly and honestly. He answers questions that are of great concern to people dealing with same-sex attractions.

This book is of real importance at the present time because of the apparent increase in the number of people who are struggling with this issue, either in their own lives or in the lives of those they love. Many are critical today of the moral teachings of the Catholic Church on same-sex attraction—despite the fact that these teachings are grounded in Scripture and the natural law and have been the consistent stand of the Church for centuries. It is easy to understand that a person who experiences such attractions will find the Church's teachings difficult and may be tempted to call them unrealistic. Father Waiss's compassion and understanding when dealing with such problems is admirable, as is his ability to explain the logic of the Church's position, and his gentle but unyielding insistence on maintaining the objective Christian stance.

Father Waiss has written a very hopeful book, one that will be enlightening to those with same-sex attractions who are already committed to leading a chaste life and very helpful to those who continue to struggle. Anyone with an open mind can surely find something of benefit in his book, and so it can even be shared even with those who reject the Church's position.

The Church is not free to alter the faith to suit popular opinion and has had plenty of experience with teaching unpopular truths. We live at a time when Catholics have to be prepared to challenge cultural currents on a number of issues. This book makes us better able to do so effectively and fairly. It combines a search for truth with a hope founded on divine grace and God's ability to change the lives of each one of us. This is a book for people who have hope and for those who need hope. It is, as well, for those whose goal it to share the hope of the Christian faith with others. I highly recommend **Born to Love** for those who are interested in following the teachings of the Gospel.

Father Benedict J. Groeschel, C.F.R.

Introduction

Catholic teaching on homosexuality is a difficult topic to speak on or to write about. This is so, not so much because it is not clear what the teaching is or where the Church got such a teaching, but because it is bound up with so much emotion, often with pain and suffering both for the individual who experiences homosexual inclinations as well as for loved-ones dear to them.

It has become a very important and urgent topic. It has become a civil rights issue for the media and culture. Homosexuality is linked to the defense of individualism and the individual's pseudo-freedom to be able to have sexual relations with anybody in any way... "As long as I'm not hurting anyone." Television and music promote it. Our grade-schoolers are being taught that having two mommies or two daddies is the same as having one of each. Our high school students see nothing wrong with it; having premarital sex or having gay or lesbian sex is just another flavor of the same fun activity, with a false simplicity akin to liking one flavor of ice cream over another. Those promoting the gay life-style are using politics to defend it at all costs in civil laws. The gay agenda has become the norm, and we are getting to the point that some believe that those who espouse traditional Judeo-Christian values will soon run the risk of being persecuted and imprisoned for hate-crimes.

Homosexuality and same-sex attraction run to the emotional core of the human person. That is why it is so hard to transcend the emotional order to speak rationally on the subject. Yet there is something that runs even deeper than this: a desire to love and be loved—so often confused with sex. So, by focusing on the true nature of love we hope to make some headway on this topic.

true identity—through the sincere gift of himself to others, that is, by existing in relationship to another "I", to both God and creatures. By being born into a web of relationships, and by forming our own, we will develop a strong and secure basis of our identity, self-worth, and dignity.

Man "cannot fully find himself except through a sincere gift of self." It has already been said that this description, indeed this definition of the person, corresponds to… the creation of the human being — man and woman — in the image and likeness of God… [to] an essential indication of what it means to be human, while emphasizing the value of the gift of self, the gift of the person.

The Book

I chose to write this book in dialogue for two reasons: first, because it is not meant to be the final word but to engage the reader in the process of understanding the subject and for him or her to move the dialogue forward beyond what is written. The reader should be an active participant, posing new questions and seeking answers to questions not addressed here.

A more important reason for the use of dialogue is to help the reader understand the very deep and personal nature of this subject. Homosexuality involves people, individual persons, each with his or her unique story and struggle. By presenting fictional characters—with a basis in experience with real people—I hope readers will learn to approach people they may know or come to know with the sensitivity of having stepped into their shoes, and to learn to love them as Christ would.

I desire that this book reaches the many Catholics who have friends, fellow students, children, siblings, colleagues, etc. with homosexual inclinations, to show them that it is possible to be faithful Catholics, faithful Christians, and faithful friends. We all need to understand the moral teaching of the Catholic Church and learn how to explain it to others in an effective, attractive, and compassionate manner.

I also hope my brother priests find this book helpful in their ministry to individuals who struggle with this cross.

Many may think that the Church's teaching on homosexuality is too much for people to swallow, at least all at once. If the Church insists on its teaching on chastity, marriage, family, and homosexuality then many will turn away, both those living the life-style and anyone who has sympathy for those in this predicament. Like many things Jesus said, this teaching is "a hard saying; who can listen to it?" (John 6:60), which risks that some will draw back and no longer want to follow him (cf. John 6:66).

Yet, we need to remember that the vast majority of those with homosexual inclinations do struggle to be chaste and these are the ones who are most abandoned, and who have the least amount of support. Our compassion should be toward those striving for true love, striving for truly lasting relationships, for a true relationship with God... then they will be open to the truth, and the Truth will set them free (John 8:31).

From the witness of their noble lives, others will be won over.

The Setting of the Dialogue

This is a continuation, or an outtake, of a dialogue between Father JP, Sam, and Margie found in the book, **Couples in Love**.

For those who need to be introduced, Sam is a twenty-six-year-old bachelor—a non-practicing secular Jew. He and his girlfriend, Margie, a Catholic woman—recently returned to her faith—entered into a joint dialogue with Father JP to discuss Catholic teachings on love, dating, relationships, sex, respect, commitment, and marriage.

In that initial dialogue, Sam brought up the topic of homosexuality because he had a Catholic friend from high school who was living the gay life-style and who was now quite antagonistic toward the Catholic Church. Father JP had offered Sam the possibility of inviting his friend over to discuss these matters in greater depth, rather than just gloss over the subject in the short time they had.

This motivated Sam to renew his contact with Jeremy, his high school friend. As they caught up on events each had experienced, Sam told Jeremy about his frank discussions that he and his girlfriend had had with a Catholic priest. Jeremy was taken aback. He was fascinated that a Jew like Sam would ever dare discuss religious and sexual matters with a Catholic priest. Sam shared some of the insights that had benefited him.

After Jeremy reminded him how the Catholic Church had alienated him with its strong teaching against homosexuality, Sam asked Jeremy, "Why would the Catholic Church be so condemnatory against homosexuality when it has a very beautiful teaching on sexuality in general?" Jeremy begged to differ. Then Sam offered Jeremy this challenge, "Why don't you and I have a conversation with Father JP? I would love to see how he would respond to your challenges. I think we'd both learn a lot from that exchange."

This dialogue is the result of Jeremy accepting that offer.

What Does the Church Have to Offer Us?

Sam introduces his friend Jeremy to Father JP. Jeremy is a fallen-away Catholic who is living with another man in a homosexual relationship. Jeremy explains to Father JP that he went to Catholic school through the 8th grade and then went to a public high school where he met Sam.

Sam: JP, I want to introduce you to my friend, Jeremy. We were in speech and debate together in high school, and now Jeremy works as an assistant floor manager at the local TV station, and is moving up the ladder quite rapidly.

Father JP: That's great, Jeremy, I'm impressed. That's a hard field to break into.

Jeremy: Well, I've always been interested in the media and theater. I guess it just came kind of naturally to me.

Sam: Yes, it always came naturally to you. You were a good actor and quite good in speech and debate too.

Failed Expertise

Jeremy: Father, Sam tells me that you are an expert in homosexuality. I have to tell you I went to Catholic school and know what the Catholic Church teaches. I just came here because my friend Sam asked me to, and because he wants to know what you would say on this topic.

Father JP: I don't claim to be an expert on homosexuality. I am a Catholic priest who fully believes in all that God has revealed in the Old and New Testaments as it has been transmitted to us through the centuries by means of the Church. I believe that both Scripture and its transmission has been guided by the Holy Spirit.

I don't intend on defending the Christian teaching on homosexuality—only a few people would be willing to listen to such a defense unless they are already in the choir. I don't think either you or Sam are in that choir. Rather, I can share my experience ministering to people with these inclinations, how I responded to their questions, and how I addressed their concerns.

Sam: JP, you know me by now. Although much of what you have told Margie and me makes sense, I have a skeptical streak. I certainly am not in the choir—not yet anyway.

Father JP: My theological and pastoral training in the seminary did not include much in the arena of homosexuality. Sure, we touched on the moral implications that homosexual acts incur. But little or no specialized training was given in how to approach, listen to, or to counsel individuals with homosexual inclinations or those living in a homosexual relationship. Like most, I had to learn from experience and often by my mistakes. Fortunately, most of those individuals were quite forgiving and allowed me to correct those mistakes.

In my years of priesthood, I have come to know quite a few people with struggles in this area. I have known men and women with homosexual inclinations, most of whom strive to be chaste. Yet I have known those who chose to enter the gay life-style, even after coming to me for counseling. I have known priests who struggled with homosexual inclinations as well as other individuals committed to living celibacy. I have known others who have been falsely accused of being gay—due to certain mannerisms—and have resented being pursued and propositioned by homosexuals.

I have also known women whose husbands have abandoned them and their children to seek fulfillment in a life with another man, and I have known men whose wives have abandoned the family for a woman. I have known priests who have abandoned their vows to God to fully immerse themselves in the gay life-style.

This is my expertise—limited at best.

You Don't Understand

Jeremy: But Father JP, I don't think you understand how it feels to be gay or what it's like to be so different, to be the butt of one joke and another; how it feels to have people hate you and to have the Church look down on you and not accept you as you are.

Father JP: Jeremy, true, I don't know what it feels like to be gay. I do accept you and respect you as you are. If we are going to have a reasonable conversation, we will all have to accept and respect each other as we are. But don't expect me to change if you don't want me to expect you to.

I think I do understand some aspects of how you feel. I too have felt the prejudice of hatred for my beliefs. Once I was walking down a street in San Francisco when a man from across the street started yelling foul obscenities and curses at me simply because I was dressed as a priest. He hated the Church and me for my association with the Church and its teaching on homosexuality.

I can understand why some homosexuals want the right to marry; they seek a lasting and permanent relationship that can fill their lives. As a priest, I have had to find a lasting and permanent relationship to fill my life, yet I didn't do it through marriage but in an intimate relationship with God and in developing fraternal relationships with my brother priests.

I can understand why some homosexual couples would want to adopt kids; they seek to find greater fulfillment and meaning to their lives by the presence of children who look to them as parents. As a priest, I have found great fulfillment in the presence of many "children" who look to me as their spiritual father.

I can understand why gays and lesbians have wanted the Church to accept their life-style and admit them into leadership roles in parish ministry; they desire a relationship with God and to be an active participant in his family. All of these are good.

Sam: But all this seems to indicate that the Church will have to change…

Jeremy: And change it will, just as the rest of society has changed. It seems like there are still those in the Church who want to turn back the clock, keep it back in the Dark Ages, and take all society with it.

Father JP: Jeremy, if it bothers you that other people don't respect you *unless you change*, then why will you not respect the Church—and Christians in general—*unless we change* what we believe and who we are? Does that seem fair?

If we are going to have a conversation, we need to have respect for each other independently of whether or not the other person freely decides to change.

Jeremy: OK, holy and reverendíssimo father…

He said this with a cynical smirk.

Father JP: Jeremy, we don't need any condescending B.S. Just call me JP… that'll be fine.

Sam: Yes, Jeremy, JP has respected me, even when I have been wrong and strong-headed. He has respected my Jewish beliefs and I have never felt humiliated by him. We should try to reciprocate. He has been comfortable with me just calling him JP.

Father JP: Sam obviously cares for you, Jeremy. Presumably, that is why he introduced the two of us.

I see in you a very sensitive soul and a noble person. You seem to have anger against the Church. But I really do not know you and would like to get to know you better.

Jeremy's Story

Sam: Jeremy, why don't you tell JP a little bit about yourself so he has an idea of your story and why it has been so hard for you to be gay.

Jeremy: OK, no problem… just about everybody knows my story anyway. I'm not ashamed of my past. In fact, I'm proud of who I am.

I grew up in a fairly normal family. I have a brother who is four years older than me. From early on, when I was still a small child, I knew I was different: I wasn't like my brother, Jeff, or like other boys my age, either.

I was very religious back then. I loved to pray in Church and at my bedside. In fact, I prayed everyday that God would make me normal, just like the other boys.

My older brother was a jock and my dad used to go to all his sporting events and brag about his accomplishments. Yet, my brother would cut out girly pictures in swimsuits from catalogues and hide them in his dresser drawer. But as a kid, I knew that was immoral—how naïve I was back then. My brother would show me the pictures, but I would turn away knowing it was sinful.

When my mother discovered the pictures, she was very upset. My brother blamed me, of course. Yet, my dad sided with my brother which hurt mom quite a bit. Later, my brother would proudly expose porno magazines to me to try to scandalize me, even once he did it in front of my dad who just laughed.

But back then I had a great love for God. I went to confession and to church and read every spiritual book I could get my hands on because I really wanted to get closer to God. But deep down inside I knew I couldn't, because I was different; because I was not attracted to the erotic porn of naked women but to men, strong muscular men. And, as a good Catholic boy, I knew these desires were sinful—extremely sinful! Hah! How brainwashed and simple-minded I was back then…

Father JP: Jeremy, did you talk to anyone about these feelings? Did you bring them up when you went to confession?

Jeremy: Frankly, I was too ashamed to tell anyone but God. I didn't think anyone else would understand. I did confess "impure thoughts and feelings" but the priest just seemed to ignore that and rushed through to the absolution. He didn't seem to have time to care about what was going on inside of me. All he wanted was to get through the line and back to his things.

If he would have shown more interest in me and what was bothering me; if he were to have asked me a few simple questions about why I was having those thoughts I'm sure I would have told him. But what difference would that have made, he would have just absolve me anyway and I would have gone back to the same "sinful" feelings…

Sam: But, Jeremy, didn't you ever talk to your mom about these things? You seemed pretty close to her.

Jeremy: Sure we were close. But mom was so holy and I didn't want her to think that her other son had similar problems to my older brother. She was all stressed out about trying to please dad and trying to save Jeff, that I didn't want her to have another burden. She was always so happy to have me by her side. She was proud at how close I was to God. This was a real comfort to her. I couldn't burden her with this.

So, I went to God. I prayed. I told him I wanted to be loved by him, by the God who loved the straight boys—I wanted to be fixed. Eventually, I quit praying because I could never live up to the expectations of a God of straight kids. My church told me—both directly and indirectly—that I was broken and more unworthy than any of my straight friends, even more unworthy than my hedonistic brother, who was at least, "natural."

Yet, I wanted to be loved by the same God who loved straight boys. I longed for that. I needed that.

Sam: But if I recall, you dated girls back then and had pretty normal relationships with them?

Jeremy: Oh, sure I did! I pretended to be normal. I dated girls in high school, but I would never - *ever* touch them inappropriately—that was a sin! It was the one thing that seemed to make my dad proud. I would have been much happier if my dad were to come to one of my school plays. But he didn't.

I would bring home some of the prettiest girls in the school just to impress my dad. And he was impressed, but these girls never really meant much to me and this caused me to resent my dad even more.

Well, toward the end of high school I did start messing around with girls. It started with a girl that was flirting with me at a party. She started taunting me for being "afraid" of her and of me being so "holy." Something got into me such that I wanted to prove to her that I was just as "sinful" as other boys. Sure it was all a show, because I didn't really feel anything for her, but

I proved to myself and to her that I could satisfy a girl. Although I felt ashamed of this afterwards, for sinning and for causing someone else to sin, I started living a double life. Pretending to be normal and this form of escape enabled the denial and repression of my real feelings. But they kept coming back.

My dreams and fantasies were male only. I did not consciously prepare for nights of lustful fantasy; they just came, especially when I was mad at my parents or teachers for one reason or another. I even got a girl pregnant, but when I told her that I didn't love her she terminated the pregnancy. When I told my dad, he was relieved and told me to be more careful, but deep down—in a sick sort of way— I sensed he was happy and proud. Fortunately, my mom never found out; it would have crushed her.

Father JP: It sounds like it crushed you instead, especially how your father reacted to your charades.

Jeremy: I love my father. He and I always got along. But he loved my brother more, that's all. I tried to show him that I was normal. I knew it would crush him if he discovered the truth, though he always kind of knew.

Eventually, I knew that being a fag was who I was, although it was against God's plan, against the religion of my mother, against the dreams of my father. My successful escapades with women only made me suffer more, by denying my true nature.

One day, in my junior year in high school, I was sitting on the radiator in the school hallway. Next to me was one of the most popular jocks in the school, Rick. He was a senior and I was trying to impress him by my ratings of girls as they passed by, when he discretely let slip from his mouth, "Jeremy, I am gay."

It was like the top of Mt. Saint Helen's, the lid, hinges, chains, locks and concrete blew off my carefully concealed Pandora's Box, out into the light of day. I felt like I was naked for everyone to see, yet I hadn't said a thing; I couldn't say anything; I was utterly speechless, which as you can tell is not me.

Rick broke the ice, as he winked at a pretty girl walking down the hall: "You are too, aren't you? I can tell."

But I told him, "Rick, I'm Christian... I'm Catholic... we don't do those kinds of things..." He just smiled and said, "Yeah, right! You, Christian? Give me a break."

I went over to his house that afternoon. We talked. Each of us shared with the other the years of repressed feelings, hurts, and humiliations. He told me how he became a jock to prove to everyone that he was normal. We hugged. We kissed. It was the first time I had experienced love.

Although I tried to go back to my old repressed self, every time I saw Rick I melted. Soon everybody knew and I felt free. Sure, there were those who called us names... who laughed at us... But most of our friends supported us because they cared about us and saw that we were happy.

As for church and faith, it was all over. I saw it for the hypocritical institution that it was. I didn't want to have anything to do with those self-righteous Bible-thumpers who only know how to condemn. They just don't know what it is like to be gay.

Father JP: Jeremy, not every Christian is a self-righteous Bible-thumper. If we are truly Christian then we are called to love others as Christ loves them. That includes loving those with homosexual inclinations and those living an actively gay or lesbian life.

Jeremy: Come on, JP, don't give me that crap; everyone knows what the Bible says about homosexuality, at least as interpreted by you high-moral Christians. The God of your Bible doesn't love lesbians or gay men.

CHAPTER **2**

What Does the Bible Say About Homosexuality?

Sam: JP, what does the Bible really say about homosexuality? I've heard some who say it unequivocally condemns it and others who say it supports it or is ambivalent towards it.

In the Beginning

Father JP: If we want to understand what the Bible says about homosexuality, we have to go to the beginning of the Hebrew Scriptures where God explains his purpose for creation:

> Then God said, "Let us make man in our image, after our likeness... So God created man in his own image, in the image of God he created him; male and female he created them. And God blessed them, and God said to them, "Be fruitful and multiply, and fill the earth..." And it was so. And God saw everything that he had made, and behold, it was very good. And there was evening and there was morning, a sixth day (Genesis 1:26-31).

The last thing God did in creating the universe, as the summit and goal of all that he created, was to make man. This says that God created us with great dignity, made to reflect God's image and likeness in a complementary fashion as male and female, and Scripture concludes that "it was *very* good."

Sam: But how do man and woman reflect God's image and likeness, since man is a physical being and God is a pure spirit?

Jeremy: Sam, the Church teaches that we are made in God's image and likeness in that we have intelligence and freewill, whether gay or straight.

Father JP: True, Jeremy, one of the ways we image God is found in our ability of knowing truth and loving another person. This is truly a touch of the divine.

But the Bible goes on to show how woman was made for man and man for woman:

> *Then the LORD God said, "It is not good that the man should be alone; I will make him a helper fit for him." So... the LORD God caused a deep sleep to fall upon the man, and while he slept took one of his ribs and closed up its place with flesh; and the rib which the LORD God had taken from the man he made into a woman and brought her to the man.*
>
> *Then the man said, "This at last is bone of my bones and flesh of my flesh; she shall be called Woman, because she was taken out of Man." Therefore a man leaves his father and his mother and cleaves to his wife, and they become one flesh. And the man and his wife were both naked, and were not ashamed (Genesis 2:18-25).*

Even the love that man and woman show by becoming one flesh expresses the great dignity of man and woman as the image and likeness of God. Love—the union of spirits—is truly divine and its physical expression is something sacred.

Sam: I remember you explaining this quite well to Margie and me. It really is a very beautiful teaching. I was particularly impressed with the "logic of love" that shows how the one flesh union between a man and woman is meant to express the life-long one spirit union in marriage. Although initially I thought this also applied to any committed relationship, you made a very beautiful argument for how sex requires a marital commitment for it to be a true expression of love.

Jeremy: Yeah, but we gay men become one flesh too! Therefore, we reflect the divine likeness as well, heh, JP?

Father JP: Not as interpreted in other passages of Scripture! God's love for his people is certainly spousal, even, erotic, but it is always viewed as God's masculine love for his feminine people, his virgin Bride:

> For your Maker is your husband, the LORD of hosts is his name... For the LORD has called you like a wife... like a wife of youth... says your God (Isaiah 54:5-6).

Christians find the definitive fulfillment of this passage in the fifth chapter of Paul's letter to the Ephesians:

> Husbands, love your wives, as Christ loved the church and gave himself up for her..., that she might be holy and without blemish... "For this reason a man shall leave his father and mother and be joined to his wife, and the two shall become one flesh." This mystery is a profound one, and I mean in reference to Christ and the church (Ephesians 5:25-32).

So, Scripture only contemplates *one flesh* as referring to the intimate union of a man and woman in marriage:

> The body is not meant for immorality, but for the Lord, and the Lord for the body... Do you not know that your bodies are members of Christ? Shall I therefore take the members of Christ and make them members of a prostitute? Never! Do you not know that he who joins himself to a prostitute becomes one body with her? For, as it is written,

"The two shall become one flesh." But he who is united to the Lord becomes one spirit with him. Shun immorality. Every other sin which a man commits is outside the body; but the immoral man sins against his own body. Do you not know that your body is a temple of the Holy Spirit within you, which you have from God? You are not your own; you were bought with a price. So glorify God in your body (1 Corinthians 6:13-20).

Jeremy: But these texts don't say anything explicit about homosexuality. They simply condemn the use of another person for selfish sexual gratification, whether by men by using their wives without love, or by prostitution. To use these passages to condemn loving, gay or lesbian relationships is to take them out of context.

The Old Testament—Choosing Interpretations

Father JP: True, Jeremy, but the Bible says more than this. This is just the initial groundwork that manifests God's original plan for creating man as male and female.

The first time that homosexuality is dealt with is with the rescue of Lot from Sodom in Genesis 19. There, God destroys a whole city due to male lust for other males (Genesis 19:5).

Jeremy: But the Sodom story just condemns a people who should have offered shelter and food to these strangers—that was the custom of the time and area—but instead they tried to abuse the strangers through a form of gang rape. That's what made these people so despicable. Although the sin of Sodom is mentioned in many passages of the Bible, none of them mentions the sin as homosexual activity.

Father JP: Even before their attempted rape of these strangers, Scripture tells us that, "the men of Sodom were wicked, great sinners against the LORD" (Genesis 13:13), "because the outcry against Sodom and Gomorrah is great and their sin is very grave" (Genesis 18:20). Peter explains that Sodom and Gomorrah were condemned for their wickedness, licentiousness, and ungodliness:

> But... there will be false teachers among you, who will secretly bring in destructive heresies... bringing upon themselves swift destruction. And many will follow their licentiousness, and... will exploit you with false words... For if God did not spare the angels when they sinned, but cast them into hell... if by turning the cities of Sodom and Gomorrah to ashes he condemned them to extinction and made them an example to those who were to be ungodly; and if he rescued righteous Lot, greatly distressed by the licentiousness of the wicked... then the Lord knows how to rescue the godly from trial, and to keep the unrighteous under punishment until the day of judgment, and especially those who indulge in the lust of defiling passion and despise authority... But these, like irrational animals, creatures of instinct, born to be caught and killed... They are blots and blemishes, reveling in their dissipation, carousing with you. They have eyes full of adultery, insatiable for sin. They entice unsteady souls... Forsaking the right way they have gone astray... These are waterless springs and mists driven by a storm; for them the nether gloom of darkness has been reserved. For, uttering loud boasts of folly, they entice with licentious passions of the flesh men who have barely escaped from those who live in error. They promise them freedom, but they themselves are slaves of corruption; for whatever overcomes a man, to that he is enslaved (2 Peter 2:1-19).

Jeremy: But this passage doesn't mention homosexuality either.

Father JP: But the "ungodliness," "licentiousness," "indulgent lust," "defiling passion," "like irrational animals, creatures of instinct," "eyes full of adultery, insatiable for sin," etc. fits more homosexual sex than it does simple inhospitality. For this reason, Jude concludes:

Sodom and Gomorrah and the surrounding cities, which likewise acted immorally and indulged in unnatural lust, serve as an example by undergoing a punishment of eternal fire (Jude 17).

The Christians knew what Sodom represented.

Jeremy: But Jude only concludes that it was "unnatural" lust, not that it was homosexual lust.

Father JP: The descriptions of the "unnatural" lust of Sodom and Gomorrah should not be taken in isolation. It should be put in the context of God's "natural" plan for man and woman in Genesis one and two, and in context of the rest of the Mosaic Law. It is the Mosaic Law that interprets the ancient events of the Patriarchs in light of the Ten Commandments:

You shall not give any of your children to devote them by fire to Molech, and so profane the name of your God: I am the LORD. You shall not lie with a male as with a woman; it is an abomination. And you shall not lie with any beast and defile yourself with it, neither shall any woman give herself to a beast to lie with it: it is perversion (Leviticus 18:21-23).

And again:

If a man lies with his daughter-in-law, both of them shall be put to death; they have committed incest, their blood is upon them. If a man lies with a male as with a woman, both of them have committed an abomination; they shall be put to death, their blood is upon them (Leviticus 20:12-13).

These passages make it very explicit that homosexual acts are considered serious sins.

Sam: JP, I was told by a rabbi—granted he was a more liberal rabbi—that these verses belong to the "purity code" of the Old

Testament and were simply condemned based on cultural biases against the pagan practices of Egypt and Canaan, not because they were intrinsically immoral. Let me read what it says at the beginning of this section:

> And the LORD said to Moses, "Say to the people of Israel, I am the LORD your God. You shall not do as they do in the land of Egypt, where you dwelt, and you shall not do as they do in the land of Canaan, to which I am bringing you. You shall not walk in their statutes. You shall do my ordinances and keep my statutes and walk in them. I am the LORD your God" (Leviticus 18:1-4).

So, God is saying to Moses, tell these people that since they have left a pagan culture and will be surrounded by another, they must avoid their religious and cultural practices, so as not to adopt their gods as well.

This section of Leviticus forbids mixing cattle breeds, sowing two kinds of seed together (Leviticus 19:19), and bans tattoos (Leviticus 19:28), all of which were done in Egypt and Canaan. So, do you think we should use these verses to ban homosexuality and tattoos?

Father JP: These passages do more than just ban Egyptian and Canaanite cultural and religious practices, they reveal to us God's love for Israel. He does not want Israel to become enslaved to idol worship, superstition, spousal and sexual abuses, etc. Rather God invites Israel to form part of his family and to experience his love, directing them toward their true happiness.

The prohibition on homosexuality is also surrounded by other prohibitions against adultery, murder, rape, and sacrificing children to Molech (Leviticus 18:21; 20:2-5). These are issues that obviously have to do with more than mere ritual or cultural purity.

Look at what else you would allow if you choose to follow this line of interpretation: bestiality and incest, and just about every other kind of sexual abuse. I don't think you want to approve all that just to approve homosexual acts.

In making any interpretation, we have to discern whether we are truly trying to understand God's Word, or whether we justifying our position with Scripture.

Jeremy: All right, so let's say that we're going to take this text of Leviticus seriously. Let's join all of the literalist Bible-thumpers, and take God at His word. Here, give me that…

Jeremy grabs the Bible from the table.

… right here, it says that "if a man lies with a man as with a woman, he is to be put to death." That's what it says. Read it for yourself. That's what your Bible says. That's what your God says. Does the Church think that all of us gays and lesbians should be put to death, JP?

Either all this bullshit about *loving the sinner and hating the sin* is a heap of steaming hypocrisy, or else you have to admit that Leviticus is a human document, based on an out-moded and intolerant system of thought, and that it no longer pertains to modern life. So which is it?

Father JP: Jeremy, I can see this is a sensitive topic for you. However, we are wrestling with these issues of the Bible together.

I really believe God inspired the Bible. Our Lord is not interested in us killing all those who commit serious sins, but what he is trying to teach us in these passages is that serious sin *kills* our relationship with God, which is Life itself. The Holy Spirit tells us that sin kills and thus *destroys the soul:*

> *Keep your tongue from slander… a lying mouth destroys the soul. Do not invite death by the error of your life, nor bring on destruction by the works of your hands; because God did not make death, and he does not delight in the death of the living (Wisdom 1:11-13).*

So, if you take the life of an innocent person, abuse a child, sacrifice children to idols, or even curse mother and father (Leviticus 20:9), you have destroyed your relationship with God in the process and will lose eternal life.

Jeremy: You mean to say that capital punishment is just a symbol?

Father JP: God had to speak the language these people could understand. But when God speaks of death, he is referring to more than just physical death. He is principally referring to the death of our relationship with him.

For example, when God placed Adam and Eve in Eden, he commanded them:

> You may freely eat of every tree of the garden; but of the tree of the knowledge of good and evil you shall not eat, for in the day that you eat of it you shall die (Genesis 2:16-17).

But they did not *physically* die the day they disobeyed this command, rather they lived for more than eight hundred years before they finally died (cf. Genesis 5:1-5). However, on the very day they disobeyed God they did kill that intimate relationship with God: they felt ashamed, they realized they were naked, they hid themselves from God, and they were cursed by him (Genesis 3:7-19). That day they spiritually died, since their intimate relationship to God was destroyed.

However, God wants us to turn from our sin:

> But if a wicked man turns away from all his sins which he has committed and keeps all my statutes and does what is lawful and right, he shall surely live; he shall not die. None of the transgressions which he has committed shall be remembered against him; for the righteousness which he has done he shall live. Have I any pleasure in the death of the wicked, says the Lord GOD, and not rather that he should turn from his way and live? (Ezekiel 18:21-23).

Jeremy: OK, but if you were stoned to death, there isn't any time to turn from your sins. Why would God insist that the people kill those who fell into sin and not give them the opportunity to convert before dying and losing eternal life?

Father JP: Three thousand years ago, the people had little concept of eternal life. God used the possibility of capital punishment to help them understand the consequences of their actions. This is why the New Testament Church continues to say that homosexual acts—any sexual act outside of marriage—*kills* our relationship with God.

Jeremy: Even so, these passages intend to condemn only exploitive, manipulative sex—whether heterosexual or homosexual—including rape, prostitution, pagan sex rituals, and abusing children. The Bible does not condemn loving, caring relationships between men or between women. When the Bible speaks of such relationships, it is very positive, such as when it describes David and Jonathan:

> *I am distressed for you, my brother Jonathan; very pleasant have you been to me; your love to me was wonderful, passing the love of women (2 Samuel 1:26).*

Father JP: True, David loved Jonathan; it is also true there is no indication of anything exploitive, manipulative, or of prostitution in their relationship; but neither is there any indication whatsoever of anything sexual. If the Bible meant to approve this relationship as homosexual it would have mentioned it explicitly. If the relationship between the two was sinful and erotic in any way, then the Bible would have mentioned that too, just as it describes David's other transgressions against the Mosaic Law, especially his adultery with Bathsheba, the wife of Uriah, whom he had murdered to hide his sin (2 Samuel 11-12), and his disobedience to God by taking a census of the people (2 Samuel 24). Yet it never mentions even a hint of impropriety between David and Jonathan. It never mentions that David lusted over Jonathan or over any other male, as he had lusted for Bathsheba. Such a homosexual interpretation is simply—if not wishful—fantasy.

Jeremy: This is not fantasy, JP—wishful or not—when you grow up with a strong emotional attraction to men as I did. On the one hand, a homosexual Christian reads Leviticus and feels that he is condemned for all eternity, just to have the feelings and desires for love. Then he reads about David and Jonathan and longs to have a relationship as intimate as they had. In reading the Bible, you are damned if you do and you are damned if you don't.

Father JP: It is not easy to read the Bible when you have strong same-sex desires. But it is important not to project onto the Bible what we want to hear. One must read it in context of the whole of Scripture with a great sensitivity to discern what God wants to communicate to us.

New Testament

Jeremy: But are you not projecting your interpretation on the Bible? The New Testament tells us how to interpret it, and it does away with all the rituals and sin offerings of Leviticus.

Father JP: The New Testament did not come to abolish the Law, but to fulfill it. As Jesus explicitly says:

Think not that I have come to abolish the law and the prophets; I have come not to abolish them but to fulfil them. For truly, I say to you, till heaven and earth pass away, not an iota, not a dot, will pass from the law until all is accomplished. Whoever then relaxes one of the least of these commandments and teaches men so, shall be called least in the kingdom of heaven; but he who does them and teaches them shall be called great in the kingdom of heaven (Matthew 5:17-19).

Jeremy: But what about how Paul tells us that the ceremonial law is out with the New Order:

> But now the righteousness of God has been manifested apart from law, although the law and the prophets bear witness to it, the righteousness of God through faith in Jesus Christ for all who believe (Romans 3:21-22).

So, the Old Law—including Leviticus—is no longer valid.

Father JP: Paul is referring to how Christian faith and baptism fulfills and replaces circumcision, as he clarifies elsewhere:

> In [Christ] also you were circumcised with a circumcision made without hands, by putting off the body of flesh in the circumcision of Christ; and you were buried with him in baptism, in which you were also raised with him through faith in the working of God, who raised him from the dead (Colossians 2:11-12).

Besides, Paul makes it pretty clear that homosexual acts are not consistent with the Gospel, just as they were not consistent with Leviticus:

> For the wrath of God is revealed from heaven against all ungodliness and wickedness of men who by their wickedness suppress the truth... Ever since the creation of the world his invisible nature, namely, his eternal power and deity, has been clearly perceived in the things that have been made. So they are without excuse; for although they knew God they did not honor him as God... and their senseless minds were darkened... Therefore God gave them up in the lusts of their hearts to impurity, to the dishonoring of their bodies among themselves... For this reason God gave them up to dishonorable passions. Their women exchanged natural relations for unnatural, and the men likewise gave up natural relations with women and were consumed with passion for one another, men committing shameless acts with men and receiving in their own persons the due penalty for their error. And since they did not see fit to acknowledge God, God

*gave them up to a base mind and to improper conduct...
Though they know God's decree that those who do such
things deserve to die, they not only do them but approve
those who practice them (Romans 1:18-32).*

So, although Paul recognizes the New Covenant has fulfilled the Old, he recognizes the sinfulness of homosexual acts
and how it kills one's relationship with God, since "those who
do such things deserve to die."

Jeremy: But Paul is just condemning the "unnatural." If heterosexual oriented men were gratifying their lust by homosexual
acts, then it ought to be condemned as "unnatural." But for gay
men and lesbian women, it is a natural orientation for us.

Father JP: Paul is not talking about orientation at all, but about
behavior: "shameless acts" and "natural" and "unnatural" relations. For this reason Paul states:

*Do you not know that the unrighteous will not inherit the
kingdom of God? Do not be deceived; neither the immoral,
nor idolaters, nor adulterers, nor sexual perverts—"male-
intercourse"—nor thieves, nor the greedy, nor drunkards, nor
revilers, nor robbers will inherit the kingdom of God. And
such were some of you. But you were washed, you were
sanctified, you were justified in the name of the Lord Jesus
Christ and in the Spirit of our God (1 Corinthians 6:9-11).*

Paul uses the same term here that the Septuagint Greek ver-
sion of the Old Testament (translated more than a hundred years
before Christ) uses in Leviticus 18:22—*arsenokoitai*—as he
does again in First Timothy, Paul reiterates:

*Now we know that the law is good... that the law is not
laid down for the just but for the lawless and disobedient, for
the ungodly and sinners, for the unholy and profane, for murderers of fathers and murderers of mothers, for manslayers,
immoral persons, sodomites, kidnapers, liars, perjurers, and
whatever else is contrary to sound doctrine, in accordance*

with the glorious gospel of the blessed God with which I have been entrusted (1 Timothy 1:8-11).

Some will argue that the word, *arsenokoitai*, is obscure in Greek and mistranslated as male-intercourse, but it is quite clear from the Greek translation of the Hebrew of Leviticus what it means.

Jeremy: Although the church reveres the Apostle Paul, he is not God. He is only a messenger whose message has been tempered with the societal, political, and cultural "norms" prevalent during the time of his writings.

Father JP: Neither you or I are God. If either of us try to impose our cultural bias on the Gospel, we would do wrong too. That is why God gave us the Holy Spirit and Church authority, to guide us into the fullness of the truth.

Jeremy: But in the past the Bible was used to condone slavery. "Playing it safe" or being conservative is what the slave owners would have wanted us to do in this country. But today we rightly condemn slavery because the biblical teachings about justice, love, and human dignity led us to see the light about how evil it is. Similarly, the broader Bible teaching strongly suggests that we should accept gays and lesbians as equal partners in the church.

Father JP: In the Bible, slavery is an image for sin. It is precisely because the Church believes in the human dignity of gays and lesbians—as loved by God for all eternity—that it challenges them to live the Gospel message. We want you—and all persons—to be truly free and happy, by becoming free from sin and all inclinations to sin:

Jesus then said to the Jews who had believed in him, "If you continue in my word, you are truly my disciples, and you will know the truth, and the truth will make you free." They answered him, "We are descendants of Abraham, and have never been in bondage to any one. How is it that you say, 'You will be made free'?" Jesus answered them, "Truly, truly, I say to you, every one who commits sin is a slave to sin. The slave does not continue in the house for ever; the son continues for ever. So if the Son makes you free, you will be free indeed (John 8:31-36).

The *Catechism of the Catholic Church* concurs:

Jesus... [came] to free men from the gravest slavery, sin, which thwarts them in their vocation as God's sons and causes all forms of human bondage (CCC 549).

Freedom and sin. Man's freedom is limited and fallible. In fact, man failed. He freely sinned. By refusing God's plan of love, he deceived himself and became a slave to sin... Human history attests the wretchedness and oppression born of the human heart in consequence of the abuse of freedom (CCC 1739; cf. 421, 601, 1733, etc.).

Sure, if you interpret the Bible too literally and selectively — just choosing the texts that support your position — you can justify slavery and just about everything else, including homosexuality. However, once one understands how the Bible uses types and images, then slavery is seen as the evil it is, just like sin in general is. Then one also understands the sin of homosexual acts too.

Sam: So you give slavery a symbolic meaning like you did to capital punishment, eh JP?

Father JP: Sam, it's not just giving *slavery* a symbolic meaning, it is finding consistency in the Bible. For us Christians, Jesus taught us to love others as we do ourselves. If we are to love the slave as ourselves, we would want them to be free physically as well as spiritually, wouldn't we, Sam?

Sam: I guess so.

Father JP: So, we can't justify slavery by selective interpretation of the Bible.

Sam: JP, going back to the ritual code, if you say that Leviticus 18 and 20 condemns homosexuality, shouldn't you also obey all God's other commands there? What about the ban of wearing clothes made of two types of cloth, such as wool and linen (Leviticus 22:11)? Isn't that condemning cotton-polyester blends? Are you not selecting what commands to obey and which ones to ignore?

Father JP: Jesus Christ tells Christians that we must obey all these commands, only to do so in a proper way. For example, Christ shows us how we ought to interpret the Bible and the passage on wearing clothes made of two types of cloths:

> And no one puts a piece of unshrunk cloth on an old garment, for the patch tears away from the garment, and a worse tear is made. Neither is new wine put into old wineskins; if it is, the skins burst, and the wine is spilled, and the skins are destroyed; but new wine is put into fresh wineskins, and so both are preserved (Matthew 9:16-17).

So, Jesus now shows us God's proper intention of Leviticus 22:11, that we should not mix or imitate religious and cultural practices, even though they have some similarities. This will be seen as Jewish converts to Christianity will try to impose circumcision on pagan converts, but the Apostles will determine that baptism replaces circumcision (Acts 15:1-31; Romans 2:28-29, etc.).

Jeremy: But isn't it true, JP, that everyone has to get to the point of deciding whether to accept what the Bible says or to accept a life that corresponds to who he is? I can say at least that in my life, after my first engagement with gay sex, I had to make a choice. Knowing what the Bible said about homosexuality and discovering how free and fulfilled I was in a relationship with another guy, I just *knew* God wanted me to be the way I am; I just *knew* that God wanted things to be different, that he didn't want me to continue suffering like I was.

Father JP: I feel for you, Jeremy, and for what you must be going through. Although we must *choose* whether to accept God's word with faith or not, it is not up to us to decide *what* God is saying to us. That message is his for us to accept or reject.

WWJD: How Would Christ Confront Homosexuality?

Sam: Another friend of mine told me that Jesus said nothing about homosexuality and it was only Paul's overzealous prudery that made Christians homophobic.

Father JP: Jesus may not have said anything explicit about homosexuality, but he did say quite a bit about sexual morality and the real meaning of human love.

First, as we saw, he reminds us that the all of the law is to be accomplished and not to be relaxed (Matthew 5:17-19). When he comes to dealing with adultery—which was a much more prevalent problem than homosexuality—he raised the bar even higher:

> You have heard that it was said, 'You shall not commit adultery.' But I say to you that every one who looks at a woman lustfully has already committed adultery with her in his heart.
>
> If your right eye causes you to sin, pluck it out and throw it away; it is better that you lose one of your members than that your whole body be thrown into hell. (Matthew 5:27-29).

So, even lustful thoughts and desires can "kill" the soul's relationship with God and cause us to go to hell, which is eternal separation from God. Jesus also raises the standard on marriage, condemning divorce (Matthew 5:31-32).

So, do you really think Jesus Christ would lighten the Old

Testament teaching against homosexuality? What about sacrificing children to idols, since Jesus said nothing explicit about that? No, from the consistent picture portrayed by the evangelists and from that of early Christian writers and from how Christians put this gospel into practice, it is clear that Christ reaffirmed the Old Testament teaching on homosexuality.

Sam: But do you think Jesus would use the Mosaic Law to condemn a gay man or a lesbian to death, as he condemns divorce?

Father JP: No, Sam. In fact, when Jesus addresses the issues of marriage, he shows that the Mosaic Law on divorce was insufficient:

> And Pharisees came up to him and tested him by asking, "Is it lawful to divorce one's wife for any cause?" He answered, "Have you not read that he who made them from the beginning made them male and female, and said, 'For this reason a man shall leave his father and mother and be joined to his wife, and the two shall become one flesh'? So they are no longer two but one flesh. What therefore God has joined together, let not man put asunder."
>
> They said to him, "Why then did Moses command one to give a certificate of divorce, and to put her away?" He said to them, "For your hardness of heart Moses allowed you to divorce your wives, but from the beginning it was not so. And I say to you: whoever divorces his wife, except for unchastity, and marries another, commits adultery; and he who marries a divorced woman, commits adultery" (Matthew 19:3-9).

The Pharisees defended divorce based on the Mosaic Law. But Jesus goes back to *the beginning* when God formed the first man and woman. The bond of man and woman as they become one flesh in marital intimacy is something sacred, something God has joined together: we must not *put it asunder* by divorce, or by adultery, or by fornication, or by homosexual acts. That is God's design for humanity.

Sam: Are you then saying that Jesus condemns gays and lesbians by his authoritative interpretation of Genesis?

Father JP: No, I'm not saying that either.

If we want to know how Jesus would react toward actively homosexual individuals, then let's read the Bible—with both faith and openness; there I think we can find a wonderful example of what Christ would do.

On one occasion, Jesus was in the Temple and the Scribes and Pharisees brought a woman who had been caught in adultery:

> And placing her in the midst they said to him, "Teacher, this woman has been caught in the act of adultery. Now in the law Moses commanded us to stone such. What do you say about her?" This they said to test him… And as they continued to ask him, he stood up and said to them, "Let him who is without sin among you be the first to throw a stone at her." And once more he bent down… But when they heard it, they went away, one by one, beginning with the eldest, and Jesus was left alone with the woman standing before him. Jesus looked up and said to her, "Woman, where are they? Has no one condemned you?" She said, "No one, Lord." And Jesus said, "Neither do I condemn you; go, and do not sin again" (John 8:2-11).

I think Jesus would have a similar attitude toward any man or woman "caught" in a homosexual relationship. Jesus would love them. He would offer them his understanding and forgiveness. He would not condemn them to death—spiritual death—but challenge them to go and sin no more.

Jeremy: So, you are saying, JP, that if Our Lord "caught" me in a homosexual relationship and I was being dragged by a bunch of Bible-thumpers to be tortured and killed, he would intervene?

Father JP: I have no question about that: he certainly would.

Jeremy: Would you, JP?

Father JP: I would hope so. As you know, we Christians can be more talk than action when we are hard-pressed to act in defense of someone under attack.

More than risking my life, I am willing to risk my reputation. As you know, gay-bashers have no mercy. Anyone who associates with homosexuals also incurs their wrath; but I am willing to risk this, just as Jesus did, eating and befriending tax collectors, sinners, and harlots (Matthew 9:10-13; 11:19; 21:28-31; Luke 15:1-7).

Jeremy: Then why does the Church condemn us?

Sam: Yeah, JP? Why don't you tell us why the Church is making a concerted effort to fight against homosexuality and the rights of gays and lesbians to marry?

Father JP: I would like to address that, but we need to take a break. Perhaps we can meet again next week and continue our dialogue.

Jeremy: JP, would you mind if I bring along a friend of mine, BillyLu? She is full of spunk and has a sharp tongue, but I think she would better argue for the gay side than I.

Sam: Oh boy, JP, I've met this BillyLu. She's a pretty tough cookie.

Father JP: If she is willing to have a civil dialogue, then please bring her along.

CHAPTER **3**

Homosexuality and God's Plan

The next meeting took place two weeks later. Although Jeremy was still adamant that the Church was unjust in condemning homosexuality, he felt drawn to Father JP's compassionate response: it both attracted him and filled him with a certain trepidation.

In seeking backing for his position, Jeremy convinced BillyLu that he needed help in defending homosexuality as a human rights issue. Although BillyLu agreed to take on the challenge, she balked at that idea of meeting at Father JP's church. At Father JP's suggestion, they decided to meet at a local pizza parlor, one that BillyLu frequented. Sam also brought along his girlfriend, Margie. Everyone began by ordering soft drinks, until BillyLu ordered a strong, dark beer. Father JP ordered the same, to everyone else's surprise.

Jeremy: BillyLu, I'm sure JP would like to know something about who you are before we begin, why don't you start by telling us your story...

BillyLu: So you all can psychoanalyze me? No thanks. I don't need any shrink telling me why I think the way I do.

Father JP: BillyLu, we're here to continue a discussion Sam, Jeremy, and I started a few weeks ago. Sam and Jeremy thought you had a lot you could add to the discussion. Perhaps they were afraid they couldn't keep up with the Church…

Sam: JP, that's a bit smug, don't you think?

Father JP: Oh, I was just joking. We shouldn't go around taking ourselves too seriously.

BillyLu: So what was the hot topic you discussed last time?

Jeremy: Basically, we discussed what the Bible says about homosexuality. JP defended the traditional interpretation that the Bible condemns us gays and lesbians.

BillyLu: So, what's new? Fundamentalism has been around for centuries and I don't think we'll ever get rid of it. So, if the Bible is your God then just go and worship it, but please leave the rest of us alone.

Father JP: BillyLu, I'm a Catholic Christian; this is my belief. And, by the way, we do not worship the Bible; that would be just another form of idolatry. We worship God and believe what he has revealed. Not that I always fully understand the logic of God's Word and Love. Sometimes I too must wrestle with it to try to make sense of it. But I believe it not because it makes sense, but because I love God and have chosen to believe his Word.

We Catholic Christians do believe that God has revealed that any sexual activity outside of marriage is an offense against him, our Creator. You may not believe it, and certainly I will not force you to believe it. However, I ask you to treat it with respect, otherwise there can be no dialogue.

BillyLu: But then I expect you to treat me and my beliefs with the same respect, that sex between any committed couple — whether heterosexual or homosexual — is just as holy as sex in any Christian marriage. I'm not Catholic; I never was Catholic; and I will never, ever become one. Are you willing to respect that?

Father JP: I will respect you and love you just as you are. I commit myself to respecting your freedom to follow your conscience and will do all in my power not to humiliate you or berate anything you believe, even if your beliefs are contrary to my own. I consider your conscience sacred.

BillyLu: Oh, yeah…? My lesbian conscience…?

BillyLu hesitated for a moment…

Well, OK… I guess I can live with that.

It was good timing, as the waiter showed up with the drinks and took the order for pizza.

CAN WE SAY THAT HOMOSEXUALITY IS INTRINSICALLY DISORDERED?

Sam: So, JP what does the Church teach about homosexuality? From what I gather, it sees homosexuals as intrinsically disordered.

Father JP: Sam, I think both Jeremy and BillyLu would find that offensive.

BillyLu: You bet I do! You bet I do! That's just the kind of hate-speech that makes so many gay kids commit suicide.

Father JP: Well, that statement is not Catholic or even Christian. So, you don't hate the Catholic Church or Christianity but a false picture of it. By the way, I also hate that picture because it is utterly false and cruel.

Margie: But Father JP, I was just reading the *Catechism of the Catholic Church* to prepare myself for this gathering, and I remember it clearly saying that homosexuality is "objectively disordered" (cf. CCC 2358). I think that is one of the reasons why BillyLu and Jeremy have such a negative picture of the Church. I mean, I would find it offensive if the Catholic Church said it was "objectively disordered" to be attracted to a Jewish man.

Margie turns her gaze from BillyLu to Sam, her Jewish boyfriend.

Father JP: But what are you talking about when you say *homosexuality?* Are you referring to the person? Are you referring to erotic sexual acts between persons of the same sex? Are you referring to the inclination to those acts? Does homosexuality refer to the attraction that a person may have toward another person of the same sex?

I am absolutely certain that is why there is so much misunderstanding about the Church and homosexuality: the same term can refer to very different realities: to a certain group of persons; to the performance of certain kinds of acts; to the inclination to perform such acts; or to the attraction of one person to another.

BillyLu: Obviously, homosexuality ultimately refers to persons who *are* homosexuals, to those who are gay or lesbians.

Father JP: If that is the case, BillyLu, then the Church teaches that homosexuals are intrinsically good.

Persons Are Intrinsically Good

At this point, Father JP brought out his Catechism of the Catholic Church *for reference, as the conversation continued.*

Jeremy: How can we be intrinsically good when the *Catechism* says that we are "objectively disordered," as Margie pointed out?

Father JP: Jeremy, because it is the person—whether homosexually inclined or not—who is intrinsically good. The great dignity of the human person is inviolable. The *Catechism of the Catholic Church* develops this at great length, as every human person has been created in the image and likeness of God (Genesis 1:26-27, 5:1-2):

> The dignity of the human person is rooted in his creation in the image and likeness of God (CCC 1700).
>
> The divine image is present in every man. It shines forth in the communion of persons, in the likeness of the union of the divine persons among themselves (CCC 1702).

We all received that great dignity at the moment we came into being—even before that, since "he chose us in him before the foundation of the world" (Ephesians 1:4). And our freedom is an "outstanding manifestation of the divine image" (CCC 1705).

The dignity of being made in God's image and likeness, of being free, can be disfigured by sin (CCC 1701), but it cannot be totally rubbed out or lost even by the slavery to sin.

Margie: So, the *Catechism* is telling us that every human being, whether male or female, whether a sinner or a saint, whether gay, lesbian, or straight, is loved by God and endowed with unspeakable dignity?

Father JP: That's a very succinct and accurate summary of the *Catechism*.

Margie: Then us Catholics should love BillyLu and Jeremy as God does, with a special affection because of their lofty dignity as children of God.

Father JP: You've got it, Margie.

SIN IS INTRINSICALLY DISORDERED

Sam: If it isn't the person, then what does the Church call intrinsically and objectively "disordered," JP?

Father JP: Ultimately, anything that harms our relationship with God and our noble relationships with others would be a disorder—in other words, sin.

The *Catechism* makes that pretty clear:

*There are concrete acts that it is always wrong to choose, because their choice entails a **disorder** of the will, i.e., a moral evil. One may not do evil so that good may result from it (CCC 1761).*

Jeremy: So, what you are saying is that it is not persons who are disordered, but the sins they may commit.

Margie: And so we are called to love the sinner—who is intrinsically good—and hate the sin—which is intrinsically evil.

Father JP: You are both correct. That is why all persons are good in themselves despite their sin, which is—by definition—a disordered act.

BillyLu: But the Catholic Church is singling out homosexual sex as particularly disordered. Our sex is the worse of all evils, so it must be eradicated by eradicating us homosexuals.

Father JP: Not really, BillyLu, for many particular sins are described as disordered, and such sins are conquered by God's grace and our struggle—not by eradicating sinners.

For example:

*There are some concrete acts—such as fornication—that it is always wrong to choose, because choosing them entails a **disorder** of the will, that is, a moral evil (CCC 1755).*

So, fornication—sex between individuals who are not married—is also a disordered action. We could list other sins, such as unjust divorce:

> Divorce is immoral also because it introduces **disorder** into the family and into society. This **disorder** brings grave harm to the deserted spouse, to children traumatized by the separation of their parents and often torn between them, and because of its contagious effect which makes it truly a plague on society (CCC 2385).

Sam: It seems like you are saying that the disorder is the repercussion that moral decisions have on people and relationships.

Father JP: That is a great observation. All our actions, even our thoughts, our looks, our failure to act, etc., can greatly impact our relationships to God and to people.

Jeremy: Like that guy who walks into the telephone pole while checking out a hot chick... Sam told me about that analogy.

Father JP: That's right, Jeremy. If a girl catches her boyfriend lusting over another woman, it can be history for him. For this reason the Church condemns pornography and masturbation with clarity and force:

> Both... the Church, in the course of a constant tradition, and the moral sense of the faithful have been in no doubt and have firmly maintained that masturbation is an intrinsically and gravely **disordered** action (CCC 2352).

Jeremy: That seems kind of harsh, JP. Doesn't the Church realize that people—especially young kids—may not be able to control themselves? Certainly, masturbation doesn't hurt anybody.

Father JP: In the same paragraph, the *Catechism of the Catholic Church* tells us that, although the act is intrinsically disordered, the particular person may not be guilty of sin or morally responsible for that action:

> To form an equitable judgment about the subjects' moral
> responsibility and to guide pastoral action, one must take
> into account the affective immaturity, force of acquired habit,
> conditions of anxiety, or other psychological or social fac-
> tors that lessen or even extenuate moral culpability (CCC
> 2352).

So, you are correct, Jeremy, that an individual may not have any guilt, but the disorder lies in the lack of control. As the boy or girl grows older and has a serious relationship—he or she is married, for example—such activity as masturbation or pornog-raphy—when discovered by the other spouse can gravely harm or even destroy a relationship.

Jeremy: If my boyfriend caught me masturbating, my Tommy would just laugh or join in.

Margie: You must be kidding! I know how offended I would be if I were married to Sam and learned that he was doing porn and masturbating. It would be a real slap in the face... as though I wasn't good enough for him.

Look at this way, Jeremy, what if your Tommy caught you with a woman or another guy instead?

BillyLu: That's what happened to me...

BillyLu said this very matter-of-factly. The rest turned to see if she would finish her thought; Margie especially wanted to hear more and her body language communicated to BillyLu that it was safe to go on; mo-ments later she continued:

Yeah, my husband caught me in bed with my girlfriend. My husband and I didn't have much of a relationship anyway, and that ended the little we had. But our fictitious relationship was much more of a sin than anything Leslie and I had going on.

BillyLu left it at that. She wasn't ashamed of what had happened but also didn't want to continue with her story. So, Jeremy interrupted the silence by calling the waiter over to order a beer for himself. Sam also needed one at this point.

Margie: OK, Father, mortal sins are disordered. I think we get that. But isn't God a forgiving God?

Father JP: Yes, Margie, he is. He reveals himself like a Father, the Father of the prodigal son who wasted all his inheritance on disordered conduct. But the Father welcomes his son back, running to him when he sees him at a distance, and smothers him with love and affection (cf. Luke 15:11-32). God wants to do that with each one of us.

Margie: But, isn't God a nurturing mother, too?

Father JP: Although revelation sometimes portrays God with maternal perfections (CCC 370), comparing his love with a mother's love (Isaiah 66:13), much more often it reveals to us that the Church is our mother. She is nurturing and full of affection. She should welcome the repentant sinner, often reassuring the sinner and making it safe for him to return to the Father and receive his love.

Margie: But we are all sinners. Doesn't that mean that we all have disordered inclinations and actions? What about our small sins, are they disordered too?

Father JP: Even small sins—what the Catholic Church calls *venial sins*—consists in a disorder that harms one's relationship with God:

> *Venial sin weakens charity; it manifests a **disordered** affection for created goods… Deliberate and unrepented venial sin disposes us little by little to commit mortal sin.*

> However venial sin does not... break the covenant with God (CCC 1863).
> Venial sin constitutes a moral **disorder** that is reparable by charity (CCC 1875).

Thus, as you said, we all are inclined to disordered action. But, as the U.S. Catholic bishops state:

> It is crucially important to understand that saying a person has a particular inclination that is **disordered** is not to say that the person as a whole is **disordered**. Nor does it mean that one has been rejected by God or the Church.

ARE HOMOSEXUAL ACTS DISORDERED?

BillyLu: JP, let's cut to the chase. What you are really getting at is that homosexuality is disordered. We're disordered, subhuman slime in your eyes. We already knew that coming in.

Father JP: I can see that you are hurt by what I am saying. But I ask you to trust me in this: I care a lot about you and Jeremy, just as I do Sam and Margie. I want you to be truly happy, in fact, I want to spend eternity with you all in heaven. I hope in heaven we will be able to all enjoy a good beer, pizza, and friendly conversation like this and not have to worry about going back to work in the morning.

Jeremy: But BillyLu is right, JP, doesn't the Catholic Church consider homosexuality disordered?

Father JP: Remember, persons as persons are never disordered, but always loved by God. Thus, if God loves and respects a person then all other human beings are called to love that person, whether a saint or sinner.

Now the Church considers sexual relations between persons of the same-sex as disordered and sinful, just as it does any sexual activity outside of marriage between a man and a woman.

Margie, would you mind reading to us what the *Catechism* says on homo-sexuality?

Margie: No, not at all, Father JP. Here we go…it says:

> *Basing itself on Sacred Scripture, which presents homo-sexual acts as acts of grave depravity (Cf. Genesis 19:1-29; Romans 1:24-27; 1 Corinthians 6:10; 1 Timothy 1:10), tradition has always declared that "homosexual acts are intrinsically* **disordered***"… They close the sexual act to the gift of life. They do not proceed from a genuine affective and sexual complementarity. Under no circumstances can they be approved (CCC 2357).*

Jeremy: Why does the Church have to single us out?

Father JP: The Church is not singling out homosexual acts. In the sections on sexual morality—on the sixth and ninth Commandments (6th: *CCC* 2331-2400; 9th: *CCC* 2514-2533)—the *Catechism* describes homosexual sins as just one sin among many. In fact, of the one hundred plus paragraphs, more than seventy paragraphs focus on the positive aspects of sexual morality.

Of the paragraphs describing sexual sins, eleven paragraphs deal with sins against chastity (such as, lust, fornication, pornography, prostitution, rape, erotic entertainment, moral permissiveness, impure looks) and fourteen paragraphs deal with sins against marriage (such as, adultery, divorce, polygamy, incest, child abuse, trial marriage, and living together). Only two paragraphs deal with the sin of homosexual sex, with the later paragraph listing it among several others.

In other words, homosexual sex is certainly disordered: it can kill one's relationship with God and hurt other relationships, as well. But you cannot say that it is singled out as more deviant than these others. In fact, divorce is condemned at much greater length than any of these other sins.

Margie: So, the *Catechism* is saying to us that all sinful activity is disordered—not just homosexual tendencies—and because of that no human being can ever be considered slime, or "trash."

Is the Inclination Disordered?

Sam: Good point, Margie. But, JP, although you mention that homosexual acts are considered disordered, I also thought that the gay and lesbian inclination was considered an objective disorder, whether or not it is acted upon. Is that true?

Father JP: The Catholic Church considers anything that would incline a person to disorder as a disorder too. Thus passions (strong emotional drives) can be either upright or disordered:

> *Passions are morally good when they contribute to a good action, evil in the opposite case. The upright will orders the movements of the senses it appropriates to the good and to beatitude; an evil will succumbs to **disordered** passions and exacerbates them. Emotions and feelings can be taken up into the virtues or perverted by the vices (CCC 1768).*

Thus if one had a strong emotional drive for sex with children or for drugs, it would be a disordered passion since it would incline the person toward disordered behavior that would hurt him and others.

Jeremy: But sometimes one is born with such desires. They are innate. It would be unnatural for a person just to ignore those inborn desires.

Father JP: Are you saying that if one has an inborn desire to have sex with children that he should just give in to such desires?

Jeremy: No, no, JP. That's different. You are harming an innocent person as a result.

Father JP: So, what makes a particular behavior disordered is not the fact that it may have arisen from an inborn desire but that it may harm an innocent person. If one has strong desires for some behavior that is disordered, then the desires are also disordered.

The Catholic Church says the same thing about ignorance. If a person is too young to know that something is wrong—like masturbation—then that ignorance may mean he is not responsible for the action because it is outside his control. However, the ignorance itself "remains no less an evil, a privation, a **disorder**. One must therefore work to correct the errors of moral conscience" (CCC 1793).

BillyLu: OK, JP, we get it. You are saying that the homosexual inclination is an objective disorder because homosexual sex is a disorder. It's not too hard to figure that out.

Father JP: Yes, BillyLu, you got it. Because "homosexual acts are intrinsically **disordered**" (CCC 2357), then "deep-seated homosexual tendencies" are "objectively **disordered**" (CCC 2358). But the Catechism goes on to say:
    This... constitutes for most of them a trial. They must be accepted with respect, compassion, and sensitivity (CCC 2358).
So, the person is never disordered and must always be accepted with respect, compassion, and sensitivity.

BillyLu: But we don't want your f—ing compassion, we want to be treated as normal. You treat us as some kind of sick-o's. Everything about us is "disordered."

Margie: BillyLu, you seemed hurt by what Father JP just said. I know I would be too if others seemed to be condescending or patronizing toward me.

BillyLu: That's right, Margie. I hate it when people look down on me as though I'm some kind of helpless paraplegic.

Margie: But, there are times when I have felt like I was being bullied by some S.O.B. but I became quite grateful when someone came to my defense and told the jerk to back off and treat me with respect and compassion. I think that is what Father JP was intending to do.

Father JP: I'm sorry, BillyLu. I did not intend to offend you or to be patronizing. I'm trying to present this teaching in such a way that you see that the Church does not try to marginalize you or anyone.

Sam: But don't you think it is unfair, JP, that the Church points out homosexual inclinations as disordered whereas other disordered desires and inclinations are never mentioned?

Father JP: But they are indeed mentioned, Sam. For example, lust:

> Lust is **disordered** desire for or inordinate enjoyment of sexual pleasure. Sexual pleasure is morally **disordered** when sought for itself, isolated from its procreative and unitive purposes (CCC 2351).

Lust is disordered, whether it is directed toward someone of the same sex or of the opposite sex. The problem is that very few people think lust is a sin at all.

Jeremy: That is true. How can you watch TV today without being bombarded with arousing images? But I don't see what's wrong with that.

Margie: Sam, I hope you don't feel that way, do you?

Sam: No, Margie...

Father JP: But even a greedy lust for money is considered a disordered desire and inclination:

> The **disordered** desire for money cannot but produce perverse effects. It is one of the causes of the many conflicts which disturb the social order (CCC 2424).

BillyLu: Well, that's all fine and good, JP. It is easy for you to say that this is a disordered desire. But, JP, you've never felt this way.

Margie: I can assure you that probably none of us have felt the way you do, BillyLu. Even Jeremy's feelings are quite different from yours.

Father JP: BillyLu, I could never feel exactly like you do. But nor have I felt like so many others who I try to understand, encourage, and guide. For example, I have never felt so angry that I could kill someone. If I did, would that make it right? We may not control our feelings but we are responsible for controlling our behavior. That is the real point the Church is trying to make.

CHAPTER 4

"But God Made Me This Way"

The pizza came, which briefly distracted the conversation. As each commented on the platters, it allowed people to catch their breath and digest the conversation that had just ended. It wasn't long, however, before BillyLu restarted the conversation.

BillyLu: How can homosexuality be a sin? Sin is something you choose.

Jeremy: Yeah, one doesn't choose to be straight, gay, lesbian, or bi-sexual. It's just who we are. So, it can't be a sin.

BillyLu: I'm not surprised that the Church condemns homosexuality, since the Church has been condemning all forms of sexuality, except to produce babies in marriage. The Church condemns sex before marriage—but that's not biblical. The Church condemns masturbation, petting, passionate kissing, and living with someone before marriage—all of this is not biblical. The Church even condemns birth control in marriage—tell me where that is in the Bible!

Jeremy: What the Church is really saying is that sex is evil.

Everything that makes one fulfilled by giving us pleasure is of Satan. But God created sex, so sex must be good. Anyone who condemns others for their sexuality is condemning God.

BillyLu: All this Catholic guilt just makes me sick. It's such BS. It's totally obvious that the Catholic Church is just trying to lay all that stupid, homosexual guilt on us, to make us feel like dirt, to humiliate us. It's all a way to control us and make us behave the way the Church wants. I can't buy into that. God made me this way and that's the way I'm going to stay.

Jeremy: I couldn't agree more with BillyLu. God made me this way so why should I change?

Father JP just let the others get everything out and waited for a proper opening.

Father JP: Before going on, we need to keep something very clear: Christians believe that God created sex as something very good, rather, that God made it sacred. We do not condemn sex outside of marriage because sex is evil; but that the sexual union is meant to reflect something very sacred, the committed and unconditional love between a man and woman, and the eternal, unlimited, and unconditional love that the Father has for the Son, that the Son has for the Father, and is personified in the Holy Spirit.

Regarding whether the Bible condemns premarital or extra-marital sex, pornography, masturbation, petting, passionate kissing, and birth control, I suggest you read Matthew 5:27-32, Romans 1:24-32; 1 Corinthians 5:1-2; 6:9-20; Galatians 5:19-21; Ephesians 5:3-10; Titus 2:5-6. I just can't make sense of these passages without seeing a consistent sexual ethic.

Sam: What if God made certain individuals with this natural inclination to have sexual relations with someone of the same sex, wouldn't it be wrong to go against that inclination? I can see it doing a lot of damage, especially if one got married, had children, only to divorce and seek one's natural fulfillment.

BillyLu: Although it wasn't something easy for my kids at first, they certainly have adjusted well to my situation. But if I had to do it all over again, I would never have married my husband.

The "Science" of Homosexuality

Father JP: Do you really think that God made you that way?

Jeremy: Of course!

Father JP: Why?

Jeremy: Because there has never been a moment that I can remember that I wasn't gay. I have always felt different, like I didn't fit in among the other boys. Besides, all the research shows that there is a gay gene.

Father JP: What research?

Sam: C'mon JP, don't you read the paper? There have been a number of studies.

Jeremy: For example, a study of identical male twins showed that 100% of the homosexual males had a homosexual twin.

Father JP: Jeremy, that study was done in 1952 by Kallman* and was discredited for how he recruited the 37 twins in the study. A more recent study by Bailey, Dunne, and Martin used

---

* Cited references can be found in the endnotes.

a larger sample size of 4,901 twins taken from the Australian twin registry that guaranteed the study's neutrality. Of the 4,901 pairs, 113 pairs had at least one who was considered psychologically homosexual, 49 identical (monozygotic) twins and 64 non-genetic (dizygotic) twins. Of the 49 identical (monozygotic) twins only 6 (or 12%) of these sibling pairs were both homosexual; of the 64 non-genetic (dizygotic) twins, only 5 (or 8%) of these sibling pairs were both homosexual.

Certainly we don't find the perfect 100% correlation that Kallman reported for genetic twins and there is little difference in the correlation between genetic twins and between non-genetic twins: both genetic and non-genetic twins had a 10 (plus or minus 2) percent likelihood of both siblings being homosexual if one was.

Perhaps there is some genetic influence, but that genetic influence is minor compared to the physical necessity we see with biological gender, eye color, skin tone, hair color, etc. The researchers themselves concluded that subjective and environmental factors must play a role in the homosexual outcome of an individual.

BillyLu: But what about all the scientific work discovering the "gay" gene that has been making press?

Father JP: We need to be careful about so-called scientific studies that we read about in the paper. Much of the work is very preliminary, often done just by one group. For a result to be scientific it must be reproducible.

For example, in 1989, Stanley Pons and Martin Fleischmann announced they had achieved cold fusion with a simple tabletop device. The press published this as a scientific milestone and the solution for cheap and environmentally friendly energy. The only problem was that no other team of scientists could duplicate their findings, and the scientific community discredited their conclusions.

Many of the studies hinting at the possibility of a "gay" gene have not been reproducible by other groups or are based on insufficient evidence. For example, a research project that began in 1993 by Dr. Dean Hamer and others found that many gay men shared a common genetic marker on the X chromosome. Fifteen years later they still have not found the heralded "gay" gene. On the contrary, the journal *Science* reported the results of the research of Rice, Anderson, Risch, and Ebers, who looked at four distinct chromosomal markers in the same genetic region of the X chromosome and found no relationship to homosexual orientation in the 52 gay sibling pairs they studied, thus discrediting Hamer's research.

IS IT A SIN TO BE BORN GAY?

Sam: But why do so many people make a big deal about the genetic link to homosexuality?

Jeremy: Well, because if homosexuality is genetic, then we are not responsible for this condition. If some of us are simply "made" homosexual, then we should have a right to act on those inclinations.

Father JP: But, Jeremy, would you say the same thing about alcoholism? Similar research is being conducted on alcoholism. Similar twin studies have been done and correlations between racial genetics and the frequency of alcoholic tendencies and behaviors have been made.

Although there indeed may be genetic factors involved in alcoholism, we still hold people responsible if they drive under the influence or if their drinking affects their family life.

BillyLu: But is it a sin just to be born this way? Whether or not it is genetic, I just know God made me this way.

Father JP: It is never a sin to be born any which way. You,

Jeremy, and each one of us are loved by God just the way we are. But God calls us to take dominion over our lives, to make choices, to strive to become people who no longer live for themselves but for him and for others.

Besides, each of us has certain weaknesses that dispose us to certain kinds of sin. For some, it may be an alcoholic tendency; for another it may be a quick temper; for still another it may be sensuality. Yet all of us are called to take responsibility for our lives and live in a way that respects others and that builds up society, not harm it.

Margie: Why do all gays and lesbians say they didn't choose their orientation and were born that way?

Father JP: That's not true, some indeed admit they had a choice in the matter. Chapman and Brannock surveyed lesbians in 1987 and found 63% of them admitted choosing their life-style, 11% were not sure, and 28% felt they had not chosen it. So, at least some do admit choosing that way of life. Other studies show that most adolescents having homosexual inclinations will lose that same-sex tendency by age of 25.

Whether or not it was chosen and whether or not it persists, God loves us into existence and confers certain gifts and tendencies on us at birth. Other tendencies we acquire by the way we are raised and by unique experiences we go through, including traumatic experiences. Some of those tendencies will wane as years go by. All of this is part of our personal make-up.

Jeremy: I've heard that some "straight" parents want to find the gay gene so they can do genetic screening like they do for Down Syndrome. Then they would abort the gay fetus before it was born.

Margie: That's horrendous!

BillyLu: Horrendous? No, it's downright criminal and evil, something you'd expect from a Nazi eugenics program. It just goes to show how "straight" parents have more fear over the idea of their children turning out gay or lesbian than the possibility of their children having a physical illness or birth defect.

Father JP: In fact, frequently those striving to discover the biological basis for homosexuality do so because they see homosexual inclinations as abnormal.

Sam: But for those for whom it is not a choice, why don't you Christians just leave them alone.

Father JP: Christianity is about helping people achieve the freedom to make responsible choices and to be able to choose to enter into a relationship with Christ. We cannot force anyone to make responsible choices or to believe in Jesus Christ, but we try to teach and encourage them to do so. We especially try to teach them how their choices impact their relationship with God, with others, and their eternal happiness.

An alcoholic—the person who is addicted to his drink—is not truly free not to drink and thus is not free to really love his family. As Christians we don't "leave them alone" because their choice often impacts others, such as spouses, children, and others. Escaping into an alcoholic stupor isolates them from God and loved-ones. Challenging them to control their drinking and renew their relationships—often by asking for pardon—gives them the freedom to live for others.

Likewise, the porn addict is not free to love. Selfish sexual gratification keeps him from truly giving himself to another. Often the porn addict is full of shame and thus hides this addiction from those he ought to love, thus he is unable to enter into true intimacy with the person he should love.

When it comes to gay men and lesbians, typically they are more promiscuous—more likely to be addicted to sex—and thus less free to love, make commitments, and enter into lasting relationships.

BillyLu: Come on, JP, gays and lesbians are not any different in sexual promiscuity. Sure, some are bad, but so are many heterosexuals.

WHAT SCIENCE SHOWS

Father JP: Again, even though one's experience may not reveal any difference, the studies show that there is. A pre-HIV/AIDS study done in 1978 found that 75 percent of white, gay males claimed to have had more than 100 lifetime male sex partners. Of those 75 percent with more than 100 lifetime sex partners, 28 percent claimed more than 1,000 lifetime partners, 22 percent claimed to have had 250-1000 partners and 15 percent between 100-250 sex partners. Perhaps since the HIV/AIDS scare promiscuity declined, but with new treatment for HIV the experts say that promiscuity is returning to those levels again.

BillyLu: But that study is old and with gay men. It doesn't apply to lesbians.

Father JP: Although lesbian relationships tend to be more stable than those between gay men, an Australian study published in the year 2000 found that 93 percent of lesbians reported having had sex also with men, and were 4.5 times more likely than heterosexual women to have had more than 50 lifetime sex partners.

Sam: If this were all true, JP, then you would expect that gays and lesbians would contract more sexually transmitted diseases, have more health problems, and live a significantly shorter life.

Father JP: Sam, that is precisely what the scientific data shows.

A Canadian study showed that gay men had a life expectancy shorter than the general male population by between 8 and 20 years. And, according to the Center for Disease Control, homosexually active men are one thousand times more likely to contract HIV than those who are not. Compare this to cigarette smokers whose life expectancy is 13.5 years shorter than the general population.

BillyLu: Oh, I hate smokers. They deserve it.

Margie: I hate it when people smoke, too. But you don't really think we should wish them to have a shorter life, do you BillyLu?

BillyLu: BillyLu: Well, no… but smokers choose to smoke and it hurts other people as well as themselves. I don't really wish them a shorter life, but they know what they're getting into, so they should not be surprised at the consequences, it's their funeral. Now I'm sure you think the same about us homosexuals, don't you, JP?

Father JP: No I don't, and you shouldn't either. We need to love and care for a smoker, and if we did, then we would try to motivate that smoker to quit. But we can never force them, but must respect their freedom. We cannot make our love for them conditioned on them doing what we want, even if that change of behavior will help them live longer.

I care for you and hope you live a very long life. More importantly, I hope you live an eternal life. That is why I tell you these things so that you make good life-choices with the full freedom of love.

Margie: If all these things about health and longevity of homosexuals are true, then why isn't this information in the newspapers?

Father JP: Perhaps because the newspapers don't think people want to hear it; perhaps because they are afraid of being attacked by the gay-activists for fostering…

Sam: Perhaps it is simply that the media has a liberal bias.

BillyLu: Back off you guys… You know, it's attitudes like that that really piss me off… The media is simply reporting the facts. It certainly has no interest in blaming gays and lesbians for all the problems of society, like you guys are.

You really don't know how much we suffer… I'm just sick and tired of all this conservative, hate-filled BS…

Father JP looked at BillyLu for a moment without saying a thing. He mulled over how to communicate to her that he did understand and care, knowing that his words would not do it.

Jeremy: Do you really care how much we suffer, JP? Do you realize what it's like to experience the humiliations we experience, the name calling, and the discrimination, simply because we are a little different and have feelings for people of the same sex?

What you're doing is just using the scientific data to manipulate us by making us feel guilty for all our problems. I resent the Catholic Church for always trying to put us on a guilt trip.

Father JP: This is not about guilt, but about truly caring about you. The last thing in the world I would want is to manipulate you.

I do care and so does the Church. There are many Catholic institutions that are offering free or low-cost medical attention for persons with AIDS. Often the Church is reaching out to them when these persons are in the last months and days of their lives, abandoned by their families and friends, suffering in a very horrible physical state. Often these are heroic caregivers—I think of Mother Teresa's nuns in San Francisco and New York—look after AIDS pa-

then it is highly suspect.

It is interesting to note that it is not Christians who are seeking to get science to back up its position on homosexuality. We find the gay and lesbian activists trying to get science to find some evidence that same-sex attraction is biological and genetic. Christians never claim that a genetic influence would make any difference on the morality of sexual activity. If genetics makes some people more passionate than others, or if it makes some people's libido more sensitive than others, the immorality of sex outside of marriage remains true for them too, although it may be more difficult for them to live.

Yet, we do appreciate good science. Knowledge brings with it a greater freedom; the more you know the more you can take responsibility for all the consequences of your actions. Christians favor good, objective, and unbiased science. It will help us make better choices.

CHAPTER 5

Civil Rights

The conversation continued, but Jeremy was tired of all the statistics and so-called scientific studies. So he changed the topic.

Jeremy: JP, you make the case that it is unhealthy for us to be queers and lesbies. I don't know where you get your data, but what if we had a vaccine for HIV and the other medical ills you say plague our community? Would you then leave us alone?

Father JP: Jeremy, I'm not here to persecute you, although you may feel as though I am by some of the things I've said. My sincere desire is to have a healthy dialogue and exchange of ideas. I hope you would agree that that is what we have been having, even though we don't agree on everything.

But you do bring up a good point. Longevity and health are not the real issues. What is, is God's plan for creation and for each one of us.

Jeremy: Well...? Doesn't God reveal to us his plan through what makes us happy?

Father JP: God reveals his plan to us in many ways. One

is through his revealed Word. Another is through his creation, which is an expression of his Word:

> For what can be known about God is plain to them, because God has shown it to [men who suppress the truth]. Ever since the creation of the world his invisible nature, namely, his eternal power and deity, has been clearly perceived in the things that have been made. So they are without excuse (Romans 1:19-20).

God reveals his plan by what makes us *truly* happy, by what gives us peace, security, healthy relationships, fruitfulness, and freedom, as opposed to what makes us unhappy, fearful, selfish, proud, etc.

Are Homo- and Hetero-Sexual Relationships the Same?

BillyLu: Well, JP, homosexual relationships make some of us happy. Everybody knows that falling in love and expressing that romantic love in a sexual relationship with that special someone is one of the most sublime and uplifting human experiences in life. To deny that opportunity to us is a crime against humanity because it denies us the right to pursue our true happiness.

Father JP: One of the last things in the world that I would ever do, BillyLu, is to try to deny you the right to seek happiness and fulfillment in your life.

I am just trying to explain what God has revealed, both by his Word and through his creation, so that you can consider these things in the choices you make in living your life. I cannot stop you from living with your partner and will not attempt to break it off — only you can do that by a free choice on your part. If you do it, I hope it will be in pursuit of true happiness and not because I or anyone else has manipulated you to make that decision.

Sam: But BillyLu simply wants to be happy, and sex is part of most people's idea of happiness. Isn't being in a same-sex relationship the same as being in a heterosexual relationship, as long as both are loving, committed, and lifelong?

Father JP: It is understandable why those in gay and lesbian relationships want us to consider their relationship on the same plane as others. They long to have the same kind of intimacy and closeness they see in these other relationships. But are they really the same? Can you really compare the two?

Is having a close relationship to a brother exactly the same as having a close relationship to a sister? Is having a close relationship to an aunt exactly the same as having a close relationship to an uncle? What about grandfather and grandmother? Mother and father? Son and daughter? Is having a close friend who is a guy the same as having a close friend who is a girl?

Margie: No, no, and no. These relationship pairs have similarities, but each one is very distinct. That is so obvious.

Father JP: Well, the problem is that it doesn't seem to be obvious to everyone, right, Sam?

But why would we want to compare a marriage of husband and wife, a mother and father, with a homosexual pair? It simply is different, even though the homosexual pair may *long* for their relationship to be the same.

Jeremy: Yet, we too can have a deep and intimate bond that is as emotionally strong as any heterosexual couple.

Father JP: But is it the same? Doesn't a marital relationship differ from a deep and intimate father-son or mother-daughter relationship?

Homo- and Hetero-Sexual Sex

Jeremy: Well yes, but we homosexuals also express this emotional relationship through sex, just as the married couple does.

Father JP: But others may wish to express their emotional relationship in an extra-marital sexual affair, or an "intimate" one-night stand, or with an anonymous prostitute? That doesn't mean that these expressions are the same as one in a marital relationship.

Jeremy: What if we have a committed homosexual relationship?

Father JP: But is it really the same?

Jeremy: Why should it be different? Our sexual experience is just as intense and intimate.

Father JP: Let's think things through; even the sexual activity is different. The act itself communicates entirely different messages.

Sam: How so?

Margie: Look, Sam, it is so simple: gay and lesbian sex can't produce babies, only heterosexual sex can. Even animals "know" that sex is for reproduction.

Jeremy: Although most animals may not have sex when they are infertile, we human beings do. This argument is pretty silly. Think of the consequences, Margie.

Are you saying that post-menopausal or infertile or "fixed" couples shouldn't have sex? Do you really mean to imply that sex that cannot conceive is bad and that the ability to conceive is necessary to validate married sex? If so then there are a lot of evil people having sex who shouldn't be.

Your argument that "sex is for reproduction" is either ridiculously illogical or you are imposing on the rest of us another hypocritical double standard.

Sam: Don't speak that way to my girlfriend, Jeremy, she deserves respect.

BillyLu: But, there is a double standard, Sam. Jeremy maybe saying things a bit too bluntly and insensitively, but he is just being logical. Either there is a double standard, or you have to declare *evil* all sex that is unable to conceive.

Father JP: We do believe, BillyLu, that the sexual union of a man and woman in marriage is more than about producing babies—it is good whether or not conception ever takes place, even if conception is physically impossible. However, let's face the facts: homosexual activity can never generate new life, no matter how intense the experience may be. So, it is not the same as the marital union.

But there's more to it than that. There are other reasons why homosexual sex is not the same as sex between married spouses, these other reasons have to do with the one-flesh union willed by God in Genesis.

For example, when a husband and wife become physically intimate, there is a face-to-face physical complementarity that makes it a truly human and communal experience, that is, a *one-flesh* experience. Their physical communion of bodies express a spiritual communion of persons through mutual, total, and simultaneous self-giving that should reflect, communicate, and deepen a spiritual communion of persons.

Jeremy: But the same happens with gay sex.

Father JP: No. In homosexual sex-acts, there is a series of sequential events, not one unifying event. In homosexual sex the first individual arouses the second, which is usually followed by the second arousing the first; or it happens that the first individual uses the second and then the second uses the first.

So, homosexual sex entails a series of acts isolated from each other, and with each act there is a de-humanizing experience of "being used" or of "using" the other for his or her own physical and emotional gratification.

These homosexual acts communicate a kind of mutual isolation and objectification. The mutual self-giving of marital intimacy is replaced by a mutual "being used by another."

Sam: But isn't it also true that some heterosexual and even married couples "use" their partner for gratification?

Father JP: There is no question that it happens. Any couple that physically expresses the total gift of self in intercourse while lacking the total spiritual self-giving found in an exclusive, lifelong marital commitment is using the other. They may gratify each other without true spiritual union, without the commitment, or without truly giving themselves totally and unconditionally — as with extra-marital sex.

But this is not what we call "love," the kind of *communion of persons* expressed in the complete and simultaneous spousal union of bodies — thus the two become one flesh (Genesis 2:24; Matthew 19:5).

The marital sexual union is truly *one-flesh* even when a couple is unable to conceive, because the simultaneous and complete union of bodies reflects the simultaneous complete spiritual union of persons that God has united and embodied in this act. This *one-flesh* act may indeed be *embodied* in the conception of a new human being, something homosexual couples will never see.

Sam: Wow! Now that you say it, I see how it fits what you explained to Margie and me a few months back. It makes sense and fits the "logic of love" you described to us.

Margie: You're right, Sam! How beautifully it fits into the definition and meaning of love.

Father JP: Jeremy and BillyLu, as I explained to Sam and Margie, love is a union of wills, of spirits, expressed through a union of bodies, such as holding hands, a hug, or a kiss. The sexual union is the most complete and total union of bodies, which ought to express a complete and total union of wills.

Margie: And it is a lie when the complete union of bodies occurs without a total union of spirits, as with uncommitted sex.

Sam: You mean unmarried sex, Margie. Remember how JP even told us that the partial commitments of engaged couples is not "totally" total, and thus even sexual acts by engaged couples are a lie.

Father JP: You see, many people long for intimacy and closeness; our society tells us that sex will satisfy that longing, but of itself sex never does. As Margie and Sam know, the sexual union is meant to express and deepen an already meaningful relationship and communion of persons based on a total gift of self. They also know that sexual acts can also be misused for selfish physical gratification or for filling an emotional hole or void.

Men and women often have sexual affairs and single people have uncommitted sex, because they feel lonely and find this *temporary* relationship satisfies their emotional "need" or hole. But in these cases the other person's body is on loan—it is replaceable, even disposable. In a true marriage, the irrevocable covenant make each other's body irreplaceable; the two bodies have become one, precisely what their conjugal union expresses.

Margie: Personally, I've come to understand that engaging in sexual acts before marriage does a tremendous disservice to the individual. Not only physically, but to their emotional wellbeing as well. My own past mistakes, even though I didn't go "all the way," taught me that. As I told Sam and Father JP, I thought that by engaging in passionate kissing and other passionate acts that did not go "all the way," that I would be closer to my boyfriend. Instead, it just produced the opposite reaction. I ended up feeling more insecure, empty, and emotionally needy. I began to become more possessive of my boyfriend and to isolate myself from my other friends. It was unhealthy for me and caused our breakup to hurt all the more. I was not free in that relationship.

Father JP: Because you were treated as an object…

Margie: And I must admit that I also treated him as an object, one I was trying to possess…

BillyLu: My God, are you guys for real? What kind of planet are you all from? Who in hell cares how unified or sequential sex is? That is pretty absurd! What matters is the love you have in your heart. You can't use another person if you love them. Why would the Church want to control such private matters as these?

Father JP: The Church doesn't go into details about how married couples show their affection and love during intercourse. The only thing the Church is concerned about is that their sexuality is treated as sacred; thus she condemns those forms of sexual stimulation that opposes human dignity, such as found in homosexual sex acts.

But there is something special, even "mystically" different, and seemingly more human about the face-to-face complementarity that unites man and woman. What the Church does say is:

The complementarity of man and woman as male and female is inherent within God's creative design. Precisely because man and woman are different, yet complementary, they come together in a union that is open to the possibility of new life.

Sex between males or between females lacks this complementarity; it fails to affirm the goodness and beauty of either femininity or masculinity, but exalts one with the exclusion of the other. This, according to the Russian philosopher, Nicholas Berdyaev, leads to profound loneliness because in the inner core of our being we "know" that a man or a woman biologically is not completely human: each of us lacks either the masculine or the feminine qualities and virtues to make us whole and fully human. This was Adam's experience before God created Eve (Genesis 2:18-23).

BillyLu: You say that the Church doesn't try to control the details of what happens in the marriage bed, but it does! It even tells married couples they cannot use birth control and oral sex.

Wow, you Catholics want to control absolutely everything, even a person's bedroom. Tyranny in all forms! How can you buy this BS?

Father JP: BillyLu, please. The Church really has no interest in controlling people's bedrooms. This is about personal freedom. However, if people choose to do immoral things—whether in their bedrooms or in public—the Church will declare those disordered acts, sins, and even crimes.

Let me give you an example. If a person committed child abuse or viewed child pornography in the privacy of their bedroom, would it cease to be wrong?

BillyLu: No, of course not.

Father JP: What about sadomasochistic sexual practices with a willing accomplice—whether male or female? Or what about sexual orgies between a married couple and their children?

Sam: Oh, man, that is really "sick."

Father JP: So, the Church has a right to declare such things "sick" or sinful because those actions treat another person as an object to be used for one's own selfish gratification.

Sam: Like contraception, right JP?

Father JP: You remembered!

Sam: How can I forget?

Father JP: And contraception is wrong for the same reason same-sex as homosexual acts are wrong: both fail to express the full meaning of love, with its total, unconditional, and exclusive gift of self. Birth control puts a condition on love: "I'll give myself totally, unconditionally, and exclusively to you… with the exception of my fertility. And I'll accept you totally, unconditionally, and exclusively… with the exception of your fertility." That's putting conditions on unconditional love—a contradiction!

Ultimately, both contraception and homosexual acts are anti-love; in addition, contraception is anti-life.

Sam: Is gay sex really the same as contraception? As long as they don't put any barrier between them, then are they not giving themselves completely to each other?

Jeremy: But without the barrier, it wouldn't be safe.

Father JP: With or without the barrier, there is no mutual gift of self; there is no complementarity; there is not mutual acceptance of the other's self-gift. In homosexual sex there is no "I give myself and my masculinity to you while accepting you and your femininity; doing so with totality in each." Likewise, there is no simultaneous "I accept you and your masculinity while giving you myself and my femininity; doing so with totality in each;" doing so while respecting the complementary equality of masculinity and femininity. In this way a married couple speaks the language of total self-giving.

No, rather, one person uses the other as an object and then lets himself be used as an object.

THEN WHY CAN'T HOMOSEXUALS MARRY?

Jeremy: You say that those acts are good and holy if they are in the right and proper place: marriage. Then why won't you just let us legitimize our relationship in marriage? That's what we want most anyway! Then the beauty and holiness of marriage would tell the world that sex itself is a very beautiful and holy activity, and that it belongs to marriage.

Father JP: Jeremy, marriage is a beautiful and holy thing. I can see how you, BillyLu, and others with homosexual inclinations would long for the intimacy and permanence that marriage represents. I can see how you would want God to bless your relationship so that he would become part of that relationship in every aspect and dimension.

But it doesn't matter so much what you want or what the world thinks but what God wants and thinks. We cannot use marriage to legitimize our actions. If a man marries a woman just to use her as a sex-slave for his gratification—even if she willingly agrees, perhaps to leave behind desolate poverty—it still would not make that activity moral, holy, or beautiful.

BillyLu: In America, we believe each and every person has a right to life, liberty, and the pursuit of happiness. I feel like I am being denied a right to pursue happiness by not being able to marry the person I love. I find it even more objectionable to be denied this right than to be denied a vote in political elections. The right to marry whomever one chooses is essential to the right to pursue happiness, so how can it be denied to a special group like us?

Margie: I know that I would find it objectionable not to have the right to choose whom I wish to marry.

Margie looks towards Sam.

Father JP: But we are not saying that you do not have a right to choose whom to marry, but how marriage is to be defined. I don't mean to be insensitive, but if someone chose to marry his dog or horse, would we have to go along with that?

Sam: But a horse cannot sign a marriage license nor does it have legal standing.

Father JP: True. But the point is how God defines marriage.

Instead, we could consider those who want marriage to include multiple partners, say that someone wanted to marry two people simultaneously, perhaps he is bisexual and wants to be married to both a man and a woman. Should we be forced to adopt that as marriage just because he thinks that it will make him happy?

Let's look at reality: in our day non-married couples—whether heterosexual or homosexual—are not denied the ability to live together, to engage in sexual activity, share economic resources, to maintain custody of children, etc.

One of the very few things unique to marriage is that it is blessed by God to reflect his love for his people and his people's for him. I can't think of any rights or actions that are denied non-married couples.

BillyLu: But other Christian churches and Jewish synagogues are performing same-sex marriages. Why not the Catholic Church?

Father JP: BillyLu, many Protestant and Jewish congregations still refuse to perform such ceremonies. But even if they did, or use grape juice instead of wine in the Eucharist, rose petals instead of water for baptism, that doesn't make it right. Some religions also allow polygamy or orgy-like satanic sex rites. Should we do something just because others are doing it?

We would never perform same-sex marriages just because everyone else is doing it. Marriage must reflect what we believe about God, Church, family, sex, and sacraments. For us, marriage is sacred, it is a sacrament closely linked to the Eucharist. It was ordained by God to be between one man and one woman as a sign and sacrament of God's relationship with his people. Thus we have no power to change it.

Jeremy: And so you don't allow us to take Communion, then?

Father JP: We don't allow anyone conscious of serious sin to receive Holy Communion. So, if a man is having sex with his girlfriend or if a wife is contracepting, neither can receive Communion until they change their heart and receive sacramental absolution.

Similarly, there are those Catholics who divorced from a legitimate marriage and later remarried outside the Church. Since their current relationship does not reflect the pure, faithful, and virginal love of Christ for his Church that is expressed in receiving Holy Communion, they too are unable to receive.

In fact, listen to how Pope Benedict speaks about Communion and those remarried outside the Church:

> The Synod of Bishops confirmed the Church's practice, based on Sacred Scripture (cf. Mark 10:2-12), of not admitting the divorced and remarried to the sacraments, since their state and their condition of life objectively contradict the loving union of Christ and the Church signified and made present in the Eucharist. Yet the divorced and remarried continue to belong to the Church, which accompanies them with

special concern and encourages them to live as fully as possible the Christian life through regular participation at Mass, albeit without receiving communion, listening to the word of God, eucharistic adoration, prayer, participation in the life of the community, honest dialogue with a priest or spiritual director, dedication to the life of charity, works of penance, and commitment to the education of their children.

Margie: So, the Church continues to provide all kinds of spiritual, emotional, and community support to those who remarry outside the Church, even though they cannot receive Communion. I imagine the same is true with people in active homosexual relationships, is that correct Father?

Father JP: That's right.

Margie: But can they ever receive Communion?

Father JP: Sure, Margie, just like the persons who have remarried outside the Church. They must promise to remain chaste—celibate—to live as brother and sister and avoid scandal.

So, if someone with same-sex attraction struggles to live a chaste life and is not engaging in sexual acts outside of marriage—or any other serious sin—then he can receive Communion. Such a person is a believer, and is struggling to live out God's plan for holiness. The same would be true for a porn-addict who struggles not to give in to his addiction.

Sam: I'm not too concerned about Communion, but I don't think it's fair to put gay "marriage" in the same category as satanic sex rites or polygamy.

Father JP: You're right, Sam, they are not the same. No, I didn't intend to make them equivalent, but only to show that just because some people perform a particular ceremony and recognize a particular union, doesn't mean everyone else should do so.

Sam: But wouldn't it just be simpler if we allowed those with homosexual attraction to get married? This way they will then be happy since we give them what they want and then they will leave us alone to be able to live our lives the way we want.

Father JP: That is a very utilitarian approach to the issue. It seems to me that what you are trying to do is minimize your own suffering or inconvenience by giving a group what they want, whether or not it really benefits them.

Suppose we had the same attitude toward the homeless, those street-people begging for money on the sidewalk. Many are just begging in order to buy drugs or alcohol. If the city were to initiate a program to set up a center far from the city, offering to give the homeless who would go there free drugs and alcohol—thus getting them off the street—would you support such a program, Sam?

Sam: No, of course not.

Margie: You wouldn't really be solving the homeless problem, just by getting the homeless off the streets. No, you would only be giving in to their addiction.

Father JP: And you wouldn't be treating them as human persons, even though you are giving them what they want.

The same is true with those with homosexual inclinations. They need our love, our compassion, our understanding, not our sanction of their sexual activity. If they want our help, we should be ready to make the sacrifices to meet their real needs.

Equal Rights or Catholic Prejudice

Jeremy: But homosexuals are not given equal rights in our society. Not only are our committed unions not recognized but we can't even show affection in public. If we do, we are made fun of and humiliated. Some have even been victims of hate crimes and murdered, simply because they were holding hands, gave another man a kiss on the cheek or a manly hug, etc. Only heterosexual couples can do so in public.

Father JP: Well, I think the problem is that we have sexualized so many ordinary signs of affection that many people overreact. Of course, it is offensive when we see people pawing each other—whatever their orientation—making out in public, or showing various lewd public behavior. This is inappropriate regardless of sexual orientation.

BillyLu: But all we want is the same protection of the law so that no one will fire us from our job because of our sexual orientation: protection from being harassed, taunted, beaten, murdered.

Margie: I want that too! Doesn't that seem reasonable, Father?

Father JP: Of course it is reasonable. The Catholic Church concurs. Margie, would you mind if I asked you again to read to us a point from the *Catechism?*

Margie: No problem, Father, I will gladly do so. Here we go...:

> The number of men and women who have deep-seated homosexual tendencies is not negligible... [which] constitutes for most of them a trial. They must be accepted with respect, compassion, and sensitivity. Every sign of unjust discrimination in their regard should be avoided. These persons are called to fulfill God's will in their lives and, if they are Christians, to unite to the sacrifice of the Lord's Cross the

difficulties they may encounter from their condition (CCC 2358).

Father JP: So, we see that the Catholic Church condemns unjust treatment and discrimination. It would be a serious sin if a person were to commit a serious injustice or discriminatory act against a homosexual person.

Sam: That's actually quite reassuring. Most people think that the Catholic Church is homophobic and discriminating against the gay and lesbian elements.

Father JP: One of the most oft-repeated commands in the Bible is, "Do not be afraid." If we were homophobic, afraid of homosexual persons, we would not be Christians.

BillyLu: But I've heard that a Catholic school fired a lesbian teacher simply because she was living with another woman.

Father JP: BillyLu, I can see how you might perceive that as unjust prejudice and denial of her rights. But we need to look at this from both sides. The employee—the teacher in this case—also has to respect the employer's reasonable demands and expectations based on its duties to others. In this case, the Catholic school has to answer to others beside itself, including the students, the parents, and the Church. They expect the school to present authentic Catholic teaching to its pupils.

BillyLu: But the teacher wasn't forcing lesbianism on the pupils or teaching anything against Catholicism.

Father JP: But parents and kids found out. When the information becomes public, then it impacts everybody, especially a community to which parents entrust their children, such as schools, athletic clubs, etc.

When parents send their children to a Catholic school they expect the principal, teachers, and staff to transmit to their children the authentic Catholic teaching, by their example and by their instruction. So, a teacher signs a contract that they are living in conformity with Catholic teaching. But the teacher breaks this contract by openly living the gay life-style, by openly living with her boyfriend, or by getting pregnant out of wedlock.

A large part of a Catholic teacher's job is his or her life-witness and the positive influence it makes on these young minds and hearts. If an individual can no longer fulfill this mission that they have voluntarily taken on, then he or she may be asked to leave.

BillyLu: So, if one keeps one's personal life hidden, then it would be OK to be a lesbian and teach at a Catholic school. So, the Catholic Church encourages people to live a double life; what is important is to *appear* to be a good and holy Catholic.

Father JP: BillyLu, appearances should reflect reality. The reality that a Catholic school expects of its teachers to reflect is that they are struggling to live in conformity with Catholic teaching. I know many teachers who have struggled to keep their hearts and minds pure—both from inappropriate same-sex and opposite-sex desires and actions—and to avoid occasions of sin.

If reality becomes public which shows some activity or attitude contrary to Catholic teaching—such as finding pornography on a teacher's computer—then the teacher will be asked to seek other employment.

Sam: Then would it ever be OK to deny homosexual persons certain rights?

Father JP: No. But it is important to make this distinction clear: although everyone has a right to work, no one has an absolute right to a particular job. Employment works by joint assent of employer and employee based on the employer's needs and expectations and on what the potential employee can offer. No potential employee can say to an employer: "I have a right to be employed and paid by you."

Thus "the Church has a right to deny roles of service to those whose behavior violates her teaching. Such service may seem to condone an immoral life-style and may even be an occasion of scandal."

An obvious example of this would be an avowed atheist: such a person does not have a right to teach religion or theology in a Catholic school.

Jeremy: But all I want is the protection of the law. In many states it is legal to fire me from my job simply because of my sexual orientation. That is not right.

Father JP: It would be wrong to fire anyone from a job simply because the employer doesn't like the race or private inclinations of an individual. That is respected everywhere. Some states have also made it explicit that discrimination cannot be made based on sexual orientation.

One should note, however, that sexual orientation is not like race. You cannot keep your race private, in the interior of your heart. Homosexual orientation is only known if it is made public. Similarly, if a person has a strong inclination for the boss's wife, but keeps it to himself, he is not going to get fired. However, if he starts flirting with her in public, and manifests that inclination then the boss is within his right to ask him to leave.

Margie: Well that's obvious, Father JP.

BillyLu: What about the lack of legal protection for same-sex couples, for example, access to a spouse's medical, life, and disability insurance. There are also rights to hospital visitation and medical decision-making privileges. Heterosexual couples get survivor benefits from workers' compensation as well as spousal benefits under annuity and retirement plans. Unmarried heterosexual couples can legally marry and receive these benefits; same-sex couples cannot.

Father JP: These benefits have changed or are in the process of changing, BillyLu. In fact most if not all current insurance policies, retirement plans, and annuities today allow you to designate a beneficiary who is not your spouse. Hospitals now require you to designate the person who is to make medical decisions for you if for some reason you become incapacitated. I am not married and I have a person designated to make those decisions for me, and it is not a spouse!

ADOPTION

BillyLu: That may be all true, JP, but we still do not have the right to adopt children in most states. Although I feel no need for this, since I have my own children, some gay and lesbian couples don't have children and want to be able to adopt.

Father JP: Some gay activists want broad laws granting gays and lesbians sweeping rights that include the so-called "right" to adopt children. But that doesn't guarantee what is truly good for society as a whole or for individuals, especially the adopted child.

Jeremy: Considering the great need for a loving, caring home for so many children in need of adoption, why is the Church so against adoption by same-sex couples? Shouldn't the needs of these children be put ahead of any ideological considerations?

Father JP: It is precisely because the Church has such a concern for children that it is absolutely opposed to same-sex couples adopting children. The Church recognizes that each child needs *both* a mother and a father, not two mommies and no daddy, or two daddies and no mommy.

Granted, it may be good for a child to have other maternal influences in his life, like a live-in grandmother, a close aunt, or a nanny. Likewise, it may be good to have other paternal influences—especially when the father is absent for one reason or another—such as a grandfather, uncle, etc. But to substitute a father with a female sex-partner who acts as a child's mother, or to substitute a mother with a male sex-partner who becomes a second father is to deprive a child of its basic human needs.

Children need both a father and a mother.

Jeremy: Isn't it better that a child have some family, even if it isn't ideal in the eyes of some?

Father JP: The truth is that there are more married couples seeking to adopt than children waiting, between 1.2 and 2.7 times more married couples waiting to adopt than children needing adoption. In fact, to meet the demand, almost half of all adoptions are now of children from foreign countries.

Even though a person has good and noble desires to have a child—perhaps to fulfill some deep emotional desire for progeny—that does not give them the right to have a child. To be a good parent, it is not enough just to have good desires and be capable of being a good provider.

For example, would you consider placing a child with a couple where both parents work 60 hours a week and the child would have to be in daycare the majority of that time?

Margie: That would certainly not be in the best interest of the child. If anything, an adopted child needs more time with his mother or father than a child born to a couple so he or she can bond with his parents. If both are working 60 hours a week, that just wouldn't happen.

Father JP: But wouldn't that be unjust prejudice against couples who both work 60 hours a week, especially if they have good and noble desires to provide for that child?

Margie: No, it's that we must put the needs of a child ahead of the wishes of the couple. It should be common sense.

Father JP: It should be, and most adoptive agencies have screening criteria that favor the child's needs. For example, these agencies screen for alcohol or drug addictions, for criminal background (especially against sex offenders), for abusive households. It would also be wise to screen for those who have been divorced and remarried, since it is a sign that their family life will likely be less stable.

BillyLu: But if a gay or lesbian couple can offer a peaceful and nurturing home, if they aren't over-working, don't have addictions or criminal background, and there is no sign of abusive behavior in the household, shouldn't they be allowed to adopt?

Father JP: First, gay and lesbian couples cannot provide the complementary emotional support and attention that a mother and a father would provide. It would be either masculinely or femininely lopsided. The child needs and deserves to have both. The child needs a caring and tender mother who nurtures and encourages; a gentle but strong father who gives a sense of security, protection, and confidence. A child needs to be loved unconditionally in both a masculine and feminine way, by both a mother and a father.

Secondly, an international study done on children raised by gay and lesbian couples found a significant higher incidence of mental illness, drug use, promiscuity, and sexually transmitted diseases. Also, the study reported greater instability in these families.

Even studies carried out in the U.S. show much higher rates of spousal abuse among both lesbian and gay couples. Domestic violence is certainly not something you want to foist on adopted children no matter how difficult they are to place. Add that to the greater incidence of suicide and unhealthy risky behaviors and most people can figure out that this is a risky experiment that is unjust to those children.

BillyLu: I've seen studies showing the opposite, JP. There seems to be a consensus that a child is much more likely to be abused by a heterosexual male than by a homosexual male.

Father JP: True, BillyLu, the gross numbers of sexual abusers are heterosexual males, but that is only because there are many fewer homosexual males.

Sam: But does that mean we should classify all gays and lesbians as potential child abusers and thus say they are unfit to be parents?

Father JP: We are not saying that all gays and lesbians are potential child abusers. We are just trying to look at all the data to figure out what is best for children.

A child in a family where at least one adult is unrelated to the child is dozens of times more likely to be abused than a child living with both parents. Although that's automatic in every adoption situation, as gay or lesbian couples have higher incidents of relationship instability, "spousal" abuse, depression, drug addiction, suicide, etc., then we are severely increasing the risk to a child when such risk is not needed. Adopted and foster children need fewer problems, not more.

Finally, studies also show that homosexual couples tend to be more engrossed in their own emotional needs, so much so, that they are unable to give the adopted child the emotional attention that he or she needs. Thus, it is similar to the overworked married couple.

BillyLu: Now, you are stereotyping us as emotionally narcissistic.

Margie: That seems really harsh, Father JP—especially toward BillyLu and Jeremy. Don't you think what you just said was an overgeneralization?

Father JP: Here we ought to look at what the research has reported and assess the emotional situation of homosexual men and women.

CHAPTER 6

The Psychology of Homosexuality

The pizza ran out at this point and it was getting late. But Father JP knew they should keep going while BillyLu and Jeremy were still engaged in the conversation. Sleep could be had later.

So, they ordered another round of beverages. This time, even Margie asked for a beer.

EMOTIONAL PEACE OR TORMENT

BillyLu: Don't you understand, JP? What happens to us physically or medically is not the most important thing for us—we want peace. A smoker doesn't quit just because the Surgeon General's warning on the label tells him that it is unhealthy—I wish he would.

Peace is what we want and having a stable marriage with children is key to acquiring this peace.

Sam: It is also true that telling kids that smoking will shorten their life doesn't prevent young people from picking up the unhealthy vice.

Margie: That's a good observation, Sam, but it doesn't resolve

BillyLu's dilemma, which is true for so many others—that people engaging in homosexual behavior are less concerned about the risks than about the inner peace they yearn for.

Father JP: But all the evidence shows that those who engage in homosexual behavior don't get the peace they yearn for. This is true whether they are "married," or have adopted children, or have produced their own through artificial or "hired" insemination.

Let's look at suicide. A person who is at peace is not thinking about suicide. However, the suicide rates among active gay males in San Francisco were 3.4 times higher than among the general U.S. male population. Another study of twins found that the twin with a same-sex partner was 6.5 times more likely to attempt suicide than his co-twin without.

Margie: Ouch, Father JP! Perhaps the reason why this is so is because the gay or lesbian person is experiencing such hatred that they just cannot endure living any longer?

Father JP: Surely it is. But we need to determine what kind of hate. Is it hatred due to outside people or due to self-hatred?

This lack of peace found in active homosexual men and women shows up in other ways too. For example those in the gay and lesbian life-style are more likely to experience major depression, anxiety disorder, substance abuse, borderline personality disorder, schizophrenia, pathological narcissism, and profound loneliness.

BillyLu: But this is just the result of intense homophobia throughout our society. If you Christians would stop persecuting us, many of these problems would disappear.

Father JP: Well, that's an interesting comment, BillyLu. Are you aware that in the Netherlands almost all traces of "homophobia"

and negative associations to the gay life style have been elimi-
nated? It is the most pro-gay and pro-lesbian country in Western
Europe, probably in the world. They have been accepting so-
called gay couples in "marriages" for years.

Yet a Dutch study—using a more rigorous design to compare two groups: one which had no homosexual experience
in the 12 prior months and another group of persons who had
any homosexual contact within the previous 12 months—found
much greater incidents in homosexuals of major depression,
bipolar disorder, panic disorder, agoraphobia, and obsessive
compulsive disorder. Lesbians in this study had higher frequency
of major depression, social phobia, and alcohol dependence.

Sam: Did the research say whether the homosexuality caused
the mental health problems or whether the mental health problems were the source of the homosexuality?

BillyLu: Now you're thinking I'm a sick-o because I'm a lesbie?
Thanks, you all. I can see I'm not welcomed here.

BillyLu started to get up and walk out. But Margie stepped in…

Margie: No, BillyLu, I'm sure Sam and Father JP didn't mean it
that way. Sam can be a little insensitive at times—I know from
experience—but that's only because he is thinking—or better
said, not thinking—in the realm of objects and science, and not
the realm of people.

Sam: I'm sorry, BillyLu, I didn't mean anything personal by what
I said. It is just that science has taught us to determine what is the
cause vs. what is the effect when we make correlations.

BillyLu

Father JP: BillyLu, you don't have to answer this somewhat personal question, but were you ever abused?

BillyLu: You got to be joking! Although my partner was abused by various boyfriends of her mother—and her mother was so weak that she wouldn't do a thing about it—I do not fit your model for lesbians, do I?

No, I have never been abused. Not even remotely. I had great parents. My dad and I had a great relationship and we did a lot of fun things together. We have the same sense of humor. We did fight sometimes; once I even knocked his glasses off... but abuse? Never.

Neither did my three older brothers lay a hand on me; they wouldn't dare, not even any sign of aggression—not that they had much in them. They were a lazy bunch always hanging around the house, watching TV and doing the minimum possible. But had they tried to even hit me or push me around, my father wouldn't have put up with it, older boys picking on their little sister.

No, I was never abused.

Margie: What about your mother, what was she like?

BillyLu: My mom was great! She stayed home with us, took good care of the house, and taught us kids all kinds of things. I was not the kind of person who told her mom everything, but she was always there for me, even emotionally. My older brothers tended to tell her *everything*—they were much more like mom. As for me, I was always very different both from my brothers and from my mom. But I think that's OK—I think it is kind of stupid to think that it *caused* me to be lesbian. I mean... millions of straight women don't have mom as their best friend. Well, neither did I.

Father JP: Did your mother pamper your brothers, or play favorites?

BillyLu: You could say that... but it was more like she avoided conflict as much as she could and my brothers took advantage of that. I think I had a decent relationship with both my parents and never sensed that I was neglected.

Margie: BillyLu, didn't you miss not having a mom who was more involved and not so passive? Did you ever long to be closer and more attached to her?

BillyLu: Not really. You know, I really think that people make a much bigger deal about things that are really nothing. It's not like my mom neglected me. I didn't feel any deep, unsatisfied longing, or anything ridiculous like that. I always knew she would always be there for me, but not as my emotional alter ego. That wasn't her and that wasn't what I needed either.

Margie: Did you ever date guys, BillyLu?

BillyLu: Sure, I dated boys like everybody else. I went to parties and drank a lot, but so did everyone else. In fact I could outdrink anybody. And I had several boyfriends but never felt connected or attached to any of them. We had sex but sex with boys never satisfied me because they didn't really care about me as a person nor did I care about them, but about the sex we got. It was just a kind of drug. Although they were using me, I also knew I was using them; so there was no way we could connect.

At this point BillyLu became a bit agitated and got up from the table and began to pace back and forth. Most thought she was upset and was going to leave, but Father JP motioned to them to let her alone.

Margie: BillyLu, did you ever talk to your mom about the guys you were dating?

BillyLu: Oh, sure… I tried a few times. She taught me how not to take relationships too seriously. When I told her that a guy was interested in me, I got the same reaction as if I told her that one of my brothers had been watching TV for 10 hours straight. It just wasn't that big a deal. She wasn't excited for me nor was she too concerned.

Once I told my mom that a boy grabbed my boobs, she just shook her head and said, "boys will be boys." It was a good lesson: "Don't take it personally and you will not get hurt."

What happened to me on a date mattered little. She was always fast asleep when I came in, no matter how late it happened to be. Dad knew things could happen, so he made sure I was on the pill before I got out of junior high.

Margie: What about moments where you felt rejected by a guy, the one who didn't ask you out on a date, or who did but said something hurtful? Didn't you have moments when you wanted to run to your mother and just cry?

BillyLu: Both my parents taught me to be pretty tough, Margie. If I had such moments or feelings I just thought of how my mother would react to that situation and it helped me to move on.

Margie: BillyLu, don't take this the wrong way, but listening to you talk it seems that you were more concerned about being rejected by your mom than by any guy.

BillyLu continued her pacing, but paused before answering Margie's question. Sam had been waiting to find out more, so he intervened.

Sam: But, BillyLu, you eventually got married, right?

BillyLu gave Sam one of those you-really-don't-get-it looks, but went on to answer his question. Perhaps because it was easier than Margie's.

BillyLu: Oh sure. In my second year of college I met George, he was a senior. What a nice guy and a good Christian. He was gentle, compassionate, and very sensitive to my needs. I felt safe with George, even though I wasn't particularly attracted to him. He was short, not very athletic, but he was head-over-heels in love with me, and that made me feel special... and somewhat obligated to him. I didn't want to hurt him by saying No.

He took me to his church. I became "born again" and met all sorts of "good" Christian women. They welcomed me. Frankly, I was more attracted to them than I was to George. But I never admitted that to anyone. That simply was not an acceptable feeling. It wasn't allowed. You couldn't be "saved" and be lesbian. So I went through the motions.

Now don't think that I was being disingenuous. I really thought I had accepted Jesus fully into my life. I sincerely thought that I was a believer. I eagerly read the Bible from cover to cover. I came to know the Bible better than just about anyone and prayed with great conviction, even to the point of impressing those longstanding Christian women.

We got married right after he graduated. I went off the pill shortly afterwards because he really wanted kids. After about a year, we had a daughter and then a son. They are great. I love them dearly, as does George. In fact, I think George loves them much more than he ever loved me, but that's another story.

But more and more I couldn't take the lie. I didn't love George, I wasn't attracted to him, and he just couldn't fill my emotional needs. Sure, I went through the motions, gave George the sex he wanted, but it was as though I was trapped in this lie, just like the sex I had with boys in high school.

Margie: Is that when you met your partner?

BillyLu: I didn't think I would ever escape the pain. But one Sunday I met this very attractive woman, Leslie, at Church. She was about my age, and the moment she looked at me, I melted. I don't know what it was.

She had kids about the same age as mine, so we started

hanging out together, sometimes at her place, sometimes at mine, sometimes at the playground. The kids played and we'd talk. I felt understood and unconditionally loved.

We became emotionally close but didn't engage sexually at first. It wasn't something either she or I was looking for. It just felt so good to be held by her. I felt safe… I felt loved as I never had before.

Sam: But how is it that your husband got upset over that? It doesn't seem like something you would have to divorce over.

BillyLu: George was clueless. Although the kids were young, they knew more than he did.

All he knew was that we had a very special friendship between us, and thought the relationship was good because the kids got a lot out of spending time with another very Christian family. You see, I felt extremely guilty about my feelings for Les. She would share similar concerns; we even studied the Bible together for answers. One day she showed me St. Paul's discourse on love—I remember it by heart:

> If I speak in the tongues of men and of angels, but have not love, I am a noisy gong or a clanging cymbal. And if I have prophetic powers, and understand all mysteries and all knowledge, and if I have all faith, so as to remove mountains, but have not love, I am nothing. If I give away all I have, and if I deliver my body to be burned, but have not love, I gain nothing… So faith, hope, love abide, these three; but the greatest of these is love (1 Corinthians 13:1-4,13).

Neither of us really loved our husbands, yet God was telling us that our lives meant nothing without love.

Sometime after that George caught Les and me in bed and the marriage was over. And I am glad. We still get along fine. He's happy now with custody of the kids. I see them once a month and we are on good terms.

Things couldn't have worked out better. I can finally be me and everyone is happy.

Margie: Now you feel safe and connected whereas before you didn't.

BillyLu: That's exactly right… and I don't have to pretend anymore to be someone I'm not, or to try to satisfy someone else's sexual desires just because that's what he wants or that it is the Christian thing to do.

CHILD ABUSE

Father JP: Now you say you were not abused as a child, but Leslie was. How do you think that affects her and her relationship with you?

BillyLu: When we met, Les had already stopped having sex with her husband, and her childhood experiences of abuse provoked that. After their second child, relations with her husband started to remind her of the events of her childhood, and the dread she had of her mother's boyfriends haunted her.

As a child, Les told her mother about the abuse but she did nothing. Her mother was more afraid of losing her sex-craved man than about her daughter, Les. She has gone through hell.

Sam: How can she stand having sex with you? Doesn't that also remind her of her childhood abuse?

BillyLu: You guys are clueless. We have a relationship. She knows I care. We don't need sex. We get sexual to express the intimacy we have for each other. No one forces herself on the other.

Margie: Why should all this matter, you guys?

Father JP: I asked you, BillyLu, whether it affects Leslie and your relationship because children who were sexually abused are more likely to exhibit inappropriate sexual behaviors, both with themselves by masturbation and sexual preoccupation, and with other children with sexual aggression. Consequently, they are more likely to be depressed, have low self-esteem, and have suicidal thoughts.

Margie: But for Leslie, that was years ago.

Father JP: These childhood traumas last for years and often remain hidden until they resurface. Many men I know suffer from precisely what Sam alluded to: their wives no longer want to have sex with them because it triggers painful memories of that abuse.

BillyLu: But our relations don't trigger such pain. They seem to alleviate the pain that had been building up for so long.

Father JP: Easing the emotional pain and injury with the strong emotional experience of sex may not truly heal her, but just mask the pain instead. It would be like giving painkillers to someone with a broken arm, instead of setting the break in a caste. A person may even become addicted to the painkillers and prefer them to the cure. But is feeding such addictions truly loving and compassionate?

Margie: No, of course not.

Father JP: As you are all aware, I presume, a high percentage of both men and women with homosexual inclinations were abused as children, almost always by men. Besides those who experienced the trauma of sexual abuse, active homosexuals are much more likely to have become sexually active at a very young age, almost always without telling parents or anyone else. Thus, they develop an intense sense of shame and guilt that they keep to themselves, often times blaming themselves for what happened to them. They often reassure themselves that they are indeed guilty because they react to their abuse by acting out sexually with themselves or with younger children.

If such a person goes into a relationship with this heavy emotional burden without first finding healing, then the person doesn't have the complete freedom to make the choice in the kind of relationships that fulfill us.

Is It a Choice?

Jeremy: Are you saying I am not free to choose to enter into the relationship with my partner?

Father JP: Well, if it is genetically determined, as you and much of the gay community have implied, then how is it free? You are telling us that you are enslaved to homosexual relationships.

Margie: That sounds pretty harsh, Father JP.

Father JP: I'm sorry, I certainly don't want to be derogatory.

BillyLu: But you have been, JP! These statements are offensive and inflammatory.

Sam: BillyLu, let's be rational. JP is offensive to you if he says homosexuality is not genetic, then he is offensive if he says that homosexuality is not freely chosen, which it wouldn't be if it were genetic.

Father JP: OK, OK... let's calm down. We all need to be careful in how we express ourselves, me included. BillyLu, I apologize for not being sensitive in how I expressed myself.

There was a brief moment of silence. Father JP took a sip from his mug, and so did everyone else. It was as if each person wanted to hide and not to be the next person to speak.

Let's take a look at children who were abused and then acted out sexually. Do you think it is a freely chosen act for them to act out sexually, either with themselves or with others?

Margie: No, Father. They have been abused. Their innocence has been taken away from them. It would be the same as if you deliberately got the children drunk several times and then leave bottles of alcoholic beverages around to tempt them. It would be a compulsive, not free behavior.

Father JP: You're right, Margie. The only way that a child can freely choose not to drink would be to freely choose to remove him or herself from the house where the abuse and addictive behavior is taking place. But that is not a valid option for children. So, the child is stuck.

The child who is acting out sexually is using this behavior to deal with the stress of the abuse. It is a form of escape from the pain, guilt, and shame, which are, the vast majority of times, compulsive, and thus not freely chosen. Often such acting out produces intense interior conflict. On the one hand, the sexual ecstasy produces enormous relief and comfort—although very temporary—and on the other hand the child also experiences tremendous guilt and horror at what has just occurred. But he is not free to stop the cycle of ecstasy and self-condemnation.

Sam: How can a person reacquire the freedom that was taken away?

Father JP: Believe it or not, true Christianity tries to teach individuals not to escape, but to take responsibility for their actions and reactions; by learning to forgive the person who has harmed them in whatever way; by learning to let go of the resentment and hurt.

BillyLu: But I have not been abused or raped, JP. My freedom has not been taken away.

Father JP: BillyLu, I don't know you enough yet. But my hunch is that you have been hurt and that you have some sadness, pain, and resentment from your past that you need to forgive and let go of.

Perhaps you have felt rejected, neglected, or hurt by someone growing up; perhaps by your mother, or your brothers, or your peers. By forgiving others you will find freedom. This is the first step to healing and true freedom.

Sam: So, JP, are you saying that homosexuality is a choice or it is not a choice?

Father JP: One does not choose one's feelings—it is not a sin to feel attracted to someone who is not your spouse—but one does choose how one reacts to those feelings; that reaction can and should be a free choice. If the reaction is truly and completely compulsive, then there is no choice and there is no freedom. Young children have very little control and thus very little choice or freedom, and thus little sin.

But there are ways to control our sexuality, for example, avoid being absolutely alone with someone of the opposite sex who is not your mother, sister, or wife. If a guy chooses to go camping with his girlfriend, then he is responsible for the unavoidable, compulsive consequences that follow.

Those with homosexual inclinations perhaps exercise freedom when it comes to deciding to move in with a sexual partner or not. There is true choice in this where freedom still prevails. Once they begin to share the same apartment, the same room, the same bed… the compulsion takes over and their freedom is diminished. But they are free and responsible for the first act of moving in together.

Since children have no control over where they live, where they sleep, or who watches over them, they have little or no freedom in their sexual behavior, especially when adults or older children have preyed upon them.

Jeremy: JP, I have always been gay, since my early childhood. I can tell you that I wish my parents had told me that it was OK to be who I was. Don't you think these children would be happier if we just left them alone, let them develop their natural homosexuality without putting them on a guilt trip for masturbating or acting out in a way that doesn't meet society's definition of gender and proper gender behavior?

Father JP: Again, I must ask you Jeremy… would that truly be a loving thing to do? Do you really think they are happier when they then feel the need to commit suicide in order to find true peace?

Jeremy, we need to love each person as they are, help them to confront the source of their pain and help them find healing, help them to find freedom. Would you allow someone who had a broken leg to commit suicide simply to alleviate his or her pain?

Margie: No, that wouldn't be loving at all.

Sam: Going back to the genetics, are you saying that homosexuality is totally an emotional reaction to traumatic experiences, that there is no biological component?

Father JP: No, I'm not saying that. There may indeed be a strong but secondary biological component. The biological component is not bad genes, nor a genetic defect, nor does it have anything directly to do with the homosexual tendency as such. Rather, the genetic component is a natural orientation toward certain gifts, talents, and dispositions. This same orientation may also lean a person toward being more easily hurt emotionally.

For example, some people are biologically more emotionally sensitive than others. This greater emotional sensitivity tends to make that person more artistic and creative, giving them a keener sense of the aesthetic. However, this same sensitivity can make a person more easily hurt by any kind of perceived or real rejection or trauma.

BillyLu: What about Les? If she really is using me to escape from the pain of her past, what can I do to help her find this freedom and healing?

Margie: WOW, that's awesome, BillyLu…

Margie said this quietly, almost imperceptibly. She couldn't believe what she had just heard: BillyLu was suddenly concerned about her friend and not herself.

Father JP: BillyLu, do with her what you have done with us: help her acknowledge the pain. If she is in denial of it she cannot freely stop the escape and take responsibility for her life. You do this by not letting her escape emotionally. Ask her about it. Engage her about it. Ask her if she retains any resentment, anger, or hatred against her abusers. Did she project this resentment, anger, and hatred onto other people, such as her husband?

Often victims of abuse are confused at first. They are afraid to confront the pain. They are afraid to let go. They need our prayers and our help.

BillyLu: Do you mean that we don't have to break up?

Father JP: BillyLu, let's take things one step at a time. Your friend needs your help.

At this point, they decided to call it a night. Everyone had plenty of ideas to chew on.

CHAPTER 7

Identity: Who Am I?

Jeremy was eager to resume the conversation with Father JP. Since their last meeting, he had been restless and unable to shake various questions that had arisen in his mind... and some inexplicable longings in his heart. A week later, Jeremy finally got Sam to arrange it so that the three could get together and resume their dialogue.

Jeremy: Father JP, judging from our last gathering—I know you may find it hard to believe—but I really feel that my homosexuality is so much a part of me that I just had to be born this way. I can't ever remember not feeling this way. I really feel it has always been my identity and that I can't do anything to change it.

Father JP: I *do* believe you, Jeremy. I can tell that in you it is something with deep roots, ones that reach almost to the core of your being. Nevertheless, the scientific research just hasn't found any overwhelming genetic component to homosexuality. But what I'd like you to consider is the possibility of your same-sex attraction not having a biological origin, even though it *feels* quite deep.

Now, you say you can't remember ever feeling that you

were not homosexual, but how far back do your memories go, not just the homosexual tendencies? What is the earliest thing you can recall?

Jeremy: Let's see… I think the earliest thing that I can remember would be… when my dad chewed me out for stealing something from the neighbors… I can't remember what it was but I do remember that my dad chewed me out good. He was quite upset.

Father JP: How old were you then?

Jeremy: I'd say… about five years old.

Sam: That's about as far back as I can remember anything in my childhood, too.

Father JP: Then it is possible, Jeremy, that you developed your same-sex attraction in those first five years of your life.

Jeremy: Well, yeah, it's possible, but if I don't remember, how can I presume that I was ever different than I am today?

Male Homosexual Identity

Father JP: Well let's look at your background, being attentive to how the first five years may have impacted your identity. What would you say that your homosexual identity is based on?

Jeremy: JP, my gay identity is based on the feelings that I remember having very early on. First, I never felt attracted to girls, I didn't do the Playboy magazine thing like my brother did, but instead always felt drawn toward men, like a magnet. I would even say it is more than a sexual thing. It's a sense or feeling that only a man is what will make me feel whole and happy. I just never felt that a girl would be anything more than a sister-like friend, not someone who would fill me or complete me.

I just can't imagine how these feelings can be wrong. Doesn't God want me to be happy?

Father JP: Of course God wants you to be happy, Jeremy. But should we base our identity just on our feelings? Shouldn't there be more to our identity than that?

Jeremy: It's not just a feeling, JP; I just *know* I'm gay. Even as a boy I *knew* I was "different," that I had a different identity than other boys—than my brother—who were the typical "rough and tumble" guys, sports fanatics, which defined their identities. I was shy and uncomfortable with their rough ways, and had little interest in sports.

Father JP: There are many boys who are shy. There are many boys who are not crazy about sports. Yet, they don't identify themselves by their shyness. Even good athletes define their identity—if it is a healthy identity—in something more than their performance on the sports field.

Jeremy: But they are who they are and I am who I am. This affects how I interact, or don't interact, with others. I had other interests than they did, and from very early on. When I was little, I'd secretly play with dolls or would put on my mother's clothes and makeup. I just enjoyed imagining what it was like to be a grownup woman. I remember I really liked that, even though I felt I had to hide it.

While my older brother was off playing sports and getting all bruised and scraped up, I stayed at home and read books. I delved into these books to try to take my mind off those hidden desires—hoping I could someday become normal like the other boys—only to find myself identifying with the female characters in the books and fantasizing...

In high school I discovered I had talent for acting and found great consolation in that. I was good at it. It helped me overcome my shyness.

Father JP: Did your parents attend your performances?

Jeremy: My mom was always there, but my dad could never find the time, although he always found time for my brother's sporting events.

Father JP: But none of this identifies you as a homosexual person. This is your particular history, talents, and interior world. This does not identify you as a unique person.

Sam: But these are certainly key elements of his personality, JP. How many men do you know who fantasize about being a woman and put on their mother's makeup and clothes? That's not something most boys do.

Jeremy: What clarified my identity as gay was falling in love with Rick my junior year. We were drawn to each other like magnets.

At first, I wanted to keep our relationship a secret. I even went to the priest to confess my impure thoughts and fantasies— never mentioning their homosexual nature. This wasn't too hard because I had been confessing my masturbation... how foolish and naïve I was, hah!

Father JP: If you were struggling, then you were pleasing God with those efforts.

Jeremy: Well that soon ended. Rick and I started to engage each other sexually. It felt right, but then the guilt came over me because I knew God and the Church disapproved, so I just had to go to confession. It was the hardest confession I ever made.

I confessed having sex but the priest asked, "Was it with your girlfriend?"

"No," I responded.

"Was it with your boyfriend?" he asked. For the second time in my life I felt totally exposed and naked.

"Yes," I responded feebly.

Then the strangest conversation ensued, "Do you feel ashamed of what you did?", the priest asked.

"Yes… well no… I mean, I don't know, Father."

"Well, maybe that was the way God made you," he reassured me. But I was in shock and confused. I didn't know what to make of it. I knew what I had done was wrong in the eyes of the Bible and Catholic teaching. How could he say that?

That was the last confession I ever made.

Father JP: That saddens me, Jeremy. He compromised the truth and his priestly vocation.

Jeremy: Well, the irony about that was that he got kicked out of the priesthood when he got caught in a homosexual relationship himself.

Father JP: Let's pray for him and for all ministers of God who struggle to remain faithful to their calling. Again, Jeremy, I'm sorry you were not given the help and support you deserved at so critical a time in your life. Obviously, he couldn't support you with what you really needed because the advice he would have given you would have also challenged his own double life.

Jeremy: Even though you may not think so, Father JP, it actually helped me. It opened me up to the possibility that maybe God did indeed make me this way.

Sam: Did you tell anybody else about your situation with Rick?

Jeremy: I didn't have to. I was talking one day to a very close friend of mine, Salleen. She was telling me about a guy she had a deep crush on, but he already had a girlfriend. Well, that weekend Salleen attended a party where this guy happened to be without his girlfriend, and she was telling me how she and this guy disappeared from the party and started "making out." All this made her so happy, but the word got out and his old girlfriend was now on the rampage.

Then, out of nowhere, interrupting her own dilemma, she asked me, "Jeremy, you're gay, aren't you?" Although I didn't say a thing, she knew. "It's OK. I'm behind you one hundred percent. Don't be afraid to be yourself." I tried to pretend I didn't know what she was talking about, but she finally got it out of me.

Of course, the cat was out of the bag and everybody knew. But instead of feeling ashamed, I felt freed, and Rick and I could be open about our love. From then on, it was clear that my identity was to be gay and that there was no changing that. People accepted us.

Father JP: So, do you see your identity as being rooted in the fact of having an attraction to men?

Jeremy: Yes, that is a defining characteristic of who I am and where I will find fulfilling intimacy.

Father JP: But, Jeremy, it seems that your identity has less to do with being attracted to men as it does with the emotional satisfaction of having men attracted to you, that men—or a man—long to be with you.

Jeremy: Now that you say it... that's true, Father, that is so true.

Sam: That reminds me of some girls I know who just love to be the center of attention. Their identity, their whole sense of importance and value comes from wooing men away from other girls, even away from the guys' girlfriends or wives...

IDENTITY BASED ON PERFORMANCE

Father JP: But such an identity—one based on having an attraction or being attractive to another—is a very fragile identity. What if that attraction weakens and goes away, would your identity also go away? What if you have an attraction toward a particular guy and then that wanes or he has no interest in you; would your identity also wane? Or what if you suddenly have an attraction for some other guy?

Sam: Isn't that why homosexuals want to marry, to give some permanence to their identity?

Jeremy: Well, yes... that's what we want, a permanent relationship.

Father JP: Homosexuals are not the only ones who tend to base their identity and self-worth on an emotional attraction or being attractive to others, some "straight" women do too, especially young women, who spend incredible efforts in the quest for beauty, seeking the physical appearance of an ideal model. There are also bodybuilder men who practically worship themselves and their bodies. But this is not truly human.

Others base their identity and self-worth on performance, such as on good behavior—being a "good" boy—or on their athletic success or success in school. Others feel a need to meet the expectations of their parents, teachers, or peers. But such a basis for one's identity and sense of value would be dangerously fragile, because as soon as one loses one's ability to perform or attract, or someone else can perform or attract better than he, then his identity and value is threatened.

Sam: Such as when the person gets old, fat, and gray.

Father JP: Yes, or if he loses his job or retires from his profession.

Worse yet is when a person has a negative identity and self-worth based on sexual abuse. In such cases, a person may blame himself, not feel worthy of anything better, and may identify himself as an object of someone else's gratification. When a person sees himself in this way, he easily lets himself be used as a means to an end, as a means for another's pleasure, and to the destructive exploitation of human weaknesses. But when the exploited person is no longer "useful" to the user, he or she is discarded and any sense of value and identity is shattered.

So, an identity and positive or negative sense of self-worth can easily become distorted when it depends on one's appearance, sexual orientation, or sexual abuse, because such an identity would be a performance-based (objectified) identity.

Sam: JP, how does one tell whether one has this kind of performance-based identity?

Father JP: Many ways. One way to tell is if one feels pressured to do things perfectly. Perfectionism is a sign that one must *perform* in order to be of value or worth.

Another sign is the feeling of being overwhelmed. Usually this is the case because we are trying to please everybody at the same time: our parents, friends, siblings, boss, teachers, pastor at church, etc. If we don't *perform* as they wish, then our identity is questioned; it is based on pleasing others by our *performance.*

We see how this can lead to all sorts of manias: expecting perfection from others, worry, insecurity, indecisiveness, fear of failure, discouragement after failures, preoccupation with success, the inability to delegate, eating disorders, excessive body-building, cosmetic surgeries, scrupulosity, antisocial behavior, etc. All of these are signs that we place our sense of value on performance.

Jeremy: But is this really the basis of the homosexual identity?

Father JP: If one bases one's personal identity and sense of self-worth on one's sexual attraction, or on the good feeling of being attractive and "loved" by another of the same-sex, or on sexual performance, then such an identity would be based on performance, on being an object for another.

IDENTITY BASED ON RELATIONSHIPS

Sam: Then where do we find our true human identity?

Father JP: As human beings, our identity is not based on what we do, or what we have done, or on what we have, but on our relationships. This is the source of our true value and importance.

Think of a little newborn child: Does an infant have any value?

Sam: Of course he has.

Father JP: But is his value based on the amount of money he earns, or on his accomplishments, or on the kinds of chores he can carry out at home?

Jeremy: No, JP. An infant doesn't earn anything, except for a small tax deduction. That doesn't come close to the expenses that child incurs.

Father JP: Yet the parents do not consider the child a burden or liability, but as a great gift to them and to the family. Why would that be?

Sam: Well, simply because the child is theirs.

Father JP: Exactly! Because the child is their son or daughter, and is the brother or sister to his siblings; he is also the grandson or daughter, nephew or niece, cousin, etc. to a whole slew of people. In other words, the child is born into an incredible web of relationships that gives that child his unique identity and value.

If we consider the child's relationship with God, then his dignity and value take on an infinite character: he or she is loved by the Almighty! A homosexual person is loved for his or her own sake independent of his homosexual inclinations.

Sam: But don't most of us identify ourselves and get our sense of self-worth based on the job we do and our accomplishments?

Father JP: That is important for men — as well as for many women, now-a-days — but it too produces a fragile, performance-based identity that fluctuates with that performance. However, the more human way of identifying oneself is by relationships (for example, "I'm Jack and Marylu's son… or my sister Sue had you as a teacher…"). If we have good, stable relationships then we have a good, stable identity.

When one's sense of self-worth is based on being willed and loved by God for one's own sake, independent of parental or peer acceptance then that form of identity hits the mark as true and secure. Then, if our identity is thus properly formed, it will endure and remain stable throughout illnesses, disabilities, job-loss, or other setbacks.

Sam: What about being dumped by your girlfriend, or boyfriend, in Jeremy's case?

Father JP: We can maintain a stable identity even with setbacks like these. Our identity is not based on only one relationship.

Of course, the more stable our web of relationships, the more stable our identity and sense of self-worth will be. That's why one should strive to have many friends and on improving relationships with parents, brothers and sisters, extended family, etc. A generous and giving person will have a good personal identity; a selfish, narcissistic person will have a very unstable identity because he has few relationships.

The homosexual identity—or the fashion model identity—is incredibly fragile, because it is not rooted in relationships but in performance and sexual attraction. It tends toward narcissism, which diminishes one's relational identity.

Sam: So, family is important for one's identity?

Father JP: One forms his initial relationships in the family. And through these relationships, one develops a proper sense of masculinity or femininity. From there, the person goes forth from his family to form other relationships—friends, peers, colleagues, and his own family. Each relationship allows a person to expand the identity he received in the family.

Sam: So, that is why the first five years are so important to a person, right?

Father JP: Yes, it forms in us the key elements of who we are and gives us a sense of our self worth. A lot of things happen in those early years.

Child psychologists tell us that little girls come to see themselves as female between 15 and 20 months; boys see themselves as male between 18 and 24 months. Between three and five years old a child learns basic social skills, both with peers as well as with adults. Many elements of gender roles and gender-related relationships are learned during this period.

Jeremy: But none of us can remember things that far back. How can I tell whether this may have affected my gay identity?

Father JP: Perhaps you can't tell due to memory limitations, but perhaps other people can—such as your parents—telling you about your reaction to different events and revealing clues about your pre-five year old personality. Most parents will say that they could see the key elements of their child's character, personality, and sense of identity already firmly established in the first five years of that child's life.

Developing Our Identity

Sam: How would a child develop a homosexual identity?

Father JP: When a child is born, he has little or no sense of any personal identity. But as he grows and matures, he begins to discover who he is and what role he plays in the family and later in the world. When he grows up with poor relationships—whether to his parents, siblings, or peers—he may focus on what pleases others and thus develop a sense of identity based on activity and behavior: a "good" or "bad" boy, athletic, studious, good at the piano, etc.

Sam: I think that happens with all of us. It certainly happened with me, and I grew up in a good family.

Father JP: Because we live in a culture and society where performance is so important, our occupation, accomplishments, and successes—or failures sometimes—play a more important role than they should in shaping our identity. Although women tend to identify themselves more by their relationships, today they too have a lot of pressure to perform and to identify and value themselves by worldly success—this describes secular feminism.

Sam: That's right, I remember how you spoke to Margie and me about this.

Father JP: Well, imagine what happens when the family has unhealthy relationships. For example, suppose a little boy grows up in a family where dad is an alcoholic. If dad is sober, the boy feels safe, even if he misbehaves somewhat due to his immaturity. However, if dad is drunk and distant from the boy—even if he does everything right—the boy feels unloved and unlovable. Dad may even get upset and angry with the boy for no apparent reason, which just reaffirms his sense of being unlovable. The boy wants to love and be loved by his father, but is afraid of dad and does not feel safe around this form of masculine presence.

The boy's identity is unstable because his relationship with his father is unstable. So, as a defense mechanism—to give himself a safer, stable identity—he distances himself from his father.

Sam: Does this non-relationship define a boy as gay?

Father JP: Sam, it's not so much a "non-relationship" as a relationship-hole or wound that goes unfilled by the normal father-son relationship. Similar relationship-holes can develop in families where the child experiences neglect or violence.

Sam: But how does this relationship-hole affect Jeremy's gay identity? You seem to be saying that he is basing his identity on his sexual attractions or on how well he performs sexually. Is his gay identity the fruit of trying to fill that relationship-hole with a sexual relationship with men?

Father JP: I can't say for sure, because each person is unique and develops his identity in a unique way.

Jeremy: Yes, I'm unique, but I'm gay... I've always been gay. That is simply who I am.

Father JP: Well, at least you have *felt* that way from five years old on; you have identified yourself as different from your brother and from other boys.

Jeremy: Isn't that the same?

Father JP: Let's look at what may have happened before you were five. I'm basing this on experience from others with homosexual inclinations, although their experience will certainly differ from yours.

Already in those early years, a child may develop a relationship hole or vacuum toward his father, perhaps because he fears his alcoholic father's harsh reaction to him. He distances himself from his father's unpredictable reactions by distancing himself emotionally from his father.

Yet he sees other boys engaged emotionally with their fathers; he sees how other boys' fathers love them affectionately and unconditionally, how those fathers are proud of their sons. Perhaps he sees how his own father is proud of his jock brother, but cannot relate to him who is more artistic—thus he is different from other boys, from his brother. The boy with the father-wound longs for what these other boys have, but sees that he is different from them—already in the first five years—because he is not loved by his father as they are by theirs.

Sam: But a boy does not have erotic desires for his father, JP?

Father JP: No, Sam, he doesn't. A boy doesn't usually have any erotic desires. That doesn't usually occur until puberty. But a boy can sense that he is different even before he is five years old.

Jeremy: And why would a boy feel so different at such a young age if it weren't due to biology?

Father JP: A person begins to form his identity by the way he perceives that he is unique and special, what makes him *different from his peers.* At first, one's sense of identity and uniqueness is based on one's relationship to family—my father and mother is different from your father and mother. If one has unstable relationships, or has relationship-holes, then the person may try to fill that hole by basing his uniqueness and specialness on being better at a certain activity, such as at a position in football, or excelling in math or science.

On the other hand, a young man may begin to feel unique and different, not being accepted by one's peers as a peer, by *not* fitting in. Perhaps he notices that he relates to boys, girls, and adults differently than his peers do. They may even make fun of him and call him names.

Sam: But how would that turn into same-sex erotic attraction?

Father JP: Puberty brings with it *a longing for a more intimate relationship outside the family,* often associated with sexual attraction and erotic desires and feelings. Well, it is not unusual for such erotic attractions, fantasies, and early sexual experiences to powerfully influence how a young man perceives himself in relation to others and to the world outside. Sexual emotions are so strong that they can crystallize this self-perception and freeze the person's self-identity in the process.

Often such a person begins to focus on the differences between him and his peers as a way of clarifying his identity. Sometimes he can become so concerned about these differences that it can become almost an obsession. Finally, as he lets more and more people know about his secret identity—coming out of the closet—he may feel great relief from the burden of keeping all this secret, even begin to take pride in "who he is."

Jeremy: But isn't this how most people come to perceive and identify themselves?

Father JP: Sam, do you identify yourself as a heterosexual male? Do you ever introduce yourself as, "My name is Sam. I'm a heterosexual male"? Or, "I'm Sam. I'm only attracted to brunettes"? Or, "I'm a strip-clubber, that's my identity"?

Sam: No, that would not be only be ridiculous, JP, it would be offensive to others.

Jeremy: But this doesn't mean we should be intolerant of other people's identity, even if they identify themselves in this way, does it? If some individuals want to identify themselves as heterosexual males or use the "gay" or "lesbian" label, why shouldn't we let them?

Father JP: The question is, Jeremy: is that their true identity? If a child identifies himself as a "loser," a "goof-off," or as a "bad-boy" should we let him use that label to describe himself? Should we let that identity stick?

Sam: No, JP, you're right there. Even I have seen how such labels stick in some people's heads and they never get over it. I think many prefer the label "loser" so they don't have to make the effort to "win."

Father JP: But think: how does a person get those labels? Doesn't it occur when other boys begin picking on that person and maliciously call him names? Doesn't it also occur when perhaps a parent or teacher gives a young man a negative label because he or she is frustrated with him?

Yet, how many homosexual men experienced this while they were young? This should not have happened and we shouldn't allow it to continue.

Jeremy: True, I was called "gay" and "fag" by other kids in grade school. Oh, how I hated that. But I worked hard at learning how to act—and I'm a good actor—such that no one knew I had this tendency.

Sam: No one except Salleen, your female friend, who exposed you in high school.

Jeremy: But then no one was making fun of me. I just knew I was different and when I realized that it was OK and I was accepted for who I was, the labels didn't bother me any more. Now I'm proud to be "gay."

Father JP: We ought to give each person the freedom to truly be him- or herself, and not let that person become imprisoned by labels. When you were in grade school, Jeremy, you fought the labels externally by acting in such a way that nobody knew what you were going through inside.

True freedom, however, is interior. It entails fighting to become a person fully, by choosing to fill the relationship-holes and wounds with healthy relationships.

Jeremy: But if I'm happy being gay, what's wrong with accepting the label and living out what everybody knows I am?

Father JP: What you may not understand is that the feeling of being different can become a deeper and a more radical aspect of our identity when the sexual urge comes into play.

Normally, the sexual experience is meant to fuse a relationship between a man and a woman in marriage such that their emotional identity is focused on this relationship and on the relationship they form by engendering children through their sexual union.

But when a young person is still at the point of discerning, "Who and what am I? What should I do with my life? What is my identity?" and also begins to experience strong emotional attractions with a longing for a relationship with a man or a woman, then it is possible for an intense sexual experience to etch an identity of being "gay" or being "lesbian" into his or her psyche. This experience can also etch the sense of being different into the same psyche, forging an identity, sense of self-worth, and esteem based on homosexual activity.

Jeremy: But what a support it is to be surrounded by people who tell you that this is your identity, that it's OK, and that for me it is not something to be ashamed of... Where would I be without the Gay-Lesbian-Bisexual-Transgender group at school? Imagine being harassed without a support group like that.

Father JP: Such support groups and programs to prevent harassment of those with same-sex attraction are something good, in principle. Unfortunately, however, many of these do more than that. Often they encourage people to base their personal identity on attraction and sexual experience, saying if it feels good, just go with it. They promote the homosexual life-style, call it good and legitimate, and try to get everyone to treat homosexuality as equal to any other relationship.

But the worst harm they do is to make it even harder for those with a fragile, performance based identity to develop the good relationships they need for a true human identity.

True Masculine Identity

Sam: You have given us an idea of how a little boy may develop a homosexual identity, but how does a normal boy develop a sense of being male and not female?

Father JP: This is an important question, because it can help us understand those with same-sex attraction and help them make up for what they may have lacked growing up.

The key in the boy's development of a masculine identity is his relationship with his father. A little boy sees his father as one to be obeyed, a person of authority, but also as a provider and source of food, nourishment, security, and much more. He should also see his father as someone who loves him unconditionally, which is usually manifested to him by his father wanting to play and spend time with him, especially when he comes home from work. This unconditional love is also manifested in the forgiveness that a father communicates to a child after he has messed up or disobeyed.

Jeremy: Doesn't a boy's relationship with his mother also play an important role in his identity?

Father JP: Certainly it does, but in connection with her relationship to his father.

For example, a boy sees his mother loving his father. Mom loving the boy seems emotionally connatural to him, that is, it is something that gives her some kind of emotional fulfillment. Whereas, mom's love for dad is more altruistic, sacrificing her own wishes to please him. Thus a boy wants to be loved like that.

Also, the boy sees how he is the fruit of the mutual gift of self that his mom and dad made to each other; if his parents have a secure relationship then he feels secure in his identity. Also, a boy sees how dad loves mom, sacrifices himself for her, works to provide for her needs and the needs of the children that she tells him about.

A boy also sees how dad serves mom by the different jobs he does around the house, ones that she may feel inadequate to do or that fit his talents better. Perhaps dad does the yard— mowing, weeding, etc.—or plumbing and repairs, or fixes the cars, etc. The boy sees how much dad pleases mom by doing these things and desires to do the same.

Jeremy: Can a mother do anything to keep a boy from developing a good male identity?

Father JP: A healthy mother will recognize and encourage her son's masculinity, even if he tends to have a more sensitive temperament. Occasionally a mother may feel drawn to confide her problems and relational issues to a sensitive or talkative child, especially if the child's father is not emotionally available for her. Such a mother may transform the proper mother-son relationship into a kind of girl-to-girl-like relationship with her son, thus thwarting the development of the true masculine identity.

Sam: But are these the only relationships necessary for a healthy male identity?

Father JP: No, of course not. A boy learns a lot and develops his identity from other relationships too, for example, in relationship with his grandparents. He interacts with them and develops a relationship with them through his parents, and learns from his parents how to interact differently to his grandmother than to his grandfather.

The boy also develops his identity through a relationship with his siblings whom he loves and is loved by unconditionally. Now this doesn't always happen automatically, but the mother and father work at cultivating the proper relationships between their children.

For instance, a dad encourages an older son to be a good example to his younger siblings, to show them how to obey, to treat his siblings—especially his sisters—with gentleness and kindness. Perhaps he shows him how to properly play with his younger siblings, showing these siblings that they are important to their older brother because they too are incarnations of the love between mom and dad.

When a little brother or sister begins school, the dad entrusts their care and protection to an elder son (or daughter), expecting him to defend his sibling against being picked on, or to go after him if he ventures into danger on the street. Thus a boy learns sacrificial love; he learns how to live in such a way as to reflect the relationship he has to others in the family.

Jeremy: But what if he is a younger brother who needs protection, or even the youngest in the family?

Father JP: He still learns something important, that his older brother or sister loves him unconditionally. He also desires the respect garnered by his older brother. Perhaps he learns how to be an older "brother" to other kids at school who don't have such a brother to protect them from mistreatment or dangers.

Jeremy: All this seems to be saying that I have an unhealthy male identity. That means you're saying that I'm sick, JP.

Father JP: Your "gay" identity and sense of self-worth focuses on performance, sexual performance at that. I would rather call that kind of identity, fragile and unfulfillable, since sexual pleasure will never fill the true longings of the human heart.

Jeremy: But if homosexuality is not a disease or an illness, then there is nothing to cure.

Sam: JP, why can we not just accept these people for who they are? Why do we need to try to change them?

Father JP: Sam—we shouldn't label people with homosexual inclinations as "these people," as though they should be separate from the rest of us. We need to accept every person for who they are, as one loved by God from all eternity.

It's not about curing or changing anybody but about loving them enough to seek their true happiness.

Are Parents to Blame?

Jeremy: I love my mom and dad and my brother dearly. Yet all this seems to imply that my parents are to blame. I don't see how I can blame them for my homosexual identity.

Father JP: And you shouldn't blame them.

Most parents do not try to make their child homosexual, nor do they usually choose to have bad relationships with that child. Parents themselves are often working with the identity and sense of value they inherited, and with the relationship-skills and ways of interacting with others they learned growing up. If your father's father was cold and distant, then likely your father picked up the same defect in interpersonal skills. He did not decide to have bad relationships and relationship-skills growing up.

Jeremy: Then you are blaming them, Father JP, because you are pointing the finger at them.

Father JP: We wouldn't blame your parents if your brother was born with a genetic birth defect, would we? Would your father be responsible for the genes he transmitted to him?

Jeremy: No, of course not. But he is responsible for his behavior, is he not?

Father JP: He is to the extent that he is aware of and has control over his character traits. Often, a person is unaware of his being cold and distant, for example. And even if he is aware, often he has no idea how a particular child is reacting to that trait; perhaps he thinks the child is coping as he did growing up.

So, we shouldn't blame parents for the homosexuality of their children, although our culture does, just as it tends to blame parents for children born with birth defects: many in our society say parents should have aborted such children instead of giving the burden of supporting them to rest of us. If we ever did discover a "gay" gene, our society would begin screening for that gene and add another excuse for eliminating a child.

Let us remember that human persons have an intrinsic dignity as persons loved by God. No one is ever intrinsically evil or bad. This calls for the rest of us to accept each person and his parents with love, and strive to help him live a normal and productive life.

Sam: If indeed every person's true identity is based on relationships, then one's web of relationships is to blame for one's homosexual identity. Are not the parents to blame for any weak and defective affirmations in those relationships?

Father JP: Sam, I would say all of us have some defect in one or more of our family relationships. But I'm also sure Jeremy's mom and dad wanted what was best for him. They tried their hardest, but his identity is based on the relationships he has to them and through them, as well as on relationships he has developed on his own. Having defects in family relationships is just part and parcel of being human after the fall of Adam and Eve.

Speaking of the fall of Adam and Eve, Pope John Paul II says that:

> God wills for them the fullness of good, or supernatural happiness, which flows from sharing in his own life. By committing sin man rejects this gift and at the same time wills to become "as God, knowing good and evil" (Genesis 3:5), that is to say, deciding what is good and what is evil independently of God, his Creator... Sin brings about a break in the original unity which man enjoyed in the state of original justice: union with God as the source of the unity within his own "I," in the mutual relationship between man and woman ("communio personarum") as well as in regard to the external world, to nature.

In other words, we cannot blame God for the weakened relationship that Adam and Eve had with him after the Fall. Nor should we primarily blame Adam and Eve for the bad relationships that form our identity. Each relationship depends on two persons who are free, and that relationship is affected by a myriad of actions on behalf of both parties. Thus each relationship is shrouded by a profound sense of mystery based on the interpersonal subjectivity of each person.

We will best take control of our identity when we try to understand how we have formed our identity but without seeking to find blame. Blame is often used to shirk our responsibilities.

Sam: Then we would have to conclude that the homosexual identity—that is, sensing oneself as having value and identity due to one's sexual attraction—could only occur if we have had a bad relationship with our parents?

Father JP: No, it could also occur if we have other bad relationships, for example, if we have bad relationships with our siblings or peers. So, a defective identity occurs whenever one's *web* of relationships does not give that person a sense of value and identity. That could happen if there are weak and defective affirmations from those relationships. But it could also happen that someone has tainted our relationship with our parents, siblings, or peers, for example, if an uncle abused a child and threatened the child with killing his parents were he to ever tell anybody. Thus the child fails to relate to his parents by hiding this "secret" from them.

There is a great variety in our relationships and how they affect the way we view ourselves. Exactly how those weaknesses in relationships affect a particular person with homosexual inclinations will be unique for each person.

Jeremy: It would seem that everybody would have some defect in his identity since no relationship is ever perfect. Is that true or do only gays have a defect in some family relationship?

Sam: I know my parents were not perfect. I think my sister and I have a reasonably good identity, although we are not perfect;

we too need to continue working at improving our identities.

Father JP: You are both right, no one has a perfect identity because our human relationships are never perfect, which also affects our relationship with God.

So, we all should work on improving our relationship with others, with parents, family members, and by making many good friends.

Sam: Reflecting on my childhood and some of the things you have told Margie and me, I think certain events affected my parents and my relationship with them.

Right before I was conceived, my mother lost a pregnancy, her first. I think because of that she was overprotective of me, and sought emotional comfort in lavishing me with attention. My dad kind of pulled away a bit and got immersed into his work. I was spoiled, until my sister came on the scene when I was ten years old.

I think I pulled away from mom at that time—like my dad had done—and sought my identity from among my peers and teachers. It was pretty much performance-based identity as the successful student.

Jeremy: You had a pretty good-with-women identity too, if I remember well, Sam.

Sam: Perhaps if my relationship with my mother had been better I wouldn't have made that mistake, Jeremy.

Father JP: Or perhaps if your mother and father had a closer relationship with each other, it is hard to tell. However, their relationship is key to your identity.

Sam: That being said, JP, can someone ever develop homosexual inclinations if his parents did everything right?

Father JP: It is much harder to develop homosexual inclinations if one's parents do everything right, but it can happen because the child's identity is dependent on other relationships besides those to his parents. Also, traumatic experiences such as sexual abuse can occur without parents being aware of the abuse.

But there are so many other negative influences on parenting that "good" parents are often misled in how to deal with their children. More than ever before, parents need to be aware of their children's emotional needs and how the media, family members, teachers, coaches, peers, may affect the identity their children are developing—especially when the extended family is not involved in their children's lives. Many times parents can get help in forming their children's identity from church and from more experienced families.

Jeremy: Well, JP, you have given me a new way of looking at my identity. I do see how my identity is performance based, but I'm not so sure that my gay identity depends on that. I can see that might have been the case had I been abused as a kid or had an alcoholic dad, but that just wasn't the case for me. I just can't see how relationships to my parents are to blame for being who I am, and I am still sure that I had this identity already when I was five years old.

Father JP: I suggest you explore a bit more how you bonded with your mother and father growing up, Jeremy. See if they will not tell you how you may have reacted to certain events that may reveal that you pulled back defensively from your father or brother or from someone else.

Jeremy: I can't do that, JP, my parents would interpret that as me trying to place blame on them for my homosexuality.

Father JP: Perhaps you can get together with your brother and reminisce about your childhood. Since he is older, he may remember some events that occurred that may explain your childhood relationships better. Ask him if he remembers how you treated him, or your friends, or your parents. As long as it doesn't look as though you were pointing the finger at him, my guess is that he will tell you what he remembers.

Sam: Is there anything I can do to purify and heal my own identity, JP? I'm sure that me pulling back from my mom in my teens must have affected her and my relationship to her and thus my identity.

Father JP: Sure, Sam, just work at trying to get closer to her. Perhaps you could go to your mother and tell her how you were thinking back on your teen years and want to apologize for pulling back from your relationship with her and perhaps for ways you were disappointed in her. Give her the opportunity to acknowledge her own responsibility in disappointing you; then look for ways of sharing more of your life with her. I'm sure she will appreciate that.

Jeremy: I just can't go for all this. Improving my relationship with my parents is not going to change my gay identity. It is not going to change my relationship with Tommy. Why are we wasting all this energy on something that is not going to change?

Father JP: Another thing I would challenge you on, Jeremy, before we part ways is this: reflect on the relationships you have in your life. Ask yourself, how stable and permanent are they? How deep and intimate are they? Are you afraid to reveal yourself or certain aspects of yourself to anyone, fearing that they may reject you or abandon you?

Do you have any relationship-holes, emotional lacunas that are longing to be filled?

Do your relationships depend on your performance, whether sexually, behaviorally, professionally, etc.? Do any of your relationships depend on you maintaining your boyish appearance? How many men have you truly been able to trust? How many men really wish the best for you?

Jeremy: You don't know how many guys hit on me, JP, because of how young I look. Guys sometimes think I'm only 15!

Sam: How you hate it when they "card" you at the bars?

Jeremy: That only happens at the "straight" bars, Sam, which I rarely go to anymore.

CHAPTER 8

Supporting the Homosexual Person

A few days later, Sam came to the church with Margie. After waiting for the line of people to finish, Sam ventured into the confessional to talk with Father JP.

Sam: JP?

Hey I'm here at church with Margie and saw nobody else waiting so I thought I'd come in to say "hi" and to ask you a question or two about Jeremy, while Margie is preparing her list of sins.

Father JP: Good to see you, Sam. Is there anything new with Jeremy?

FRIENDSHIP

Sam: Well, he doesn't want to come see you any more. The idea of change, of breaking up with his partner and moving out is just too much for him right now.

But even still, he and I have been spending a fair amount of time together, in fact, too much time, if you ask me.

Father JP: Sam, you are doing well. Jeremy needs support and precisely the best support are male friends who don't view him as an object. Try to mentor him as you would a younger brother who has made very big steps to change his life.

Right now, he needs your friendship. It is good for him to develop a lot of good male friends who treat him as "one of the guys."

First, try taking interest in some of his kinds of things. For example, you know that Jeremy likes the theatre, so perhaps you can go with him to see a show. If possible, go with him and a few other guys you know who also enjoy theatre. Thus he can develop solid masculine relationships that don't depend on stereotypical or culture-bound ideas of what it means to be masculine.

Sam: That's fine, JP, because I like theatre too and I do certainly know a few other guys who do. But some of my best friends and I also enjoy watching a good football game now and then. Wouldn't it be excluding Jeremy not to invite him?

Father JP: You don't have to invite Jeremy to everything. However, if you do get together with some of your buddies, don't be afraid to invite him to join you. Reassure him that it's OK to not like sports or football, there's nothing unmasculine about that.

If he accepts because he enjoys your company, then after-wards you can give him some hints—just one or two—on how to be more natural. He'll be very grateful.

Sam: Well, thanks JP, but I'm concerned... I feel like Jeremy is clinging to me. Is this healthy and, more importantly, is it healthy for him that we remain friends? He seems very needy and I am worried that I may be a temptation for him, what do you think?

Father JP: Don't worry about being a temptation for him. He longs for and needs male friendship; if he has that he will not desire male sexual contact.

But you do need to set boundaries. Let him know that you have a girlfriend who also needs your time and attention. Let him know when to call you and when it is too late to talk. Let him know these boundaries without making him feel that he is a burden to you.

Perhaps you can initiate the phone call or initiate doing something together instead of waiting for him to call you. Then he knows you really care about him and you want to spend time with him: you are not always saying "No."

Sam: What about showing each other signs of affection? Every time we get together he wants to give me a long hug; I don't feel comfortable with that.

Father JP: You're in the teaching mode, so teach him—you're his mentor. Let him know how guys give each other affection, with a handshake, a high five, or whatever is the latest greeting. Tell him it is OK for a guy to give a close friend a hug, but normally you only do so when you haven't seen that friend for ages.

Also, let him know that a punch in the arm, or a slap on the back is not offensive, but the masculine way guys who really know each other acknowledge the other. If he grimaces or takes offense then the other guys will not view that positively.

Sam: JP, Jeremy doesn't seem too interested in sports: should I invite him to play with me and some of the other guys? Do you think it might embarrass him?

Father JP: He needs to enter more into the male world, and sports are a good part of that masculine world, but you don't want to introduce him to it in an artificial or superficial way. Playing sports that he is not interested in may only reinforce his feeling that he is "different." So, let him know that there are many guys out there who are not super coordinated or who are not big into sports. However, if he is interested in learning then invite him to join you.

If he accepts the invitation, let him know how to introduce himself to the others playing sports. If you're playing baseball, then he should introduce himself to the others as one who never played baseball in school—perhaps track or soccer was more his sport—so that he may play a position that doesn't require as much throwing.

If you can anticipate this a little in advance, perhaps you can teach him some of the fundamental skills yourself. Or, if his hand-eye coordination is not up to this, then perhaps you could try biking or hiking with him.

Sam: But you can't expect a person like Jeremy to make himself like baseball, JP, can you?

Father JP: No, and you shouldn't. But many times we don't like something because we are unfamiliar with it. So, just offer him the possibility of becoming more familiar with the sport should he want to. Even if it is biking or hiking, he can relate to men better if he has some sport that he does on a regular basis.

How Should Straight People React to Homosexuals?

Sam: I also know some other people at work who seem to be gay. Frankly, I don't feel that comfortable around them. Wouldn't it just be better for them, and for me, to leave them alone?

Father JP: They are your co-workers and they need your friendship. We all need friendship, but someone with same-sex attraction particularly needs healthy, non-erotic, same-sex relationships. We all need to know that we are loved just for who we are, not for anything we can offer the other person.

Sam: I have learned a lot from these conversations with you and Jeremy. Should I use the knowledge I have gained to offer them help to overcome their homosexual tendencies?

Father JP: Sam, if you offer to help them, you may turn them away. You will be saying by that offer that you will only really love them if they change.

The first thing we need to do is to offer them our friendship. Perhaps even ask them to help you. Perhaps you can ask them to help you grow professionally. As they see that you appreciate the good they have to offer perhaps they will ask you for help in some aspect of their personal life.

Try to treat your possible homosexual co-worker just as you would everyone else, especially in areas of affection. If you shake hands with your male co-workers, shake hands with him; if you pat your other co-workers on the back, then do the same with him. Make sure you don't give the impression of excluding him from anything; if you don't invite him to something because it doesn't correspond to him for some reason, explain it to him in a positive way, perhaps doing something just with him ahead of time.

Sam: What is the best way to respond to them if they bring up the subject of their homosexuality with me? Should I pretend like it is not a big deal?

Father JP: But it is a big deal, Sam, it is a big deal to your co-worker. To imply that it isn't is to imply that who he is and how he sees himself is not a big deal.

Look at it this way: suppose your co-worker approached you and revealed to you that he had a very serious form of cancer. On the one hand, you shouldn't overreact and suggest he's going to die. Yet, on the other hand, you shouldn't pretend that it's not important, that he'll be all right no matter what happens. No, that would be belittling the cancer and lack sensitivity to how it affects him.

Homosexuality is a big deal to your co-worker and if you take him seriously as a person you will take this aspect of his life seriously.

Sam: Then what should I do?

Father JP: Listen to him. Show interest. By showing him that what he has to say is important to you, you are saying that he is important.

Don't cut him off as he tries to explain what's going on inside of him—often it is very hard for him to get it out; he may have a lot of built up pain, hurt, anger, and stress. Don't try to fix him, just listen. When he asks you what you think, give him your perspective, but always remind him that it is *his* life—neither you nor I can live it for him.

Don't be scandalized by anything. He may tell you details about his sexual exploits that you find quite horrid; don't react negatively, but tell him you care about him and how important this is to him but prefer not to get into these kinds of details. If he asks you "why," just say that you have an oversensitive imagination in these matters.

Sam: Wouldn't my listening attentively to them mean I accept and approve their homosexuality?

Father JP: When someone comes "out of the closet" and reveals his or her decision to live a gay or lesbian life-style, often that person is trying to get us to approve all that he or she has decided to do. We shouldn't let him use this to manipulate us into accepting homosexual relations and activity as something wholesome or good for him or society. Yes, we must always understand and love the person for who he is, but that does not mean that we love and approve everything the person does. If our co-worker was doing drugs, we could still love the addict but without approving his drug use.

Let him know what your position is. You can tell him something like, "Hey, I'm Jewish and our religion has always considered homosexual acts as offensive to God. However, I care a lot about you as a person and will always try to treat you with respect. I will never try to coerce you to believe what I believe..."

Mutual respect is the only basis for dialogue. Although it would be wrong to out-and-out reject him, either implicitly by ignoring him or explicitly by saying, "I don't want to have anything to do with you;" even so, it would also be bad to give in with sympathetic indifference: "What you do with your life doesn't matter to me... I will support you in whatever you think or feel you ought to do." Such attitude fuels destructive behavior such as infidelity, abandoning one's children, and destructive addictive behaviors.

Sam: How does one maintain the proper balance? This is like walking a tightrope.

Father JP: Stick to the truth but with charity (Ephesians 4:15). Without truth, we ignore his wound; without charity, his wound never has a chance to heal. A good friendship can do a lot toward healing these kinds of relational wounds.

Truth will lead us to recognize that homosexual activity—like all sin—is a negation of God as Creator. You should try to explain to your friend that you are against homosexual practice but that you are not going to shun or fear him on that account. Even if he refuses to accept this truth, your charity and profound respect will open new horizons for him. By listening attentively to everything he has to say, for example, you are telling him with deeds that what he says is important because he is important.

Sam, I would recommend that you, as a Jew, share with him how your friendship with God helps you with your anxieties, insecurities, etc. If one were Christian, I would recommend he or she share how a friendship with Christ gives us help. So, talk about other aspects of your Faith and don't bring up the topic of homosexuality again until he's ready and perhaps brings it up himself; you don't want to pick the fruit off the tree when the fruit is still green.

Sam: I've noticed that some people avoid using terms like "gay," "homosexual," or even the word "sex." Is this more discrete approach better? Is it more respectful?

Father JP: Try to use the terms he uses; stepping around the issues or avoiding using the words he uses can give the impression that you see yourself as better than him—since you don't use vulgar language while he does.

But, it is also good to use terms with precision. "Same-sex attraction" or "SSA," "homosexual inclinations" and "homosexual feelings" are more precise terms than just "homosexuality," which is broad and can confuse things since "homosexuality" can be applied to many different aspects of the person's life and struggle. The term "gay" has connotations of advocacy that favors and supports the whole life-style, including gay "marriage" and adoption.

Sam: What about topics that guys like to talk about, such as sports, cars, or girls? It often times seems that my homosexual co-workers are clueless about these topics.

Father JP: Bring him into these conversations too. It would be rude to imply, "What do you know about this?" Even just changing the topic implies you don't think he has anything to add. It is important to treat a man as a man and a woman as a woman. Ask him his opinion about these topics and don't embarrass him if he says something foolish—afterwards when you are one-on-one with him, correct what he said, or give him something to read that will expand his knowledge in the particular area.

Even more important, acknowledge when he says something good and insightful. Since he is likely to be more sensitive to how a woman thinks, ask him his opinion about a situation that can help other guys with their relationships. All this will help him feel normal and not excluded while avoiding making him feel like he is a pet project or something.

Sam: Thanks, JP, these are good pointers. I think they will help me to become more sensitive to the needs of everyone—since these ideas don't just apply to dealing with homosexuals. I know a single friend who is living with his girlfriend, and a married co-worker who's messing around with a woman.

Father JP: It is so true, Sam: we need to be present to all people, whether they are saints or sinners, and encourage them to freely choose to do what is right.

BEFRIENDING THE PRODIGAL DAUGHTER

Margie came into the confessional after Sam finished. She introduced herself. After confession she asked Father JP for some advice in dealing with BillyLu.

Margie: Father JP, thank you for confession. I always feel so much peace afterwards.

If you don't mind, I have a few questions for you.

Father JP: I don't mind at all, Margie. What can I help you with?

Margie: Well I had lunch with BillyLu last week and we discussed a few things from our pizza gathering a few weeks back. I just tried to listen and be supportive. I see that she really wants help and seems to appreciate my being there. I do want to help her but I don't know how.

Father JP: You are doing a great job just as you are: continue

4444434

being a good friend, that's what she needs.

I just talked with Sam about this too. I'm sure he will share his "notes" with you.

Margie: I'm sure he will, he almost always does. He shared a lot about his conversation between you, him, and Jeremy last week. I found it fascinating how our identity could be formed more through relationships than through our behavior and activity. I never considered applying that to homosexuality.

Father JP: Perhaps you can discuss some of those things with BillyLu.

Margie: But what if I don't get it all right and end up confusing her?

Father JP: Then you and BillyLu can come by together and I'll give you a session too, just as I did with Sam and Jeremy.

Margie: That would be great, Father!

One concern I do have: you say that I should befriend BillyLu. Certainly I should avoid being an occasion of sin for her. What if she were to start fantasizing about a relationship with me? I wouldn't want that. I think she might be developing an attraction toward me as she did with those Christian women when she became Christian.

I guess the bottom line is, how far should we go in trying to reach out and help a person who is still actively engaged in the homosexual life-style?

Father JP: The answer is simple, Margie: we need to go as far as Our Lord would go.

I like to think of Christ's parable of the Prodigal Son (Luke 15:11-32). In it Our Lord describes how the younger of two sons requested and received his share of the family inheritance and then goes to a far-off country to waste his inheritance on loose living. After going hungry and becoming an indentured servant he comes to his senses and decides to return to his father's house, ask forgiveness, and beg to become a servant in his father's house. But his father receives him back as a dear son, throwing a party to celebrate. The elder brother is angered at this, refusing to go to the party or celebrate his brother's return.

Most of us react like this elder brother toward the homosexual prodigal son. We don't want to have anything to do with our homosexual brother or sister and we tend to assume that our Father, God, would disown him too; but God doesn't, does he?

Margie: No, he doesn't. But neither does the elder brother venture away from home to get his brother to return.

Father JP: But perhaps he should. The elder brother is not a model of virtue, is he?

Margie: He certainly is not. But do you think God would want us also to go to a far off country in search for his prodigal son or daughter?

Father JP: Yes, I do. In effect, this is what Our Lord did. He leaves his home in heaven and goes to a far off country by becoming man:

> Have this mind among yourselves, which is yours in Christ Jesus, who, though he was in the form of God, did not count equality with God a thing to be grasped, but emptied himself, taking the form of a servant, being born in the likeness of men. And being found in human form he humbled himself and became obedient unto death, even death on a cross. Therefore God has highly exalted him and bestowed on him the name which is above every name (Philippians 2:5-9).

Having this mind, then, we should go to the far-off country to befriend the prodigal son or daughter. If Jesus received sinners and ate with them (Luke 15:2), then we should too. The prodigal daughter may be in the throes of wasting away her father's inheritance, but we should accompany her and try to earn her trust. As she runs out of money, we will be the one who helps her find the farm that needs a hired hand. There in her misery, we will ask her about what it was like in her father's home, draw her out until she tells us: "How many of my father's hired servants have bread enough and to spare, but I perish here with hunger!" (Luke 15:17). Perhaps we will suggest that she return to her father's house, even giving her the words that she could tell her father, "Father, I have sinned against heaven and before you; I am no longer worthy to be called your [daughter]; treat me as one of your hired servants" (Luke 15:18-29).

Margie: But, Father, can I really do that with BillyLu? I mean… I feel like I'm that prodigal daughter, since I strayed from God and my faith when I was in college, wasting away my inheritance. I too sought to fill my stomach with the garbage that the pigs ate, giving inappropriate affection to boyfriends who just wanted to use me. How can I tell someone like BillyLu how to live her life— I'd be such a hypocrite?

Father JP: We are all prodigal sons and daughters, Margie. What makes your testimony so powerful is precisely the fact that you have been there, you know what it is like. You have abandoned your Father's house but you have returned. You know the pain, sadness, and hurt, but also the joy of having been forgiven. You have the capacity of sharing that joy with BillyLu and others.

As Pope John Paul says:

Conversion and contrition… a radical change of life… are (not just unpleasant self-denial but) even more a drawing near to the holiness of God (which means becoming more able to know the truth and to love and be loved) a rediscovery of one's true identity, which has been upset and disturbed by sin, a liberation in the very depth of self and thus a regaining of lost joy, the joy of being saved (cf. Psalm 51:12), which the majority of people in our time are no longer capable of experiencing.

Margie, Perhaps you could share with her some personal experience of having had comforting female love in your spiritual relationship with Our Lady as your mother.

Margie: I never thought about it in this way, Father. That is a beautiful way of looking at it. I will try to do that with BillyLu, to be her friend, to listen to her and accompany her in her journey in life. I don't know if I will be any good at it.

Father JP: I think you have already helped her a great deal. Just continue along in this vein.

Think, as her friend we would accompany the prodigal daughter back to her father's house and witness her father welcome her back. The father would certainly thank us too and invite us to join in the celebration and the great "joy in heaven" for the repentant sinner (Luke 15:7).

You may also want to reflect on how Christ treated the woman caught in adultery (John 8:3-11) or on his encounter with the sinful Samaritan woman (John 4:7-27). I imagine Our Lord dealing with a person with homosexual inclinations as he did with each of these women. In each of these situations Our Lord shows us that *the dignity of man*—his value in God's eyes—is infinite: each one of us willed by God for his own sake. Nevertheless, he calls these women to sin no more, even though others may carry a great deal of the responsibility for their sin. Taking responsibility for our part in sin is a way to take responsibility for our own lives and a way to recover our dignity of free subjects. Then we will feel eternally loved by God and our freedom will be restored.

Our Lord, who asks us to share in his mission, reminds us: "Those who are well have no need of a physician, but those who are sick do; I have not come to call the righteous, but sinners to repentance" (Luke 5:31-32). Therefore, we too are sent to the sinner.

Margie: But how should I do this? What if I don't know what to say to BillyLu?

Father JP: Don't worry about what you are to say, the Holy Spirit will guide you (cf. Matthew 10:19-20; Luke 12:11-12).

Look for ways of spending time with BillyLu. Perhaps it will be for lunch or dinner, or to grab a cup of coffee together. Ask her about her life, including relationships she had growing up, whether with her mother, father, brothers, high school friends, past boyfriends, girlfriends, partners, etc.

Margie: What? Should I talk to her about relationships with her partners? Are you sure? I think I would feel uncomfortable having her tell me about her sexual encounters.

Father JP: Avoid details about the sexual stuff, but get her to share with you the dynamics of their communication and relationship. You don't really need to comment on it much; often just letting her describe things to you will be enough for her to see "the good, the bad, and the ugly."

As you get to know more about all her relationships, you will help her discover the various ways she has been manipulated or used for the other person's needs—as we all have been in some form or another. Perhaps, she will even see how she may be doing the same toward her partner. Tell her you're aware of the problem of partner-abuse in homosexual relationships and that you hope that she has not been a victim of such abuse.

Margie: If she wants to introduce me to her partner, should I then point out how her partner manipulates her or point out her partner's defects to her?

Father JP: No, in fact, do the opposite. She will become defensive if you point out the defects of someone she cares about. So, don't do that. But if you identify her partner's good traits and qualities, then she will tend to react to defend herself: "But you don't really know her..." or "You should try living with her a few days..." or "If you only saw how she really treats me..."

I'll tell you a secret: I give the same advice to parents who are disappointed in the boyfriend or girlfriend of one of their children. I tell them to point out the good traits and qualities of the person the child is dating, and watch how the child then identifies the defects.

Margie: What about inviting BillyLu and Jeremy to volunteer with Sam and me in assisting disabled children, do you think that would be good too?

Father JP: That would be an excellent idea, Margie. By giving oneself in some form of service to others, a person learns to get out of him- or herself in order to meet the needs of others, and thus learn to be 'for' the other in interpersonal 'communion.' This is key for all of us in developing an identity based on relationships.

This could help each of them discover how suffering actually unites us to Christ. It may also help them see their homosexual inclinations in a new light, as an opportunity to die to oneself, or as a special martyrdom (witness) to the chaste and sacrificial love we see in Christ. If one has been rejected by parents, siblings, or peers, it is consoling to know that "Jesus is present... as the *one who has been rejected.* In this way [Jesus] would identify with" him, as Pope John Paul says.

PARENTS' ROLE

Margie: That's great, Father. I will certainly try to do that. I hope God will use me to help BillyLu.

I have one more question... I don't know if you have time.

Father JP: Sure, I'm in no rush.

Margie: Well, Sam also told me that you say parents are not to be blamed for the homosexuality of their children. Yet, at the same time if they are good parents it is highly unlikely their children will develop same-sex attraction.

Since Sam and I are considering marriage, I certainly don't want our children to have to worry about this struggle. What does it take to prevent this from happening to our children?

Father JP: You shouldn't worry about preventing homosexuality but in cultivating a good family environment in which your children can develop good relationships and thus develop a healthy identity too.

In this regard, parents can help a child develop his or her relationship with God and discover how God is always watching over us, listening to our concerns, and ready to take our cares into his hands. A child should learn to serve God and please him, and that our mean and selfish acts hurt our relationship with him. However, we must avoid excessive guilt, and help the child experience God's loving forgiveness. A child should come to realize that God loves each one of us just as we are; that each person is a gift in and of himself; that God gives each of us gifts and talents for our special calling in life and that the first source of our happiness should be in our relationship with the Lord.

Margie: I'm working on my own relationship with God, because I know we cannot give to our children what we do not have.

But the parent-child relationship also seems to be key for developing a healthy identity. Can I do anything to guarantee the development of good relationships with my children?

Father JP: Although it takes effort, it is pretty simple to develop a good parent-child relationship: try to sincerely receive each child as a gift, and not as a burden.

Parents show a child that he or she is a "gift" by their unconditional acceptance, affection, and love, independent of the expenses, efforts, or even troubles that may accompany the child. The child should come to learn that his parent's love is not conditioned on good behavior or performance. Constant badgering or disapproval can make a child feel rejected or inadequate, motivating him to seek his personal identity outside the family.

Margie: Although parents need to prize and treasure each child as a gift, don't they still need to correct the child when he misbehaves?

Father JP: Certainly, Margie, but with balance. Parents must look for ways to motivate the child to use his or her freewill to do good.

Margie: But motivating a child demands a relationship of mutual trust.

Father JP: Exactly! Good parents will try to foster an atmosphere of trust, making each child feel safe to talk about his worries and concerns, even when he has misbehaved. Oversensitive, worrisome, or alarmist parents make a child fear the possibility of being yelled at or corrected. Even being overly anxious about having too little time may make a child feel that he may be adding additional *burden* to the parent's problems. Thus, good parents are available and welcoming to their children.

Parents should encourage secure same sex friendships in

their child. If these are not developing, parents should try to find out why and then take steps to try to strengthen them in their child.

If a boy manifests feminine mannerisms or lacks hand-eye coordination, the father should commit himself to a daily plan to develop a supportive, positive relationship with his son, including finding activities other than sports for the two to bond.

Margie: So, you are saying that children should feel safe to talk to their parents about everything? I know some parents who never mention sex to their children and who dodge the question when their children try to bring it up. Should parents talk to children about sex?

Father JP: Yes, parents need to be comfortable speaking about everything to their children so that their children will feel comfortable telling them everything, especially in the area of chastity and modesty.

Parents are the ones responsible for giving their children a good Christian education in chastity and modesty, one that is appropriate to the child's age. This will be exemplified by the parents themselves, including safeguards and limits on television, Internet, music, etc.

Margie: Don't kids resent it when parents control their access to media? I know that I did, giving my mom a hard time when she asked me to turn off my music in the car when were driving together; the music just had a few four-letter words in the lyrics.

Father JP: Young people like to know their parents care, even though it means that they don't always get what they want.

Nevertheless, we should be careful not to become puritanical, pitting the spirit against the body. Children should learn that the body and sexuality are good, because God created them. Parents need to be ready to respond calmly and with a positive tone to a child's spontaneous curiosities about the human body and sexuality so as not to cultivate an obsessive aversion to one's body and sexuality as if it were the embodiment of sin. Rather, parents should foster a healthy respect for the sacredness of the body and sexuality as a "sacrament" of the person and of the gift of him- or herself to another.

Margie: How do you know when a child is old enough for a particular topic? Certainly parents don't want to spoil the innocence of their child by giving the child too much information too early.

Father JP: Parents should talk to other parents. I recommend parents to befriend parents who have children a year or two older than their own. Then they will learn what issues the other parents are having with their children and how they resolved those issues. This will give the parents with the younger child an idea of what things they will face in a year or so, before they become an issue with their child.

Margie: What about helping children develop relationships with their peers, since those too seem to be important to a child's identity? I have read that children whose friends are exclusively those of the opposite sex have a greater risk of becoming gay or lesbian.

Father JP: You're right, good parents work at helping a child develop good male and female friends. This starts with the parents giving good examples with their own healthy friendships outside the family and by affirming the masculinity and femininity proper to those relationships. Then it is a matter of putting a child in the types of situations and activities that will encourage such relationships, such as sports, family picnics, reunions, vacations, etc. Also, parents should help children avoid unhealthy forms of isolation and escape, such as too much isolated reading, music, video games, TV, Internet, etc.

A good way to do this is to put them in a social context: we listen to music, play video games, or watch TV as family relaxation and entertainment—never in isolation. Then a child will less likely feel the temptation toward self-entertainment, which can lead to self-gratification. Even having family time for each to read his or her book together quietly with everyone else is a good practice.

Margie: What if some of those peer relationships turn sour, perhaps when a child experiences rejection by another child or group of children, name-calling, or other forms of humiliation by peers? Should we come to the child's defense or should we just ignore it and not make a big deal of it?

Father JP: But it can be a big deal to a child. Besides, parents and teachers are obliged to teach bullies how to treat others with charity.

If a child experiences name-calling by peers, parents can help a child deal with it and avoid humiliation by coming up with some ready-made comebacks that are clear and even strong. Parents can also encourage toughness in the child, learning not to take it personally, since maltreatment from peers is not unusual and even inevitable. If necessary, parents should request the school to take steps to eliminate peer bullying, and even transfer the child to another school should the bullying not stop. Parents can also help a child understand and forgive the bully; understanding the possible *why* of his bullying. This helps the child to let go, not to take it personally, and to forgive the bully. This is crucial to emotional healing.

Parents should be especially attentive during the pre- and early adolescent stages for any out-of-the-ordinary behavior. For example, a parent may notice a child's tendency towards isolation, having few friends, breaking off long-standing friendships, or a child who now rarely speaks at home, etc. Interest in the child's long-term welfare will move the parent to investigate and to act if necessary.

Margie: Can a mother or father be too involved or too controlling in trying to prevent bad or unhealthy situations for their children?

Father JP: Certainly, due to fear of what can happen to their children, parents can be overly protective and thus prevent their children from fully developing into mature adults.

Parents are called on to set their children free. This means cultivating self-control of one's emotions—which parents teach by their own example of emotional self-control—and in the good use of one's freedom. If you are too controlling and manipulating of your children, they never learn to exercise their freedom.

By "honoring" young people—that is, *acknowledging their freedom as persons*—we affirm their natural and God-given gifts as a male or female. Parents do this by really listening with respect and calm, and encouraging them to give of themselves freely to parents, siblings and friends, etc. A warm "thank you" after a child does a chore or does something for a sibling acknowledges that the child chose to obey and to carry out the action. From this he learns that fully being a person means being a free subject of action and relationship.

Margie: What particular role does the father play in cultivating a good identity? I would only marry Sam if he can be the kind of father that our children would need.

Father JP: Certainly the father plays a very important role in the development of a child's personality and identity. Therefore, a father should be active and participate in his child's education and development. As Pope John Paul II says:

> The place and task of the father in and for the family is of unique and irreplaceable importance. As experience teaches, the absence of a father causes psychological and moral imbalance and notable difficulties in family relationships, as does, in contrary circumstances, the oppressive

presence of a father, especially where there still prevails the phenomenon of "machismo," or a wrong superiority of male prerogatives which humiliates women and inhibits the development of healthy family relationships.

In revealing and in reliving on earth the very fatherhood of God, a man is called upon to ensure the harmonious and united development of all the members of the family: He will perform this task by exercising generous responsibility for the life conceived... by a more solicitous commitment to education, a task he shares with his wife, by work which is never a cause of division in the family but promotes its unity and stability, and by means of the witness he gives of an adult Christian life which effectively introduces the children into the living experience of Christ and the church.

The father does this principally by his presence, affection, and accessibility, which is even important during the toddler years. The father shows a more masculine kind of physical affection, fatherly play (rough-and-tumble physical games), etc., which are important for a child to relate to the outside world. A child, particularly a boy, finds it hard to bond with his father and to identify with his masculinity if he fears his father, doesn't get any hugs from him, or never wrestles or plays around with him. Little girls learn how they bring out the tender and gentle side of men by how their father reacts to their smile and feminine beauty.

The father's effort to create a healthy father-son bond will help the boy develop his masculine identity. His role in the family is to help his children discover their special gifts and talents, and how those talents and gifts fit a child's particular calling from God.

If the father is not present to the child at these early stages, then the child can develop a relationship-hole, what is called a father-wound, that affects his identity.

Regarding how Sam would do as a father, look at how he interacts with children and ask about how his father interacted with him. You should be able to tell a lot by that.

Margie: I've been very impressed how well he does with kids. He enjoys playing with them and they with him. I can see that the choice of a man in marriage matters a lot.

Father JP: Of course it does, but the woman also plays a key and essential role. In fact, many times she has the ability to motivate her husband to be a good father.

A good mother and wife should be affectionate and supportive of her husband, allowing and affirming him in his role as a father, never supplanting him. A mother who is overly controlling, critical, possessive, and overprotective of a child tends to squelch a child's personal freedom and subjectivity; this prevents a child from becoming an active subject of relationships. Boys tend to cling to an overly protective mother who induces in them a fear of getting hurt (physically and emotionally) and then they may identify with her feminine traits, whereas girls tend to reject this "control" and become attractive to the independent (although distant) father.

A woman must also avoid burdening a child with relationship problems in the marriage. She must love her husband, support him, and draw out his freedom. If she needs help in their relationship, she needs to seek counsel from someone outside the family.

PARENTAL VIGILANCE

Margie: You mentioned that a very large percentage of those with homosexual inclinations were abused when they were children. Is there anything a parent can do to prevent this? I imagine that this is one of the greatest fears that a parent can have.

Father JP: If you build an atmosphere of trust, where children feel they can tell you anything, then your children will come running at the first sign of something wrong. Parents should encourage their children to tell them if any adult or child does something or shows them something inappropriate or which makes them feel uncomfortable. Secrets only produce more hurt. Often an abuser will scare the child, threatening to harm them, their parents, or siblings should they tell their parents. Or the abuser makes the child feel at fault for what has happened and thus the child hides his fault from them.

Sometimes even a general threat from a father, "I'll kill anyone who touches my daughter," can cause the girl to be afraid of reporting an abusive situation because she fears that her father will murder her uncle or brother. Thus the girl prefers to bear the burden of the abuse rather than the burden of a potential killing.

Children should know that if anybody touches them in a way that makes them feel uncomfortable, it is OK for them to say, "No," and to get away from that person immediately. They should always feel that it is better to speak out and even admit one's fault than to keep a secret, which becomes a secret with the devil.

Margie: I understand that sexual predators often look for boys who appear insecure, lonely, or awkward with their bodies, etc. Can we do anything to prevent that?

Father JP: Parents can help their children develop a sense of confidence, that they are never alone, and an awareness of their special God-given gifts, including the gift of their body. Children can learn that they are God's precious children, that God is always looking over them, and that he has placed a special guardian angel to watch over and protect them.

Parents can also help children not to be overly concerned about how they look or how clumsy or awkward they may be with their bodies by teaching them to laugh at themselves and their mishaps and to appreciate the special gifts they do have, such as artistic ability, intellectual aptitude, etc. Then the child will confidently engage and even confront the world, and will not be easily preyed upon.

Margie: Are there telltale signs of perverts who abuse children? How can we identify a potential abuser so that we can keep our children at a safe distance from them?

Father JP: This is not easy, Margie. Often abusers are trusted family members, friends, or members of the school or church staff. They often win over the trust of the parents before winning over the child. The stereotype of the crazed dirty-old-man who lurks around playgrounds offering kids candy… is just that, a stereotype that is far from reality. Most sex-offenders come across as very nice people—like the guy next door. Abusers are able to carry out their crime precisely because they seem trustworthy to the parents.

Parents need to be alert and not wait for physical signs that something has happened to their child.

Margie: What kinds of things should I look out for?

Father JP: If you notice that a child has an aversion to a particular person, explore that with the child. The abuser often seems— to the parents—friendly, fun, safe, and trustworthy, but the child may react with fear and disinterest.

Abusers often offer kids very attractive gifts to win them over—parents should teach their children to tell them about such gifts, even though the person tells them, "Don't tell your parents… they might not let you keep it."

Margie: Is it common for priests or church ministers to be sex-offenders?

Father JP: Sadly, it has happened. However, by far most

priests are faithful to their commitments to celibacy and are safe. However, a few have caused serious harm to those entrusted to them and to the whole Church. Of these few, according to the John Jay Report on the crisis in the Catholic Church, 80% of the victims of priestly impropriety were adolescent males, not children.

Sadly, experts report that 10 percent of all boys and 20 percent of all girls are abused by the age of 18. Yet an extremely low percentage of the abusers were priests. Most abusers actually do not come from a church setting at all but from among the victim's own relatives: an uncle, cousin, or stepfather. Being married doesn't prevent one from being an abuser. The highest rate of sexual abuse is from a stepfather or stepmother.

Teachers, police, and athletic coaches have a higher rate of sexual abuse of minors than Catholic priests; married clergy have a higher rate of abuse than celibate clergy. A report by Dr. Charol Shakeshaft of Hofstra University shows that an American student is a 100 times more likely to be abused by an educator than by a priest.

Finally, most of those who abuse children were themselves abused as a child—although that does not excuse it. However, we do see from this how sin tends to perpetuate itself.

Margie: All this is kind of scary, not being able to control what happens to your own children. Perhaps it would be better to remain single and then one wouldn't have to worry about all this.

Father JP: It is also scary what we can do with our own freedom. God himself takes that enormous risk with each of us. As Pope Benedict has said:

> [T]he truth of God's love comes to men and women in history, inviting them to accept freely this radical newness... God lays himself open, one might say, to the risk of human freedom.

We should imitate God, focus on what we can control and

encourage others—children included—to exercise their freedom well, each of us taking responsibility for our own lives.

Margie: Thank you, Father JP, this has been reassuring. You have given me ideas that will help me later on in marriage as well as in dealing with BillyLu.

CHAPTER **9**

Taking Control of Our Identity

More than a month went by, without any dialogue with Father JP. Jeremy continued getting together with Sam, and BillyLu with Margie.

During that period, however, Jeremy's brother Jeff was in a serious automobile accident and was close to death. Jeff was in a coma for three days before regaining consciousness.

Sam was there to support his friend and recommended to Jeremy that he needed to see Father JP. Jeremy finally agreed, but only after Sam agreed to go with him.

RELATIONAL TRAUMA

Sam: JP, as I told you on the phone, Jeremy's brother is in the hospital. I thought Jeremy needed to talk to you… it has impacted him more than he realizes.

Father JP: How is he doing, Jeremy? I've been praying for Jeff and for you, since Sam called.

Jeremy: He's doing much better. He came out of the coma, but is still pretty beat up. It is going to be quite a long recovery. I want to thank you, JP, for all your prayers.

159 ❧

Father JP: You're welcome, Jeremy.

Sam: JP, Jeremy was been on a bit of an emotional rollercoaster. I think his brother's accident has brought up a lot of emotional pain. He has been dealing a lot with his mom and dad, and his relationship with his partner has also been rocky. I was hoping you might be able to help us sort all that out.

Father JP: I'll help where I can... Jeremy, would you mind telling me what's going on, especially with your relationship with your brother?

Jeremy: I'll try, JP. I don't know if I can make sense of all this. I just feel so stupid...

Father JP: Just do your best. We'll understand if you can't get it all out.

Jeremy: When I got the call from my mom that Jeff was in the hospital and that he might not make it, I felt like I was hit with a ton of bricks. I was hurt... I was sad... I was angry, all at the same time. This just doesn't make any sense.

Father JP: Why did you feel hurt, Jeremy?

Jeremy: Well, I don't really know why. It may seem kind of silly, but my brother's accident made me feel as though he was abandoning me for good. He never seemed to have cared about me in the past, even though I cared about him. He never wanted to spend time with me, even though I did everything I could to be around him. He always excluded me.

It was if he had said to me, "Jeremy, you will never see me again. I'm history and your longing to be with me is history, too!"

Now I know my brother wouldn't deliberately get into an

accident just to hurt me, but it sure felt as though he did... I must be losing it.

Father JP: So, you were hurt and sad because you feared that you were losing someone with whom you longed to have a relationship, right?

Jeremy: Yes, JP.

Father JP: And you were angry with Jeff because you felt he was doing this to hurt you?

Jeremy: I knew he didn't deliberately do this to hurt me, but it felt like he had.

Father JP: So, you became angry with him.

Jeremy: Yeah, I was angry with him... but I think I was more angry with myself, blaming myself for my brother's accident.

Sam: Why would you do that, Jeremy? You were not driving the car when your brother got into the accident.

Jeremy: No, you're right, Sam. However, I felt that if I had not been such a big sinner then perhaps God would not have removed his protection from Jeff. I wanted to blame God for this, but then all the guilt came back upon me.

Father JP: You are not to blame, Jeremy, you are not to blame.

Jeremy: That is easy for you to say, JP. But it doesn't take away what I'm feeling. And when I saw how sad and fearful my mom and dad were, thinking that they might lose their son—their only son, in many ways—I felt that it was all my fault.

Father JP: Jeremy, what were you doing when you got the phone call?

There was a moment of silence that seemed to take forever...

Jeremy: I was at home... with Tommy... we had just finished... having sex...

Jeremy started to cry. Both Father JP and Sam put their hand on Jeremy's shoulder to reassure him.

Father JP: Jeremy, you are not to blame. I can see that God allowed this to happen because he loves you and he wants you back in his family.

Jeremy: But why, JP, why?

Father JP: Sam mentioned, Jeremy, that all this affected your relationship with your boyfriend. How so?

Jeremy: Well, I just couldn't go back to him after this. After going to the hospital, I started to spend a lot of time with my parents, and with my brother. I spent many nights sleeping alongside his bed, waiting and trying to help. When I had to go home to shower or eat, I just found it easier to stay with my parents than to return to my partner.

Sam: Did you blame Tommy too?

Is Change Possible?

Jeremy: No, he had nothing to do with this. It was my sin that caused all this pain and hurt in the family, not his.

But I wish I could just change everything, make it better. Can I do anything to change the situation between me and my brother? And between me and my father and mother?

Father JP: You can change neither your brother, nor your father and mother. The only person you can change is yourself.

Jeremy: But is change really possible, Father? I would like to change but I don't see how it is possible after all that I have been through.

Sam: If you want to change, Jeremy, JP and I are here to help you. But we love you just as you are.

Jeremy: I do want to change. Last time we spoke, Father JP, you gave us the impression that a gay or lesbian person can change his or her identity at will. I've been this way all my life, at least since I was five. You don't really believe we can change our identity? Isn't that something beyond our control?

Father JP: Since our true identity—*the sense of who we are in relationship to God, to others, and to the world*—is based on relationships, to the extent that we can enter into new relationships, heal old ones, and give priority to some over others, we can take control and transform our identity.

Jeremy: But I am happy with my gay identity, even though it is based on performance, as you say.

I was miserable trying to pretend to be straight, trying to satisfy girls to whom I wasn't attracted and whom I didn't love. Why should I try to change my identity now if I feel fine with it as it is?

Father JP: It's not about pretending; it's not about changing but developing your true identity. By developing relationships and relational skills, one can freely take control of his identity. Since each person is born with an incalculable dignity, it corresponds to that dignity not just to react to one's feelings; one should be afforded opportunities to choose his life, and to freely develop his identity and heal it if necessary.

We do indeed need to love and accept each person as he is. But that doesn't mean we accept everything a person does, especially when it hurts them and hurts others. For example, Sam, suppose you knew a lot about cars and Jeremy wanted to buy a particular car that looks nice but really is a lemon. Would you just step back and say nothing?

Sam: No, of course not. No friend would do that.

Father JP: Likewise, true love means that a friend will intervene in decisions that will affect his friend's health and happiness, which are much more important than a car purchase.

We can't change anybody; each person must choose to change himself. We must love each one whether or not he makes any changes, yet, we should also give him the knowledge that he may use—if he chooses—to take more control of his life.

Ex-Gay Movement: A Fraud?

Jeremy: After wrestling with guilt and shame for years, I came to realize that I couldn't change, because the homosexual condition is unchangeable.

Father JP: To say you can't change is to say that you are not free. Do you really believe that your life is not in your hands? Do you believe that all your actions are a consequence of necessity and fate? I hope not, because freedom is one of the greatest treasures that God gives us.

Jeremy: I'm not saying that I am not free, but my homosexuality has conditioned my freedom so that I don't have any choice in being who I am.

Father JP: Do you believe that it is impossible to live a chaste life, that a person cannot choose this?

Jeremy: It's not impossible… but it is a hard choice to make and many people find that such a sacrifice is not worth it.

Father JP: Yet, one has the power to freely choose it. That is what we want to offer people, the means to be able to choose not to give in to their sexual urges, to choose chastity, which is nothing else than to live out God's plan for human sexuality. We want to make it as easy as possible for those who want to choose it, to be able to do so.

Jeremy: But, JP, the ex-gay movement has been exposed as a fraud. Is there any 12-step program that would get you to have sex with a man? No way: if you are straight, you'd die first. The ex-gay poster boy has been caught in gay bars as recently as this fall. Those who witnessed it recognized him and reported the incident—he was not there seeking other converts but satisfaction for his out-of-the-ordinary and out-of-the-mainstream sexual needs. There are countless other ex-gays who have returned to the life-style after failed attempts to change.

Father JP: We are all human, weak, and can all fall. It wouldn't take 12 steps to get me to fall; probably one or two would be enough.

But let's face it, the fall of a handful of men who fell back into the life-style does not mean that it is impossible to change. Even the best programs for reforming alcoholics or drug addicts only see success rates between 60 and 70 percent.

Jeremy: But just the fact that the ex-gay movement is trying to fix us means God made a mistake. Can't people just accept our homosexuality as God's gift to us?

Father JP: Jeremy, I'm not trying to fix you or to heal you, but encourage you to develop your relationships. As one who has been providing spiritual guidance for many years, I can help you heal and deepen your relationship with God. Also, I can help you in your relationship with others too.

I don't know exactly what you are referring to by the "ex-gay movement," but studies have been done on re-orientation therapies and found them effective, at least for some. The fact is, some people do not want a gay or lesbian life-style and have found psychotherapy and support groups helpful in dealing with, controlling, and redirecting their homosexual desires and tendencies.

Even Paul seems to indicate that such change is possible, since he says: "And such were some of you" when he mentions male-intercourse among the unrighteous deeds of those who will not inherit the kingdom of God (1 Corinthians 6:9-11), as well in Ephesians 2:3, 5:8.

Jeremy: But are these ex-gays just avoiding homosexual activities because of fear and shame, or is it a real change in their attraction? It would be wrong just to repress or deny our *natural* sexualized longings, or to disguise these longings as a simple matter of "choice."

Father JP: You are right that to simply repress or deny our emotions does not heal us. But there are choices we can freely make, and that is what we all need to learn to do. I want you to be truly free so that you can declare your actions truly your own and not the product of genetics or of how you were raised.

Now, if it is OK to help people struggling with obesity, smoking, alcoholism, or drug addiction to change—not by repression, but by developing healthy life-habits that help them restrain some desires—then why is it a crime to help those with homosexual inclinations learn to live a chaste life without repression and denial?

Sam: Jeremy, I want to ask you a tough question: Is your identity so fragile you cannot bear the possibility that others actually choose not to be gay?

Jeremy: Sam... you think that I'm just some emotional weakling? I resent that. You straight guys are always looking down on us as some kind of freaks of nature.

Father JP: We need to treat each other with respect. Jeremy, what I think Sam was trying to say is if you are to insist that we respect those living out the homosexual life-style, then why can't you respect those who freely and legitimately choose to live a chaste life, despite their same-sex attractions, channeling their sexual desires with healthy life-habits?

Jeremy: Because it implies that we are defective if we don't live that way. You are implying that we are sick and that we need to change.

Sam: But it is true that some drug addicts have found healing and have changed the direction of their lives. Even if a particular addict should choose not to change, it doesn't give him the right to deny those who want to change the right to enter a rehab program. That too would be wrong.

Jeremy: But you are marginalizing us as pariahs to society, just like the low-life drug addicts. Don't you realize how much that hurts?

Father JP: Jeremy, Sam doesn't intend to hurt you. He really cares about you; otherwise he would never have introduced the two of us. What he wants for you is to have a greater and more complete sense of freedom. You can more freely choose who you want to be by choosing to heal and enter into relationships; relationships with God, with family members, and with others.

Healing Our Relationship with God

Jeremy: You seem to be saying that we are truly free to heal our relationship with God and with others. But if I believe that God already loves me just as I am, then why do I need healing?

Father JP: Because we all sin. Sin is nothing else than the injury or killing of our relationship with God. Sin is not sin because we do anything that really harms God or because of the objective value of what we do, but because he indeed loves us and our actions do affect our relationship with him.

Jeremy: Why would God care what I do with my body? How does me masturbating or having sex with my boyfriend affect my relationship with him? Doesn't God have more important things to worry about?

Father JP: God cares about what we do with our bodies because he loves us. He wants us to be happy. He wants us to enjoy eternity with him in heaven.

Our actions impact our relationship with him and impact our happiness. Look at Adam and Eve: God wanted to share his intimate friendship and his own divine life with them. But they disobeyed his commandment and ate the fruit of the Tree of Knowledge of Good and Evil. Why did God care what they did with that fruit? Because God would then have to allow Adam and Eve to experience the consequences of their decision: death, pain in childbearing, toil in work, and the tendency of men to treat women as objects (Genesis 3:16-19).

Our actions also impact the relationships we have with our loved-ones. For example, an unfaithful husband may say to his wife, "Why should you care what I do with my body?" She does care, because she loves him; she has given her whole life to him. Now, he has shattered their relationship and broken their covenant by what he did with his body. Also, if his children learn about it, it would destroy their respect for him and likely they will no longer want to have any relationship with him.

So, God cares because God loves you.

Jeremy: So, if I have already broken or killed my relationship with God, then what difference does it make what I do?

Father JP: Because God still loves you and longs for you to respond freely by loving him in return. Thus he desires your freedom from sin.

Consider God's Old Testament People. They broke their covenant with God so many times, returning to worship idols, even to the point of sacrificing their children to Molech. But after chastising them God forgave their sin and welcomed them back into his friendship.

What God seeks is that we acknowledge our sin, repent, and try to amend our lives.

Jeremy: How do I know what I do actually hurts or kills my relationship with God? If it doesn't feel bad, then how can it be so bad?

Father JP: There are times when we rationalize our actions and fool ourselves about whether they are good or bad. In such cases, God has to somehow reveal it to us.

God had to send the prophet Nathan to David for this purpose. David was walking on the roof of his house and spotted a beautiful woman bathing. He asked for her and he committed adultery with her. When he learned that she had become pregnant, he had her husband killed in battle, and he then took this woman to be one of his wives.

Nathan came to David to tell him of God's displeasure with

him. David acknowledged his sin and he knew that he deserved to die for it. However, God accepted his repentance and forgave his sin (2 Samuel 11:1-12:14).

Jeremy: So, you are being Nathan to me, telling me that I have displeased God and am alienated from him because of my engaging in gay sex?

Father JP: It is your sin that displeases God.

Remember the woman caught in adultery? Christ does not want to condemn you but to invite you to sin no more.

Christ offers us the opportunity to confess our sin and receive forgiveness. This restores our relationship with God and brings us back into his family.

Sam: Is that all one has to do to restore one's relationship with God? It seems kind of shallow.

Father JP: We have to work on corresponding to God's grace. Repentance and forgiveness are the first steps, but then we need to reform our lives in such a way to correspond to that forgiveness.

Think again of the example of the man who was caught by his wife in an adulterous relationship. It shattered their relationship. However, after he realized what he was losing—the love of his life and the children who were so dear to his heart—he repented. He begged her to forgive him, and she did, receiving him back into the family and into the marriage.

So, would it then be OK for him to spend time with his former mistress, as long as they refrain from sex?

Sam: No way! His wife would insist that he break all contact with her. If he were truly sincere, he would look for ways of building up his relationship with his wife, building up trust, taking her out, lavishing affection and attention on her.

Father JP: That's exactly what we need to do with God.

Sam: JP, this example makes me think that the woman, had she known that her fiancé would be unfaithful, would never have married him. Although she has no ability of foreseeing this, God does. Why would God, knowing that we are going to sin gravely, still decide to create us and befriend us?

Father JP: God respects our freedom and wants us to love him in return, but freely, not under constraint.

God knows that sometimes the only way to get us to love him freely is by letting us go, letting us fall into sin. I think of the parable of the Prodigal Son (Luke 15:11-32). The younger of two sons asks his father to give him his share of the inheritance. The father could have refused to give him what he asked for. But he did, even though he knew his son would waste it. However, emotionally his son had already left home, perhaps resenting the superficial "goodness" of his older brother. He blamed everyone else, especially his father, for his unhappiness and sought to escape. The father simply loved him and let him go, hoping that he would come to his senses and return.

Thus, God can turn our sinfulness into something good, but we have to freely decide to cooperate... freely decide to work on becoming a good and loving son of our father, God.

Jeremy: Are you saying that if I were to go to confession and receive absolution from my sin, would that be enough to change me, to suddenly make me good?

Father JP: As a person, Jeremy, you are already good. God already loves you. Going to confession is a way to acknowledge our responsibility for our sinful ways and to return to a healthy relationship with God the Father; that relationship is his grace.

Sam: But is that all there is to it, JP?

DEEPENING OUR RELATIONSHIP WITH GOD

Father JP: God is calling you to more. In the parable of the Prodigal Son, when the prodigal son resolved to return to his father's house, he made plans to say to his father, "Father, I have sinned against heaven and before you; I am no longer worthy to be called your son; treat me as one of your hired servants" (Luke 15:18-19). He knew that he didn't deserve to be his father's son. He was happy just to be a servant or a slave in his father's house.

But when he arrives, his father doesn't even let him get his full confession out; he welcomes his son back as a son, running up to him while he is still at a distance, giving him a big embrace, smothering him with kisses, and clothing him with the robe and ring of a son (Luke 15:21-22).

So, besides confessing our sins, we need to accept our sonship and build up our relationship to God as Father.

Jeremy: How do we do this, Father? I have never felt close to God as Father. I could never please him by keeping myself free from sin. How can I expect him to accept me back as his son? I have never been a good son and don't feel I have it in me.

Father JP: To be a good son of the Father we need to do what good children do. First, we need to entrust our lives to him with faith. Children believe that their father will provide and protect them no matter how they behave. We need to do the same, by abandoning our worries, our success and failure, our future and our past, into his paternal hands.

Faith in Our Father God also means believing all that God reveals to us and transmits to us through our Mother, the Church, not because we make sense of it all—although it does make sense if we understand the big picture. We believe because we have decided to trust God and that he is not going to make us believe in something false.

Faith also means obedience to all his commandments, trusting that God knows what is best for us. We let Our Father God direct our lives because we believe that—as our Creator—he knows what is best for us, his creatures.

Jeremy: What if I believe, but I'm not ready to believe absolutely everything that the Church teaches or I'm not ready to obey all God's commandments?

I want to believe, JP, that God loves me and is welcoming me back, but some of the things the Church teaches just don't make sense to me. I just can't accept the Church's insistence on no sex until marriage or that masturbation is a sin.

Father JP: Our Father God is patient. He will wait as long as it takes until you are ready to return completely. He does not want to force you to accept his commands and believe his revelation because you feel forced. He wants you to reenter his family, and be ready to develop a relationship with him, with his Son—Jesus Christ—and with the Holy Spirit, as well as with all your brothers and sisters in the Church.

Sam: So, returning to God with a contrite heart for all your sins is not enough.

Father JP: It just entails so much more than confessing our sins to God. Our Father God would not be happy if we are not on good terms with the rest of the family, like his Son.

Jeremy: Then, I take it that our relationship with Christ is also important.

Father JP: You bet it is. It helps us develop our full, transcendental identity.

Jeremy: Then, if I have developed a relationship with God the Father, what more must I do, Father JP, to develop a relationship with Christ?

Father JP: Christ invites us to be his friend, his brother:

No longer do I call you servants, for the servant does not know what his master is doing; but I have called you friends, for all that I have heard from my Father I have made known to you (John 15:15).

To develop our friendship with Christ, we need to spend time with him in prayer, to open up our heart to him and tell him about our joys and sorrows, our hurts, our disappointments, as well as our successes. Everything we would like to tell a friend we should bring to our dialogue with Jesus Christ—EVERYTHING!

Jeremy: So, you are saying that our relationship with Christ can be as close as a good friendship and that all we need to do is open up our heart to him in prayer? That seems too easy.

Father JP: That is the start, Jeremy. We also should take up our cross daily (Luke 9:23-26), because he showed us how much he loved us by dying on the Cross "Greater love has no man than this, that a man lay down his life for his friends" (John 15:13).

His sacrificial love is intimate, complete, total—a spousal kind of friendship! And it calls us to respond in like manner: "By this we know love, that he laid down his life for us; and we ought to lay down our lives for the brethren" (1 John 3:16).

So, by developing a friendship with Jesus Christ, we will never be disappointed in any other friendship, because Christ will be the firm basis of our identity. It will help heal the loneliness, sadness, and male insecurity produced by brother- or peer rejections and will be an ongoing source of confidence, strength, and happiness. If you knew that you had a friend who loved you so much that he volunteered to suffer and die for you, then you would come to know your true value and worth.

Jeremy: I can't imagine someone loving *me* like that... loving *me* without getting anything back in return... giving up everything for *me*... without getting "his"...

Father JP: Jeremy, Jesus died for you. When he was agonizing in the garden of Gethsemane, he thought of you in your sinfulness and said Yes to his heavenly father.

Jeremy: Then why would he allow me to suffer all that I have suffered these long years of loneliness, of hurt, of longing for love and not receiving it. If he really loved me, then he would have prevented this from happening.

Father JP: Perhaps he knew that this was the only way you'd really respond to his love, that you had to experience pain and hurt so you would know how good it feels to be healed and forgiven and so that you would share that with others. Perhaps he knew that you would reach an even more intimate loving relationship with him only after such an experience.

Jeremy: And what about the Holy Spirit, Father JP? Don't we also need a loving relationship with the Holy Spirit if we are to have a solid "transcendental" identity, as you call it?

Sam: You guys got me lost. I mean, I can follow how important it is to have a relationship with God, but I don't go for this Trinity stuff.

Father JP: Patience, Sam. Although you don't understand the Trinity—neither do I fully, it is a mystery—I hope you can understand and appreciate how important it is to have these multiple relationships to God.

God reveals himself to us as Father. Even the Psalms of the Hebrew Scriptures reveal God to us in this manner. Let me read you some passages from the Old Testament:

Of old thou didst speak in a vision to thy faithful one, and say: "I have set the crown upon one who is mighty, I have exalted one chosen from the people. I have found David, my servant... my hand shall ever abide with him, my arm also shall strengthen him... He shall cry to me, 'Thou art my Father, my God, and the Rock of my salvation.' And I will make him the first-born.... My steadfast love I will keep for him for ever (Psalm 89:19-28).

Sing to God, sing praises to his name... his name is the LORD, exult before him! Father of the fatherless and protector of widows... God gives the desolate a home to dwell in (Psalm 68:4-6).

As a father pities his children, so the LORD pities those who fear him (Psalm 103:13).

Sam: That is fine, JP, I can believe in a God who is father, but that doesn't mean that he's a Trinity.

Father JP: You're right. But besides our filial relationship with him, the Hebrew Scriptures also calls us to relate to God as the Spouse of his people:

For your Maker is your husband, the LORD of hosts is his name... For the LORD has called you like a wife... For the mountains may depart and the hills be removed, but my steadfast love shall not depart from you, and my covenant of peace shall not be removed, says the LORD (Isaiah 54:5-6, 10).

They also reveal God's Wisdom to us as Friend:

Say to wisdom, You are my sister... and intimate friend (Proverbs 7:4-5).

This means that we are also called to have a spousal friendship with God, which is distinct from being a son or daughter of God.

Sam: OK... but I don't quite see where you're going with this.

Father JP: Well, there is a third kind of relationship we should have with God. In Genesis 1, God's Spirit is the source of all creation and is the source of all gifts and powers to man, whether to Joseph, Moses, David, and so many others in the Old Testament (cf. Genesis 41:38; Exodus 31:3, etc.):

> Because the Spirit of the Lord has filled the world, and that which holds all things together knows what is said; therefore no one who utters unrighteous things will escape notice, and justice, when it punishes, will not pass him by (Wisdom 1:7-8).

> There shall come forth a shoot from the stump of Jesse, and a branch shall grow out of his roots. And the Spirit of the LORD shall rest upon him, the spirit of wisdom and understanding, the spirit of counsel and might, the spirit of knowledge and the fear of the LORD (Isaiah 11:1-2).

> The Spirit of the Lord GOD is upon me, because the LORD has anointed me to bring good tidings to the afflicted; he has sent me to bind up the brokenhearted, to proclaim liberty to the captives… to proclaim the year of the lord's favor (Isaiah 61:1-2).

This means that we relate to God as Spirit, as spousal friend, and as father. This gives each person a Trinitarian identity.

Jeremy: And so, Sam, Father JP is trying to show us that there are three persons in God and so we need to have three kinds of relationship with God: a son-father relationship, a spousal-friend relationship, and a relationship with the Spirit of God.

But, Father, how in the world are we suppose to develop a relationship with the Holy Spirit?

Father JP: That is an impressive summary, Jeremy; you are getting it. I ask you, Sam, to have patience with us—although you may not believe that there are three persons in God, I hope you can a least see how even the Hebrew Scripture reveal these three kinds of relationship between God and his people.

Sam: I think I get what you are saying, JP, although I don't know whether I fully agree with your analysis and conclusion. I think

I'd like to go home and reflect on these Scripture passages on my own.

Father JP: That's fair, Sam.

Regarding developing our relationship with the Holy Spirit, Jeremy, really it is quite simple. First is to welcome him, that is, to acknowledge and welcome the Life and gifts that he gives each one of us personally and individually:

*Now there are varieties of gifts, but the same Spirit...
but it is the same God who inspires them all in every one.
To each is given the manifestation of the Spirit for the common good. To one is given through the Spirit the utterance
of wisdom, and to another the utterance of knowledge...
to another faith... to another gifts of healing... to another
the working of miracles, to another prophecy, to another
the ability to distinguish between spirits, to another various
kinds of tongues, to another the interpretation of tongues. All
these are inspired by one and the same Spirit, who appor-
tions to each one individually as he wills... (1 Corinthians
12:4-11).*

Once we acknowledge those freely given gifts—and each person receives different gifts (cf. 1 Corinthians 12:14-41)—we need to use those gifts we have received in the service to others. If God has given you a sensitivity for the needs and sufferings of others, then you must show that compassion in serving them in their needs. Thus, by using the gifts and authority given to us to nurture New Life in others we serve God and enter into a deeper relationship with God as Spirit.

Sam: That's a bit abstract and vague, JP. Could you give us some specific examples?

Father JP: You're right, Sam, this can be a bit abstract.

Think of it this way. Suppose God's creative Spirit gave you a talent for playing the piano. You welcomed that gift by trying to cultivate it, practicing long hours as a child to learn the skill well.

One day you're playing the piano with great emotion for a group of people, when one of them is moved by the beauty of the music you're playing and suddenly "sees" that there is a God. That beauty—beauty of that intensity—just wouldn't make any sense unless there was something higher that was the source of that beauty.

This is reflected in the Hebrew Scriptures, how the artisans of the Ark and of the Sanctuary were guided by God's Spirit to do beautiful works that drew others toward God:

> And Moses said to the people of Israel, "See, the LORD has called by name Bezalel... and he has filled him with the Spirit of God, with ability, with intelligence, with knowledge, and with all craftsmanship, to devise artistic designs, to work in gold and silver and bronze... for work in every skilled craft. And he has inspired him to teach, both him and Oholiab... He has filled them with ability to do every sort of work done by a craftsman or by a designer or by an embroiderer in blue and purple and scarlet stuff and fine twined linen, or by a weaver–by any sort of workman or skilled designer" (Exodus 35:30-35).

Sam: In fact, one of my friends did have an experience like you described. He was moved by the beauty of a piece of music that he heard and was converted from being an atheist to become a believer. Of course, it's not that simple, but his sensitivity to and experience of beauty was the vehicle to lead him to God.

Father JP: Well, if you were the channel for the grace of that conversion, then you would have a new relationship with God through that experience. Seeing a new convert striving to live as a believer would encourage you to be more faithful to the grace you have received and encourage you to be an example to him.

Thus building up our relationship to God—our *relationships* to God—and our relationships to the angels and saints—our holy brothers and sisters who are with God—we develop a great, secure identity and the sense of our true self-worth.

Since Joseph was such loving and gentle earthly father to Jesus, many also discover that—as a friend and brother to Jesus—they can enter into Jesus' relationship to Joseph and find there what they didn't have growing up.

HEALING OUR RELATIONSHIPS WITH OTHERS

Jeremy: But our masculine identity does not just rely on our relationship with God. It also depends greatly on our relationships to other human beings. I can't imagine having a relationship just with God.

Father JP: Right you are, Jeremy. As human beings we are born into a web of relationships and are called to make and engender many other relationships throughout our lives. This will give us an even clearer and firmer masculine identity as a human person.

This is also a good part of the path for healing one's identity, moving beyond the identity based on performance.

Jeremy: But I have always had lots of relationships and lots of friends, JP. Why would I ever develop a homosexual identity?

Father JP: Let's go through a few things you have revealed to us. Now, if I bring these things up it is not to criticize you, but to help you see how your past affected your relationships. Are you OK with that?

Jeremy: I guess so.

Father JP: First, you mentioned how you knew you were not attracted to naked women when your brother exposed you to porn. Now, did you tell you mom or dad that?

Jeremy: No. I was too embarrassed and ashamed about that. If they learned that I was gay back then they would have freaked out.

Sam: How about your brother, did you tell him?

Jeremy: Are you kidding? He made fun of me and even called me "gay." I certainly wasn't going to expose myself to any more ridicule.

Father JP: Well, did you tell anyone? A friend, the priest, a grandparent?

Jeremy: No. I was afraid, just like any other kid would be.

Father JP: What this says to me, is that you were not yourself with anyone. You had to keep this to yourself, but that meant you kept it from others: from you mom and dad; from your brother, friends, and relatives.

Jeremy: That is why I just had to come out of the closet, Father. It was eating away at me inside.

Father JP: But it also meant that your relationships were kept at a superficial level. If someone loved you, they were loving this person that you were pretending to be, not your full and true self. Because of that, your "false" identity that you were pretending to be in order not to be rejected, embarrassed, or ridiculed was based on trying to be the kind of person you thought they considered loveable. But this was insecure and frightening: "What if they found out the truth, would they still love me?"

Jeremy: That is so true, Father. I was frightened. I couldn't be myself. Indeed, I was so very isolated, even though I could pretend to be so content and happy.

Father JP: And all that continued, with a good part of you remaining hidden and secret from everyone, from all your friends and family, until Rick exposed your secret. Then you finally felt understood, there no longer was any hidden secret, you could be yourself with him, and you achieved apparent intimacy with someone for the first time.

Jeremy: Wow, Father, you're right on! I finally had an identity because I finally had a relationship with a male who seemed to accept and affirm me!

Sam: But where is Rick now, Jeremy?

Jeremy: He dumped me after he graduated from high school and went to college. He told me that he couldn't live without a relationship; it was the first weekend at college that he was in bed with another guy—no, with several, in fact... It was the saddest day of my life when I learned that. I have to admit... I seriously considered suicide, but I guess I was too scared to face eternity.

Father JP: So, you achieved a certain fleeting identity by your relationship with Rick. And when Salleen also became aware of your homosexual inclinations, then you felt safe to be yourself with everybody. But when Rick dumped you, your weak relational identity was shattered and you were left with the homosexual identity, both in your own mind and in the mind of everyone who came to know of it.

Jeremy: That is right on the money, Father JP.

Sam: Wow, that does make a lot of sense. So, how do you

heal that?

Father JP: Well, a good part of the process of healing your relational identity is by healing those relationships. You need to forgive anyone you were angry at and to let go of any resentment or hurt you may still be harboring.

The first step in this process is to acknowledge those feelings of hurt and anger, and then to decide to understand those who have hurt you and begin the hard work of forgiving and letting go.

John Paul II stated that to not forgive those who have hurt us is to become prisoners of our past.

Jeremy: Father JP, I have wanted to forgive. I do love my parents and my brother a lot. However, every time I think about the past, my emotions get riled up and all the resentment comes back, and they just overwhelm me. I just can't forget.

HEALING OUR EMOTIONS WITH THERAPY

Father JP: Sometimes the emotional wounds can run so deep that we find forgiveness next to impossible. We need to take our anger and resentment to God, asking him to forgive the person who has hurt us, that he would do so on our behalf. Even Jesus does this from the Cross when he says, "Father, forgive them; for they know not what they do" (Luke 23:34).

It may take a therapist to help us resolve our emotional pain. We want to make an act of the will to forgive or to not give in to our anger, insecurities, sadness, and fears, but our emotions paralyze us, keeping us from being able to act and from forming new relationships and our full identity. Thus our emotions lead us to do the very things we don't want to do, as Paul tells us (Romans 7:13-25).

Also, we often escape from our emotional pain through denial. As time passes, the emotional pain only grows underneath the surface until we can no longer cope with it. This leads to loss of concentration, memory, and clear thinking until our emotions finally take over.

Jeremy: Isn't therapy a kind of mind-control in which you give another person control over you in order to reshape your personality?

Father JP: Therapy ought to be a truly human interaction between an individual and his therapist. One must enter into this as a subject who decides for himself. A good therapist does not try to control your life, but respects your conscience, helps you to get to know yourself better, to get to know your emotional triggers, conflicts, and the therapist can strategize with you on how to deal with different emotional situations. But, it is the client who is in full control of his destiny, making the choices that lead to recovery. To be fully human a person must decide for himself.

We may not decide to have certain feelings, but we can decide how we want to react to them after they do come. We can also decide to develop the ability to act independently of those emotions. The individual must always freely choose his future and be convinced that he has the power to determine it.

Sam: Why is it so hard to heal the emotions? Isn't our decision to love and give ourselves to another the key to building up a relationship and healing our identity?

Father JP: You are correct, Sam, the decision of our free will to give ourselves as a gift to another is key to building up relationships. However, as human beings, our emotions influence our decisions.

For example, loneliness—the absence of human affection for which we long—can cause us to become very self-absorbed and seek substitutes for that affection in self-gratification or in anonymous or superficial sexual relations. The emotion almost becomes compulsive wherein we have little control over our actions. Thus, the loneliness, which should move us to get out of ourselves and seek to be with others and to establish new relationships overwhelms us and accomplishes the opposite.

So, emotional loneliness can be a great barrier to establishing relationships. A therapist can help us identify the onset of this emotion and teach us how to control it and direct it in a healthy manner.

Jeremy: I imagine that there are other emotions that produce barriers to relationships. For instance, doesn't anger also make healing and establishing relationships more difficult?

Father JP: Yes, one must overcome anger in order to heal a relationship. Also, sadness, depression, anxiety, and mistrust all tend to lead to narcissism, which is a kind of pathological self-absorption that leads to excessive anger and is the principal reason why relationships collapse and why people abandon God and religion.

Jeremy: How would healing my anger and loneliness help me overcome my homosexual desires and achieve a more masculine identity?

Father JP: Healthier relationships will come with the healing of your emotional conflicts related to relationships, and healthy relationships will impact your homosexual inclinations. For example, if you are angry with your father it may stir up your desires for comfort in a male relationship. Or if you have profound loneliness, you may seek consolation in an anonymous sexual relationship.

Again, this is where a good therapist can help. He can help you see how certain emotions and cognitions predispose you to behave and feel in a particular way, especially in helping you understand the source of your emotional conflicts and to come up with strategies to resolve them in a healthy way.

To achieve a more masculine identity, one must learn how healthy men relate to other men and how they properly relate to women. If you are accustomed to having girl-to-girl-like conversations with women, then it will help to learn how to put up proper boundaries so you interact with women like a man and then develop a masculine, brotherly relationship toward women.

Sam: But isn't there a therapy specifically to overcome homosexuality? Wouldn't it be best for Jeremy to focus directly on the emotional orientation that produces the homosexual attraction?

Father JP: There are therapists who specialize in helping people with same-sex attraction. However, since healing comes with dominion over emotions and improved relationships, most therapists don't focus on curing the homosexual inclinations directly.

Focusing on the sexual orientation just gets us focused too much on ourselves, and it highlights our failures, which lead to discouragement and embarrassment when we don't get immediate results. Striving to overcome our same-sex attraction can even become an obsession, making it almost impossible to make any progress.

That is why good therapists tend to work on the source of our insecurity, sadness, anger, anxiety with peers, loneliness, compulsions, etc., unraveling our complex array of emotions and helping us with a strategy to conquer them.

Jeremy: Can one really get over homosexual inclinations in this way? It seems like an unsurpassable mountain to me.

Father JP: Jeremy, be patient. It takes time to heal past relationships and strong emotional triggers. We'll have to work on them one at a time. Also, it takes time to develop a network of good relationships. Both are essential. But I assure you, both can be done.

As you begin to live your new identity, as you enter into relationships with men and women with more honesty and genuine intimacy, the new patterns of thoughts, emotions, and behavior will develop and supplant the old ones engraved in your heart.

Sam: But what if a therapist refuses to help the individual wanting to change? Perhaps he says that change is impossible. What do you do then?

Father JP: If you go to a therapist and tell him or her that you want to change from being gay to become "straight," then most will tell you that is impossible or even unethical.

It would be better to ask for help in developing healthy relationships and overcoming the emotional barriers to them. You can ask for help in forgiving your father, or in detaching yourself from a controlling and manipulating mother, in overcoming your anger or your sense of inferiority, in healing sexual abuse as a child, or in overcoming your sexual addiction or substance abuse. Most competent therapists will be more than willing to help you in these areas. Then you will develop a healthy identity as you develop good healthy relationships.

Although having a therapist experienced in gender reorientation can be helpful, it is not absolutely necessary. In either case, the therapist will still need to help the person identify and overcome past peer rejection and isolation, mother- or father-wounds, weaknesses in confidence, anxieties, depressions, anger, loneliness, poor body image, obsessions, compulsions, etc. In this way the therapist can help unravel the person's complex array of emotions and reaction mechanisms and help him understand himself better.

Jeremy: Does it matter whether or not the therapist is Catholic or Christian?

Father JP: What is most important is that the therapist is qualified, and understands and respects your Catholic and Christian faith, especially regarding the Church's teaching on homosexuality.

I once encouraged a college student to see a psychiatrist for some severe anxiety problems that were affecting his schooling. He went instead to a therapist at the university—because there was no charge for the service. But the therapist was completely atheistic, anti-religion, and especially anti-Catholic. The therapist ridiculed me to this young man and encouraged him to "release" himself sexually in any manner that felt good. After a few weeks of unsatisfying experimentation, he came back to me and we resolved his issues more satisfactorily.

What you need, Jeremy, is a therapist who will work with you while respecting your faith, especially one who appreciates how a relationship with God is a good portion of a healthy identity and who will support that; one who will complement the spiritual guidance you get from your church.

A therapist who advocates homosexuality or who argues against Church teaching on homosexuality will likely produce more internal conflicts rather than resolve them.

Sam: Isn't it better to go to a psychiatrist rather than to a psychologist?

Father JP: A psychiatrist or a knowledgeable primary care physician can be very appropriate for the diagnosis and treatment of depression, obsessive-compulsive disorder, severe anxiety or panic attacks, etc. Psychiatrists can be particularly helpful in finding appropriate medication to treat the emotional ailment. In most cases, psychiatric treatment complements rather than substitutes therapy. Some psychiatrists complement appropriate medication with their own therapy to heal emotional issues.

Healing Our Social Network

Sam: JP, I've heard that programs like Alcoholics Anonymous are very effective for different kinds of addictions, are there any programs like that for homosexuals?

Father JP: I don't know how much they use the 12-step program of A.A., but there are several programs serving the homosexual community looking for support in living chastity.

One is a Catholic group called *Courage* that aims at helping those with homosexual inclinations live chaste lives, develop their relationship with God through prayer and the sacraments, learn to serve others, and develop a fellowship with others so that they know they are never alone. They also challenge homosexuals to become good examples for others while encouraging and supporting each other in living chastely.

Exodus International is another group with an extensive network of Christian programs and services to support people with same-sex attraction. It creates a support network helping those with homosexual inclinations develop their relationship with Jesus Christ and fellowship with other Christians.

Homosexuals Anonymous is also doing good things, but there are other groups such as *JONAH* for Jews and *Evergreen* for Mormons.

Both Exodus International and Courage have support groups for parents with children living a homosexual life-style.

Sam: Why would one join such a group as these? Homosexuality is a pretty intimate thing. Wouldn't sharing all these intimate feelings and emotions in a group just reinforce the tendency?

Father JP: The group dynamics of these organizations provide a strong emotional and social reinforcement to a person's desires to overcome this burden. They put a strong emphasis on developing a relationship with God and relying on him to restore their lives. They also put a lot of emphasis on taking responsibility for one's own life and repairing any damage caused by past decisions.

Finally, they foster a kind of accountability to keep one on track, or get back on track if one slips up. It is especially encouraging to be around other men or women who are struggling and who are filled with the joy, freedom, and personal fulfillment that come with a successful struggle.

Sam: All the effort that this takes to overcome homosexual inclinations seems to indicate that it is not easy to change.

Father JP: No one says it is easy. Was it easy for you and Margie to change, to go back and keep your relationship clean and chaste?

Sam: No, JP, but it doesn't take all this effort. We didn't need a therapist or a 12-step program to straighten out our dating practices.

Father JP: But it took two persons who were motivated to change and to treat each other more as persons. It also helps to have a network of friends who support you on living chastely, which is not easy to find these days. Also, both of you have been coming to see me from time to time so as to clarify doubts and get ideas on how to live your relationship as God wants.

This is exactly what these programs do for those with homosexual inclinations, with the principal difference that they specialize in the special needs, tendencies, and challenges that individuals with same-sex attraction face.

These groups provide a mechanism for peer accountability as well as mutual support. Also, these groups provide access to spiritual paternity in that they provide mentors or sponsors who can aid the person with homosexual inclinations on their particular path to holiness.

Jeremy: Does the Church require me to go to one of these programs and get therapy to change?

Father JP: No, of course not. If motivated, you may be able to sort out your emotional and relational issues on your own. What the Church requires is that all of us live chastity in thought, word, and deed.

However, you may benefit a lot from these means. Likewise, if you had cancer, the Church doesn't *require* you to see the doctor and go through an operation to be healed. However, for most people this is the most obvious way because it will help them recover most readily and be able to be there for their family and for society.

It is good to know that some people get a lot from therapy, while others get a lot from group support sessions, and some people seem to need both. There have always been a small percentage of people who have enough self-motivation to do it on their own.

How Does Therapy Differ From Spiritual Direction?

Jeremy: What about me just seeing you for spiritual guidance? How would that differ from therapy and support group sessions?

Father JP: I'd be fine with giving you spiritual direction, Jeremy. Spiritual direction, however, will focus on helping you develop your relationship with God, especially through prayer and the sacraments. Secondarily, it will help you in your relationship with others, since we must learn to see Christ in others and serve him through them.

Therapy focuses on resolving emotional conflicts that limit your freedom and put up barriers to relationships with others. It can help you identify your emotional reaction mechanism and challenge you to direct your emotions in more positive ways. In this way you get to know yourself better, take more dominion over your life, so as to be able to better give your life to God and to others. It would thus complement the spiritual direction that you receive.

Support groups, on the other hand, make use of our social

nature to motivate us to keep up the fight. When we know that others are counting on us and that we are in this battle together, it is easier to overcome discouragement and keep on fighting.

Jeremy: Will spiritual direction cure me?

Father JP: Jeremy, spiritual direction is not meant to cure, but to direct you. It will help you learn to carry the cross of your homosexual inclinations, in a similar fashion as though you were diagnosed with cancer: the spiritual direction is not there to cure the cancer but to help you bear it in a Christian manner, picking up your cross and following Christ. Your same-sex attraction may endure for some time, even years, but you can learn to carry it with a Christian spirit.

And if you have some falls, spiritual direction can help you start again and see the humiliation as God's tool to find you and welcome you back as the lost sheep that was found:

What do you think? If a man has a hundred sheep, and one of them has gone astray, does he not leave the ninety-nine on the mountains and go in search of the one that went astray? And if he finds it, truly, I say to you, he rejoices over it more than over the ninety-nine that never went astray. So it is not the will of my Father who is in heaven that one of these little ones should perish (Matthew 18:12-14).

Jeremy: Is that all that spiritual direction does, help me learn to bear my homosexuality without complaining? That seems like a waste of time and energy. I think I'd rather just go with the therapy.

Father JP: Jeremy, spiritual direction does more than just help you bear your contradiction. It can help you deal with many aspects of your life.

For example, both spiritual direction and therapy can help you with the aspect of forgiving someone: the therapist will help you deal with the emotions and cognitions that make it hard to forgive, whereas, the spiritual director will help you understand how forgiveness (or lack thereof) affects one's relationship with God. The sacrament of reconciliation is particularly helpful in the resolution of deep resentment caused by peer or parental rejection.

Jeremy: OK, I can certainly benefit from that. But is that it? Isn't there anything more that spiritual direction will help me with?

Father JP: A good spiritual director should help you develop your prayer life and cultivate a strong sense of divine filiation and other supernatural relationships. The more one develops an identity based on his or her relationship with God the Father, Jesus Christ, and the Holy Spirit, the less peer or parental acceptance, body image or sexuality will hold sway.

As John Paul II explains:

Precisely in and through prayer, man comes to discover in a very simple and yet profound way his own unique subjectivity: in prayer the human "I" more easily perceives the depth of what it means to be a person.

In prayer one comes to experience the healing and liberating friendship of Jesus, particularly when one feels rejected, isolated and lonely. Again, John Paul II says:

And [human] love can be deepened and preserved only by love, the love which is "poured into our hearts through the Holy Spirit which has been given to us" (Romans 5:5) [i.e., love from God].

Jeremy: Father JP, do you think I need therapy? Frankly, I would prefer continuing with you in spiritual direction.

Father JP: You can do both, Jeremy. I think you may benefit quite a bit from some therapy as well as from spiritual direction.

I was thinking that therapy could be especially helpful to you in your relationship with your brother. You give me the impression that you are very emotionally tied to your brother, too much so, in fact. Because of that he may feel as though you are too needy and clingy, and thus he tries to avoid contact with you.

Jeremy: Yes, you are probably right.

Sam: Jeremy, I have also felt that you are very emotionally needy toward me as well.

Jeremy: Do you feel that I've been clingy as well?

Sam: Some of the time I have, Jeremy, but only some of the time.

Father JP: Don't worry, Jeremy. If you were to get some therapy, both to explore the roots of this as well as to develop strategies to overcome this, you will be able to develop more friends, perhaps even with your brother, Jeff.

Jeremy: That would be awesome, Father, really awesome.

Sam: Yes, it certainly would be, Jeremy.

Jeremy: Then, can I start spiritual direction with you now, Father JP?

Father JP: Yes, but it is getting late and we have already covered a lot of material.

Jeremy: But can I do a confession before I leave?

Father JP: Sure...

At this point, Father JP asked Sam to step outside for a few minutes as Jeremy went through the last eight years of his life. He came out beaming, full of great peace.

Female Homosexual Identity

Having followed Father JP's suggestion, Margie had been meeting with BillyLu quite regularly. Margie shared many of the things about the homosexual identity she had picked up from Sam and Father JP. They also discussed things about BillyLu's life, including the relationships she had in her life with her mother, father, brothers, high school friends, past boyfriends, girlfriends, partners, etc.

Then turmoil occurred: BillyLu's partner kicked her out of their house... Trying to help pick up the pieces, Margie arranged for her and BillyLu to meet together with Father JP.

Margie: Father JP, thank you for getting together with us on such short notice. I wanted us to meet, because BillyLu is quite depressed. I thought you could help us through this.

Father JP: What's wrong, BillyLu? Is there any reason for you being so down?

BillyLu: You bet there is, JP, and it's all your fault.

Margie: She is blaming you, but especially me, for unsettling her life. You see, her partner kicked her out of the house.

Father JP: Why?

BillyLu: Because she was jealous of my friendship with Margie. Even after I told her that Margie was "straight" and that she was practically engaged to her boyfriend, she wouldn't believe me. She accused me of having an affair.

   She also gave me an ultimatum: "Either stop meeting with Margie and that 'homophobic' priest or we're through."

Father JP: She doesn't trust you, does she?

BillyLu: Why should she? I'm the one who has been meeting with another woman.

Father JP: What if you invited her to join you and Margie. I'd even be willing to have her join our dialogue.

Margie: I already suggested that...

BillyLu: Sure you did, but she wouldn't hear of it. She doesn't want anything to do with people who may challenge or threaten our relationship. She gave me a week to decide...

Father JP: Is this the first time this has happened, BillyLu?

BillyLu: No... It happens from time to time. Usually, it is after Leslie starts flirting with another woman at a gay bar. Longing for her attention, I start doing the same. Then she gets jealous and we fight. A couple of times it has been pretty ugly... yet she always takes me back. It's the game she plays.

   But this time, I'm the one to blame by spending so much time with Margie.

Father JP: BillyLu, it's up to you to decide whether or not to continue to play this game. No one can make that decision for you.

I can see that you still have a large hole in your heart and that you really long to fill it, but I'm also sure that Leslie cannot fill it for you. I'll pray that you make the right decision, one that will bring you true peace.

MORE OF BILLYLU'S STORY

Margie: Father JP, I thought that BillyLu would benefit from the topic of relationship-based identity that you discussed with Sam and Jeremy. I think it would help me a great deal too.

BillyLu: I'm confused, JP. You seem pretty calm and levelheaded. I got myself into this relationship with Leslie. It seemed like it was just the right thing to do. Now, it seems to be falling apart. I don't know… You seem to have *all* the answers. Certainly my husband is not going to take me back. So, where does that leave me? I just don't know who I am anymore.

Perhaps you can help me figure out who I am and where I should be.

Margie: Father JP, as you described to Sam and Jeremy how performance-based identity can be so fragile and can lead to all sorts of manias, I was thinking you could help each of us discover her identity and how we can take more control of it.

Father JP: BillyLu, how do you see your identity? According to your description, you seemed to have had good relationships with both your parents and with your brothers. You should have a strong relationship-based identity. But you don't, do you?

BillyLu: There were a few things I've shared with Margie that I didn't tell you last time.

First, I was an extremely tough girl growing up, much tougher than my three older brothers. My dad was always quite disappointed in my brothers… But I was different. I'd be out and about with my dad, cutting hay, splitting wood, or other outdoor stuff.

At school, I preferred playing with the boys rather than with girls.

Father JP: You were a tough girl growing up, and now you seem to be continuing that way of being. Is that how you picture yourself?

BillyLu: I was tough because my brothers weren't. My dad was so happy when I mowed the field or when I cut and split a cord of wood. All the while my mother pampered my brothers and escaped into her alcoholism. Dad had no respect for mom or my lazy brothers, and certainly showed it with his foul language. He never used that language with me.

In school my brothers were often picked on and beaten up. This humiliated dad. Yet, when I was picked on, I fought back and always won, even when the boys fighting me were bigger. Dad was proud of his little...

Margie: Your dad really loved you, BillyLu, didn't he?

BillyLu: Sure, Margie, as long as I lived up to his expectations. It felt very good when he showed that he was proud of me, while frequently he was critical of mom—for her drinking and of her appearance—and of my brothers for their laziness and wimpiness.

Margie: Was your mother unattractive?

BillyLu: Oh no, she was a knockout when they first got married. I looked at the family pictures and I'm amazed at how beautiful she was.

But for some reason she let herself go. She got fat and stopped caring about how she looked.

She remained quiet and dutiful, never showing much of any emotion. She continued to tend to the "woman's" work like cooking and sewing and making the house pretty. She and my dad never showed much affection towards each other. She just didn't show any empathy or compassion, although she was always around for us.

Father JP: Perhaps she didn't think she could meet your dad's expectations, that she could never be beautiful enough for him, so she just stopped trying.

BillyLu: She stopped trying for all of us. Looking at the family album she gained weight with each ensuing pregnancy.

When I was born, I think dad was disappointed that I was such a plain looking girl. Mom never bought me dresses, afraid that I'd disappoint dad even more, so I wore my brothers' hand-me-downs.

Margie: But your dad was always complimentary toward you, why was that?

BillyLu: Because I was so much like him: tough, competitive, hardworking, sharp-tongued… He spent more time with me than with my brothers, as we worked together in the garage or in the yard, or watching sports on TV. When he was spending long hours at work, I'd continue the yard or garage projects, which would please him immensely.

Father JP: Was your dad ever upset with you, BillyLu?

BillyLu: Hardly ever… until senior year in high school. I was doing extremely well in basketball, having the best stats in the league. It looked like I was going to get a scholarship to college. Dad was at every game rooting me on.

Then I got injured. When I came back I just wasn't the same.

Dad began to bark orders at me during the game, and then criticize my play afterwards as we drove home. He cursed and cussed in the foulest way I've ever heard. He even threatened to disown me as his daughter.

I tried and tried to get my game back, but I just got worse. I hated myself for it... I just wanted to die.

After the season was over, dad returned to normal, only now he was criticizing me just like everyone else. Now I too was no longer good enough for him.

Father JP: I can see how this made you feel as though your world had been undone, BillyLu. How did you rebound from all this?

BillyLu: Well, not only my world was undone, in fact, it was destroyed. But that was only part of it. Shortly after that, I was reading a magazine in bed when my mom came into my room; she was drunk. I was looking through one of my dad's Playboys, which I tried to stash before she noticed, but she did anyway.

"I used to look like one of those models," she told me. "But after having your brothers, I didn't look the same. Fat, depressed, I couldn't please your dad. He needed a perfect beauty queen.

"I was overwhelmed trying to meet your brothers' needs and your dad's at the same time. Your dad started bringing home his porn magazines and leaving them out and opened on the table for me to see: trying to 'inspire me,'" she continued.

"Dad was disappointed with you at first. He wanted a beauty queen. He blamed me for you being so ordinary. But his attitude changed when you became the tough, hard working person he wanted to see in the boys.

"Now, BillyLu, you're in the same boat as I am," she concluded. We both knew what it was going to be like after I failed dad.

Margie: Didn't you break down and cry?

BillyLu: I wanted to. But when I saw my mother begin to sob, in her drunken stupor, it just turned my stomach. I pushed her away.

I was never attached to her anyway. I had written her off very early on. I just knew she was never going to be there for me so I stopped making the effort to please her and be closer to her, it just wouldn't make any difference anyway.

Father JP: Were you surprised by what your mother revealed to you?

BillyLu: No, not really. I kind of already knew.

Margie: Why do you think she told you all this?

BillyLu: I'm sure it is because she felt like a failure and was looking for some empathy. She felt bad for me because of dad's rejection, but she was still more interested in herself than in me.

Father JP: BillyLu, if you don't mind my asking, why were you looking at your father's Playboy.

BillyLu: I had discovered my father's magazines early on. "They horrified me at first. It was my first exposure of heterosexual sex and I found it frankly ugly, distorted, degrading, and even terrifying. I was repulsed at seeing women being treated as objects. Their eyes spoke volumes to me, about the terrible vacuity of meaningless sex and subsequently of the lives of these models. They were women trapped in this horrible abuse.

Margie: I also find porn disgusting and degrading, BillyLu. I can see how discovering your dad's addiction may have affected your perspective of men, especially of the possibility of a sexual relationship with them.

BillyLu: In many ways these magazines became iconographic of what heterosexual sex and penetration represented: I saw it as something threatening and disgusting, as a vehicle of tyrannical and exploitative domination, with the man always on top and imposing himself on the woman.

Margie: But then, if those magazines were so disgusting to you, why were you looking at those magazines when your mother walked in? If that had happened to me, I would've distance myself as far as I could from both those magazines and from my father.

BillyLu: For some reason, Margie—I can't tell you why—I was still drawn to those sickening magazines. Something about them just fascinated me. Perhaps it was because I still loved my dad at that point, and admired his sense of confidence and self-possession, and how he admired and treated me—he was not abusive toward me at all. Compared to my mom—she seemed like such a sad specimen of a human being—he was not too bad. Sure he had his weaknesses, but overall I looked up to him.

Father JP: It seems to me, BillyLu—but I may be wrong—that you admired and loved your father in a certain sense because he treated you as he treated other people he admired and respected… that is, as he treated men.

BillyLu: No… I mean Yes… Oh, wow… I don't know.

Margie: Why do you say that, Father? What difference would that make?

Father JP: I'm just wondering whether this may have created a certain ambivalence in BillyLu. On one hand, she loved and admired her father yet felt this great emotional repulsion for something he did. Our heart and head try to work out and make sense of any ambivalence between emotional repulsion and attraction we may have toward persons we love.

BillyLu: Perhaps the fascination with my dad's porn, then, did come from me trying to work out that ambivalence. Something deep inside of me was telling me that I didn't want to be loved and admired... as a man. What did those attractive models have that I didn't? Why didn't dad see how empty and lonely those women were?

Father JP: Perhaps because he was escaping from his own loneliness.

BillyLu: And perhaps I wanted to escape from mine. So, I too felt drawn to porn... captivated by the fantasy that I could be loved as a woman?
　　No... that just can't be right... but I was drawn to it anyway and it totally disgusted me at the same time... and I was disgusted with myself because I was drawn to it.
　　But I hid all this from everybody.

Margie: Except from your mom...

BillyLu: She stills thinks I was just reading them for the articles! I can't believe she can be so foolish.

An Identity Longing for a Relationship

Father JP: Reflecting on your sense of identity, it seems to me very much related to your performance. Your boyish identity was based on what would please dad and avoid his negative criticism.

BillyLu: But why would I be so attracted to women, especially very erotic women?

Father JP: Because you are very much a woman in that you have a natural longing for an identity based on relationships. Your attraction for lustful women seems to me a real longing for a relationship and intimacy with your mother.

Margie: What? Why would a desire for a deep and intimate relationship with one's mother lead to an attraction to erotic women?

Father JP: Perhaps, what BillyLu saw in those attractive women was her mother. Her eye for such women was also perhaps trained by being around her father; typically a child notices what her father notices. As a father reacts to an attractive woman, the child looks to see what her father notices. Before you know it, the child is noticing those attractive women even before the father does.

If the child sees her father get excited over porn, perhaps she too gets excited to see her father that way.

BillyLu: My dad never would show me his porn, but I do remember walking in on him in the act and he quickly put aside the magazine. Then, when he wasn't around, I did a little exploring and found his hidden vice.

Father JP: Returning to your identity, I really think you had a great longing for a deeper relationship with both your father and mother. Your father was distant from you and the whole family, escaping into his eroticism and criticism. You got "closer" to your father by trying to become like him in every way possible: in his work around the house, in his love for sports, and in his lust for women. But this very fragile relationship led to a very fragile identity.

Some women with same-sex attraction seem to long for the intimacy they see men having with women; perhaps they long for the intimacy that their father appeared to have with their mother, or the intimacy they see their brother having with a girl-friend or wife, or the intimacy they see their male peers having with their girlfriends, etc.

Also, women with homosexual inclinations may become overly preoccupied with the lack of intimacy seen between their parents, and the father may engage in emotional intimacy with them that should have been given to their mothers.

Margie: What about her relationship with her mother? How would that affect her identity?

Father JP: BillyLu, you seemed to have pulled away from your mother very early on, probably to avoid the hurt of rejection. Because of that, you may have pulled away from your window into the world of the feminine, leaving you less able to develop healthy relationships with men and women.

Yet, you continued your incredible longing for the warmth, love, and nurturing embrace of your mother you never "knew."

BillyLu: You are right, JP, I was distant from my mother—no question about that—and dad never really let me into his heart with any intimacy: I always had to prove myself to him.

So, I take it you think this kept me from having a healthy relationship with my former husband, George.

Father JP: Well, didn't you admit that? If I recall, you said that you felt kind of obligated to marry George, that you were not really attracted to him, and that you stopped having sex with him after awhile. Does that sound like an intimate relationship?

BillyLu: No, it doesn't, because it wasn't. But that was all I could expect from him.

Father JP: But is that all that he expected from you, BillyLu?

BillyLu: This is just too much, JP. Do I have to go through all this torture?

Father JP: I know this is painful. I wish I could alleviate it for you. But it is like birth pangs that you must go through to be able to embrace the joy of new life.

Pushing People Away with Fear, Anger, Resentment

Margie: Father JP, I explained to BillyLu the best I could how we develop a good, secure, positive identity by cultivating a web of good, healthy, and secure relationships. Would you help us understand how one can do this when one has no experience of true intimacy and self-sacrificing love?

Father JP: Did you explain to BillyLu how to heal and deepen her relationship with God?

BillyLu: Yes she did, but I'm not ready for confession. I have tried to pray; I want to experience the embrace of a loving father who loves me just as I am. It's just that I find it easier to see God as a nurturing, affirming mother who births me into the world of spirit than as a loving and law-giving father. I just can't seem to be able to live up to the expectations of God as a male parent. The Biblical image of God as mother is more uplifting: "As one whom his mother comforts, so I will comfort you" (Isaiah 66:13).

Father JP: God has many qualities and the Bible uses many images to describe these qualities. One such "maternal" quality is expressed by the Hebrew word *rahamim,* a word etymologically derived from the word for *womb.* The word refers to God's compassion and mercy, the kind of loving compassion and concern that a mother would have for the helpless child she nurtures and protects in her womb.

Although, BillyLu, the Bible applies feminine images to God, he is never called mother in the Bible. God reveals himself as a tender, understanding, compassionate, merciful, loving... *father.* Jesus revealed to us that we should address him as, *Our Father.*

We all need a relationship with God as a father who loves us just as we are.

BillyLu: But the Bible also portrays God as a judging and condemning lawgiver, whom his people never seem to be able to please. The mother image is less threatening. I want to experience a father's forgiveness for those times I haven't lived up to his expectations; I want this relationship, but there just seems to be a barrier between me and God.

Father JP: Let's take it slowly. We are physical and emotional beings, and when those emotions lose their proper order toward the good of the person, they can put barriers in the way of our relationships.

For example, the emotion of fear orients us to avoid situations that can cause pain and hurt. But if we fear to open ourselves up and risk intimacy, because we fear being hurt again, then we avoid going deep in our friendship and sharing our deepest secrets.

Perhaps fear of God's wrath, fear of God's punishment, or fear of God's possible disapproval, causes you to put up a wall to keep him out of your life.

BillyLu: More than fear, I feel anger. Anger at my mom for not being the warm, welcoming, and embracing mother I needed; anger at my dad for having had expectations of me I couldn't meet; anger at God, for... for having made me this way...

It looked as though her eyes wanted to well up with tears, but they remained dry...

Margie: It's OK, BillyLu, it's OK. You're with friends. We love you. It's OK to cry…

BillyLu: Oh, F- it. I'm turning into such a sissy.

There was a silent pause before Father JP broke the ice.

Father JP: I envy you, BillyLu.

BillyLu: What did you say, JP?

Father JP: I said, "I envy you." You are so lucky.

Margie: Are you making fun of BillyLu? How can you say that she is so lucky?

Father JP: I'm serious, because, if she can let go and forgive her mother and father, she will have a "free ticket" to heaven.

BillyLu: But I can't go to heaven, JP, especially after everything I've done. The way I have abused alcohol and sex, the way I have ruined my marriage and family, especially how I have damaged my kids. How could God ever forgive me?

Father JP: Because Christ said it. Our Lord said to the woman caught in adultery, "Has no one condemned you…? Neither do I condemn you; go, and do not sin again" (John 8:2-11). Are you any worse than she?

BillyLu: Hell, yes. She didn't damage as many people as I have. How could God forgive me for what I have done?

Father JP: What about Adam and Eve? They "damaged" more people—all of us, in fact—and much more. You wouldn't be suffering this inner turmoil or this attraction to women if it weren't for them and their fall. All have sinned in them; all of the sin of the world can be traced to them (Romans 5:12-21; 1 Corinthians 15:22,45-58).

Yet, God had no problem forgiving them.

If you decide to let go and forgive all those who have "messed up" your life, then Our Lord promises to forgive you your sins:

> Judge not, and you will not be judged; condemn not, and you will not be condemned; forgive, and you will be forgiven; give, and it will be given to you... For the measure you give will be the measure you get back (Luke 6:37-38).

Forgive, then Christ will have no choice but to fulfill his promise. Forgive and you shall be forgiven. Isn't that an awesome promise? But you must choose to forgive.

BillyLu: Why is it always the one who is hurt who has to forgive? This just ticks me off. I feel it's a huge injustice that I am the one who has to forgive. Just because Christ did it so perfectly, and so much better than I ever could, just makes it worse.

But I can't. I just can't. I've tried. I've tried to let go, to forgive and it doesn't work. Sure, it's an awesome promise. But what if you can't forgive? Then you're just screwed. I just don't know if I can let go of all this anger.

Father JP: You can also choose to deny and suppress your anger, but then it just eats away at you inside until you explode. Often those who deny and suppress their anger use drugs, alcohol, and/or sex to keep the anger from surfacing.

Another choice is to express your anger with acts of violence, whether verbal or physical. Judging from what you told me, your dad was a very angry man who displaced his disappointment in himself on the rest of the family. Your mom suppressed her emotions with alcohol.

In any case, anger is a barrier to relationships and thus a barrier to fostering a true sense of identity. Anger pushes people away, whereas forgiveness opens us up to others and welcomes them into our lives.

BillyLu: But is anger ever justified, Father?

Father JP: Anger is a God-given passion to repulse evil and injustice, especially injustice toward one's family. Thus, it is something good; even Our Lord was angry at the unjust situation of buying and selling in the Temple, his Father's house of prayer (Mark 11:15-17).

So, it isn't being angry or feeling anger that is the problem, but holding on to the anger after the injustice or evil has passed. Often one holds on to anger as a self-protection against the sadness, emotional pain, or anguish, or even guilt or shame over being angry at one's father or mother.

Self-Imprisoned with Loneliness and Pride

Margie: Father JP, I can see myself erecting barriers in my relationship with Sam. For me, it's not anger but fear. I can see how this puts distance between Sam and me: I push away fearing that he may ask me to marry him. Other times, it has been fear that God may ask more of me.

Are there other ways we erect barriers to push people away?

Father JP: Sure, Margie, it is a very easy thing to do. Not only do we push people away with fear, anger, and resentment, but sometimes we lock ourselves up through profound loneliness, selfishness, and pride, which are also barriers to relationships.

BillyLu: But I'm not lonely. I have a partner and I have many friends at work.

Father JP: Just because we are around a lot of people, doesn't mean we are not lonely.

I think of a young man I know who drinks a lot. He has a lot of drinking buddies; they laugh a lot and have a good time together, but he is a very lonely man. He needs to drink to drown out the pain of that loneliness. Superficial relationships—the lack of true intimacy—only reinforces the loneliness.

BillyLu: You're right, my mother was a very lonely woman. She had no real friends—not in my dad, or my brothers, or in me. No wonder she drank so much.

Father JP: No wonder she couldn't be there for you. But we need never be lonely. If we are, then we are not engaged with Our Father, God, who treasures us as his child. He wants to wrap us up in his arms, mercifully welcome us back as the father of the prodigal son. But if we are lonely, then we are still in a land distant from Our Father.

If we experience loneliness, it is God's reminder that no relationship or set of relationships is meant to be the ultimate source of peace and joy. Only our definitive relationship with the Triune God will give us that, as St. Paul says: "My desire is to depart and be with Christ, for that is far better. But to remain in the flesh is more necessary on your account" (Philippians 1:23-24).

Also, if we are lonely, then we are not communicating with our best friend, Jesus Christ. He is always there for us, even though we may choose to ignore him.

So, loneliness is a self-erected barrier we need to overcome: it keeps us from having deep, intimate friendships with others as well.

Margie: What about developing a relationship with Mary, the mother of Jesus? I have found my relationship with her to be very comforting and encouraging to me in my struggles. Will such a relationship help us to overcome our fear and loneliness?

Father JP: It certainly will, especially for you, BillyLu.

Psychologists—and common sense—tell us that a child's relationship with his or her mother is key for the development of trust, for bonding in relationships, and for the sense of security. If a child has a bad relationship with his or her mother, then the child may lose the ability to feel safe in the world. Many children placed early on in day care suffer from this.

Perhaps you can try to become small again, become a little infant, and crawl into the crib of Jesus. When Mary picks up the child Jesus to hold him and nurse him, she will pick you up as well. You can learn a lot by this form of prayer: you can learn to trust, to bond, and to feel secure.

BillyLu: I always thought that we just go straight to God? I don't go for all this "mariolatry" stuff.

Father JP: Many persons, especially with homosexual inclinations, are unable to go straight to God because they see God as a severe father figure who demands perfection. They are especially intimidated when they fail in striving to remain chaste; they can't avoid imagining a disapproving and critical God.

The virgin Mary fosters a relationship with God. She is a good disciple of Jesus and teaches us how to love the Father as Jesus did—not to be afraid of him. God has a passionate love for us:

> Sing for joy, O heavens, and exult, O earth…! For the LORD has comforted his people, and will have compassion on his afflicted.
>
> But Zion said, "The LORD has forsaken me, my Lord has forgotten me."
>
> Can a woman forget her sucking child, that she should have no compassion on the son of her womb? Even these may forget, yet I will not forget you. (Isaiah 49:13-15).

The virgin Mary can help us understand how much God loves us—just as God had loved her:

For he who is mighty has done great things for me, and holy is his name. And his mercy is on those who fear him from generation to generation (Luke 1:49-50).

BillyLu: Now, I feel so guilty, Father JP. How must my own children feel? They don't have a mother. Their mother has abandoned them. Will they ever be able to trust another person, or have intimate, bonded relationships with others?

Father JP: BillyLu, it is good that you have a great concern for your children. But, from all that we have been talking about, what do your children need?

BillyLu: Some good relationships to ground their identity, right?

Father JP: You got it! And the most important relationship you could help them with is to be a mother to them, to be the kind of mother you wish you had growing up.

All your efforts in trying to do this will help you discover your true self. You will discover that you really are a woman, a mother—that is something you could offer your children.

BillyLu: But what if they don't accept me back? Perhaps they too are angry with me… disappointed in me…

Margie: Just like your father!

BillyLu: Yeah. How I hated that. I wish he just would have loved me for who I was…

Father JP: But, I'm sure your children are much more likely to forgive and accept you back than your father was. All they want is for you to try to love them just for who they are.

One of the biggest barriers to establishing a relationship with your kids is your pride. If you just worry about *your* guilt, and about how *you* are ruining their lives, and how they are rejecting *you*, or their being angry with *you*, then forget it, you will never have a deep relationship with them. You will remain like your mother—more interested in herself than in others.

We all have to work at forgetting about ourselves and giving ourselves as a gift to others, then we will establish the communion of persons we call a relationship.

Margie: Pride and selfishness gets to all of us, Father JP, and it interferes with our relationships. I know this is true when it comes to my relationship with Sam. It is even more so with my relationship with my parents. That's why I just need to be on my own at this point in my life.

Father JP: Pride affects all of us and puts barriers to deeper relationships. It affects our relationship with God, our relationships with our family, and our relationships with our friends and colleagues. Sometimes pride shows up when we compare ourselves to others, when we think about how much we have done and how little the other person has; how intelligent we are and how imbecilic the other, etc. Comparisons of persons always interfere with relationships because they close us off to unconditional love—by putting conditions on our gift of self to others—thus they close us off to relationship.

Pride also affects us when comparing ourselves with others: sensing that we come up short, we see ourselves as useless, unattractive, or unlovable. Feeling we don't have anything to offer others, we retreat from relationships with God, family, and friends. We think we don't deserve their love and friendship, so we don't make any effort to give ourselves to others.

Comparisons don't let the beauty of our own unique and unrepeatable identity be seen, because we also have to contrast it with something else.

SELF-PITY, DEPRESSION, SELF-HATRED

BillyLu: I guess I'm just angry with myself as much as or more than I am angry with my parents and with God. I'm ashamed of my life. I see myself as a total failure: to my parents, to my husband, to my children. Can I ever forgive myself for all that I have done? I feel so small...

Father JP: When you say you are angry with yourself and you start insulting yourself what you really seem to be saying is that you hate yourself.

I think of how Jesus Christ linked murder, anger, insults, and hate to the need to forgive:

> You have heard that it was said to the men of old, "You shall not kill; and whoever kills shall be liable to judgment." But I say to you that every one who is angry with his brother shall be liable to judgment; whoever insults his brother... and whoever says, "You fool!" shall be liable to the hell of fire. So if you are offering your gift at the altar, and there remember that your brother has something against you, leave your gift there before the altar and go; first be reconciled to your brother, and then come and offer your gift...

> You have heard that it was said, "You shall love your neighbor and hate your enemy." But I say to you, Love your enemies and pray for those who persecute you, so that you may be sons of your Father who is in heaven (Matthew 5:21-24,43-45).

If these elements are truly linked together, BillyLu, then there is very little, if any, difference between self-anger and self-hatred.

So, my question for you, BillyLu, is: Do you hate yourself?

BillyLu: Wow, JP, that is pretty strong stuff. But you are right: I think I do. I just can't let go of the guilt I feel. Sometimes I wish I could just crawl into a hole and die.

Father JP: Think about this, BillyLu, nobody can embrace an identity that he or she hates. If you are angry with yourself and hate yourself—your identity as a woman, as a wife, as a mother—then you will never be able to give yourself to your children and to others.

BillyLu: I just don't see how I can let go. If I look in the mirror and look at this story of mine—my messed up life—how can I not hate the person I am? How can I not feel guilty?

Father JP: And your partner welcomes you into her life just as you are, giving you an escape from the guilt, shame, and self-hatred with a kind of emotional "high"—she doesn't hate you; she isn't ashamed of you. You hope she is right, but when you come down from your "high," I bet you feel worse than you did before.

BillyLu: I certainly do, and then I turn to drink to escape that feeling until I can get emotionally "high" again.

Father JP: This gets you locked into a downward spiral of compulsive self-destruction and self-hatred. It is an addictive cycle that seems to have no exit.

You may think that you are escaping from your pain, but in truth you are just running away from your own self, rejecting the identity you hate.

BillyLu: But I want out, Father. Is there any way out?

Father JP: There is—love. Get out of yourself, forget about yourself, give yourself to your children and to your husband, if that is still possible, and you will find freedom. It is pride that keeps you locked up in the prison of shame.

BillyLu: So, are you saying, Father, that my guilt feelings are really pride, that keeps me from truly loving? I don't think I have ever loved anyone...

TRUE FEMININE IDENTITY

Father JP: You seem to be getting it, BillyLu. Pride is the tendency to focus on ourselves, on what we want, and it is a turning away from others and their needs.

So the way to grow in your identity as a woman is by learning to give yourself to others, by identifying the needs of others and making them your own. This is God's special gift to women: the sensitivity toward the needs of others. If you, as a woman, can use your gifts and talents to discern and meet those needs in others, you will be able to forgive yourself. You will see that you are freed from self-absorption and it will fill you with joy and peace.

Margie: How does one develop this identity as a woman, Father? Both BillyLu and I need to learn to get out of ourselves and make the needs of others our own. However, we live in a society that belittles that feminine genius, and prizes independence and self-reliance.

Father JP: It normally happens quite naturally. When a girl is still quite little, she already begins to express her nurturing spirit. Part of this comes from seeing her mother nurture siblings and even her father. Another part of this is responding with joy to the gift of another, especially when a little girl's father brings her a surprise—her very spontaneous joy motivates her father to give even more. Seeing how her father "melts" and becomes gentle when he is around his "little girl" teaches her how to be a motivator, drawing others out of themselves—especially men—by her sweetness, generosity, service, and beauty. All of this is reinforced by the appreciation her father shows her for her service to him.

Margie: Isn't this why girls naturally like playing with dolls, Father JP, I mean, since being nurturing comes more naturally to us? Why do we ever lose this natural nurturing tendency?

BillyLu: I don't think I ever had it.

Father JP: Sure you did, BillyLu, it just was never reinforced by your mother or your father.

Typically, a little girl finds her nurturing tendency reinforced by her family and, in the past, by society too. A little girl also develops her nurturing identity through her relationship with her siblings, younger cousins, or through her interaction with other young children. As she nurtures and cares for them in their needs she develops a woman's heart.

BillyLu: But what if one doesn't grow up in that kind of environment? My mother was so un-nurturing, she cared for us but in a very distant sort of way. She treated us more like burdens, objects, rather than giving us tender care.

And as you know, dad wasn't any help in this matter. He was more interested in having a son he could be proud of rather than a nurturing daughter—he never "melted" with me; he never brought me surprise gifts. He only gave me gifts as incentives and rewards for my accomplishments.

Father JP: You deserved to have been loved unconditionally by both your parents, but, as you experienced, that doesn't always happen. Sometimes we experience this unconditional love through our grandparents instead, or through other relationships. Ultimately, you need to learn it.

I would encourage you, BillyLu, to find some good mentors in this. Perhaps Margie's mom could coach you—if you want to develop your feminine genius, which Pope John Paul II saw so important to our society today:

> In our own time, the successes of science and technolo-
> gy make it possible to attain material well-being to a degree
> hitherto unknown. While this favors some, it pushes others
> to the margins of society. In this way, unilateral progress can
> also lead to a gradual loss of sensitivity for man, that is, for

what is essentially human. In this sense, our time in particular awaits the manifestation of that "genius" which belongs to women, and which can ensure sensitivity for human beings in every circumstance: because they are human! — and because "the greatest of these is love" (cf. 1 Corinthians 13:13).

BillyLu: I can't do this, Father JP. I don't want to do this. I hate the idea of being the sheepish, subservient housewife. I need to be appreciated for who I am.

Margie: But you and I *are* women and being feminine has nothing to do with being sheepish and subservient but with being loving and nurturing.

The world is overly masculinized and needs our feminine genius. Can you imagine a world that relies exclusively on male competition and performance while having no room for gentle compassion or nurturing love?

BillyLu: But that *is* our world, Margie.

Margie: But it doesn't have to be that way. In a sense, the young people of tomorrow need a better world, one with the full complement of femininity.

Feminine Beauty

BillyLu: How can I be feminine when I'm so plain, so ugly.

Margie: No you're not, BillyLu, and I say that emphatically! I'm sure your husband agreed; otherwise he would never have married you.

BillyLu: Even so, I hate it: how men lust over women just because of large breasts, a slim waist, and slender legs—something I could never become. I would never degrade myself by trying to live up to some male stereotype of feminine beauty. Can't they just love us as we are?

Father JP: BillyLu, I'm sure you resent being treated as an object of lust and not as a person to be admired just for who you are.

But being an object of lust is not the reason for your beauty. God gave you an elegant feminine figure that exudes grace and beauty precisely to draw people—especially men, although not exclusively so—to God by drawing them out of themselves and moving them to give themselves generously to others.

God endowed you women with feminine beauty, not to arouse men but to attract them. But they need to see the artist who crafted you; if you keep the focus on yourself and not draw people to the artist, then you will offend the artist.

Margie: But some women are less beautiful than others. Yet all of us women long for men to show us attention and to be attracted to us. How can we compete with the "super-models"?

Father JP: Your feminine beauty is not limited to the physical. The sexy body of the "super-models" will degrade over time and no longer provoke the erotic. True feminine beauty will mature with age, it will continue to motivate others, enhanced by one's womanly and motherly manner.

You attract and draw men to love by your feminine charm as well. Your gentle appreciation, your confident faith in others is even more attractive than the physical; when you are motivating, and not seducing, you are truly woman.

BillyLu: What's the difference? Don't women motivate their man by seduction? How disgusting that is to me!

Father JP: Seduction plays on a man's lustful emotions to get him to do what she wants. It is a form of manipulation that doesn't respect a man's freedom but treats him like an object.

True motivation is one that inspires men to freely give themselves; it acknowledges the emotional nature and only pushes those emotional "buttons" gently enough so that the man—or her children for that matter—can retain their freedom as they do what they are motivated to do. True motivation provides emotional incentives that always respect the freedom of the other person, always leaving room for the person to choose not to do what is being encouraged.

In the end, a motivated man always feels happy to be able to do that deed of service, even though he finds it unpleasant, humiliating, over his head, or disagreeable in some way.

Seduction brings out the animal in a man; motivation brings out the father; it also brings out the brother, husband, and friend in a man. In a word, feminine motivation makes a man out of a man.

In the beginning in Genesis, Adam was alone (Genesis 2:18) and focused on himself. When God formed woman, Adam looked upon her beauty with awe and admiration (Genesis 2:23), discovering his manhood—his call to get out of himself and become husband and father (Genesis 2:24). True manhood is free of selfish lust (Genesis 2:25).

A seductive woman is one men lust over; the charming woman is one that men cherish.

Margie: But, Father, doesn't this ideal woman only makes sense when there are ideal men out there looking to love and respect women in this way? Most men only seem to be interested in women with "hot" bodies.

Father JP: Sadly, much of what you say is true. However, there are more noble men out there than you think.

In addition, although you are not the "ideal" woman yet and you don't find many "ideal" men around, strive to be that woman. Such a woman brings out the best in men who have good will.

The man, who is only reacting to his lust by seeking women with "hot" bodies, is just a little boy who wants his immediate gratification without any responsibility. The boy wants to play and not to work.

Women are called to teach men how to become fathers— real men—which means to motivate them toward deciding to take on the responsibilities that forming a family entails. We need more women like the woman of Proverbs:

A good wife who can find? She is far more precious than jewels. The heart of her husband trusts in her, and he will have no lack of gain. She does him good, and not harm, all the days of her life… She rises while it is yet night and provides food for her household… She girds her loins with strength and makes her arms strong… She opens her hand to the poor, and reaches out her hands to the needy… Strength and dignity are her clothing, and she laughs at the time to come. She opens her mouth with wisdom, and the teaching of kindness is on her tongue. She looks well to the ways of her household, and does not eat the bread of idleness. Her children rise up and call her blessed; her husband also, and he praises her: "Many women have done excellently, but you surpass them all." (Proverbs 31:10-29).

Margie: I would love to become that kind of woman, wouldn't you BillyLu?

BillyLu: Oh, I don't know about that. The idea of becoming the subservient housewife who never gets a break from her work, who is always at the beck and call of a lazy husband, popping out babies and sewing prudish dresses… Hell, no. That's not for me.

Father JP: Think about your mother, BillyLu. She actually seemed to have given in to your father's objectifying view of feminine beauty by neglecting her health and appearance, by giving in to the thought that her self-worth depended on meeting your father's sick obsession for the erotic.

What if she were the strong woman, who had a sense of confidence in her identity as a woman? What if she were to have stood up to your father, banished the porn from the house, used her physical beauty and gentle encouragement to draw your father into being more generous with each one of you kids, teaching him how to meet the emotional needs of each one.

Margie: BillyLu, wouldn't you have preferred that? Don't you think you'd feel better knowing that you fought not to be like your mother, but tried to become the woman she wasn't?

BillyLu: Yeah, perhaps, but I think it is bit too late for me.

Margie: Perhaps we can work on this together, BillyLu. You can help me and I'll try to help you.

At that they called it a night, with Margie and BillyLu agreeing to get together to follow up on all that they had discussed.

CHAPTER 11

Second Thoughts

When Leslie learned of BillyLu's and Margie's visit to Father JP, she was livid. But instead of ending the relationship with BillyLu, she decided to take up Father JP's challenge to meet together. In fact, she was the one to call and arrange the meeting for the next day.

Again they met at the pizza restaurant to have their joint discussion, with Leslie, BillyLu, Margie, and Father JP—who was the last to arrive after finishing an appointment at the rectory.

Leslie: Father JP, it is so nice to finally meet you. I've heard so much about you, that you are quite intelligent. Actually, you are much younger and more handsome than I had pictured you. BillyLu, you should have told me.

Father JP: Thank you, Leslie, I am also happy to meet such a charming and attractive young woman as yourself.

Margie: Father JP, would you like to order something to drink; we started without you.

Father JP: Thank you, Margie, I certainly would…

Father JP orders a beer and then resumes the conversation.

And have you all begun discussing anything? Have you chosen the topic yet?

BillyLu: We were just reviewing some of the issues that we had discussed with you in earlier conversations—bringing Leslie up to date. We wanted to wait until you arrived before we dug in and tried to resolve anything.

Father JP: Good! Where would you like to begin?

Sodomy—Not the Sin of Sodom

Leslie pulled out her legal pad where she had a number of questions outlined for the group.

Leslie: Father JP, perhaps we can begin with the Bible. BillyLu was telling me that you say that the Bible condemns homosexuality. I've done a bit of research and found that most Christian scholars today consider the Bible neutral on the topic.

Father JP: BillyLu, we really didn't discuss the Bible much, did we?

BillyLu: No, we just discussed some comments on your discussion with Jeremy.

Father JP: That's what I thought. Sometimes I forget what I say to whom...

Leslie: Anyway... Nowhere in Scripture does the Bible condemn homosexuality as we understand it today.

Father JP: Of course it doesn't condemn *current* forms of homosexuality, Leslie, because it describes the forms of activity and sin that were common at the times the Bible was written. But neither does the Bible condemn *current* forms of abortion, warfare with guns and explosives, or sadomasochism.

What the Bible does describe, however, is how God condemned Sodom and Gomorrah for its grave sinfulness and it condemns men lying with men (Leviticus 18:21-23).

Leslie: But the fact is, Scripture doesn't actually identify the sin of Sodom with homosexuality. In fact, in Luke 10:12 Jesus identifies the sin of Sodom as the sin of inhospitality.

Most scholars conclude that it was a cultural bias against homosexuality that associated the destruction of Sodom with gay sex: the culture was so biased against and trying to squelch any activity that prevented or slowed the growth of the population — they needed a greater number of warriors for war. So, they let God punish homosexuality with utter destruction.

Jesus clarifies all that for us, explaining how the sin of Sodom was a failure to welcome travelers. It has nothing to do with sex.

Margie: I've heard this interpretation, too, Father JP.

Father JP: Let's read what Jesus says… here, we go… In this passage, Luke is describing how Jesus sent out the disciples to teach:

> Carry no purse, no bag… Whatever house you enter, first say, 'Peace be to this house!' And if a son of peace is there, your peace shall rest upon him; but if not, it shall return to you. And remain in the same house, eating and drinking what they provide… heal the sick in it and say to them, 'The kingdom of God has come near to you.' But whenever you enter a town and they do not receive you, go into its streets and say, 'Even the dust of your town that clings to our feet, we wipe off against you; nevertheless know this, that the kingdom of God has come near.' I tell you, it shall be more tolerable on that day for Sodom than for that town (Luke 10:4-12).

This is the passage you were referring to, is it not Leslie?

Leslie: Yes, that's the passage.

Father JP: Well, in reading this passage I can't see where Jesus says that the sin of Sodom was inhospitality. All that it says is that the town that rejects the Gospel of those disciples will be punished worse than Sodom was, which was utter destruction.

BillyLu: But isn't rejecting the traveling disciples who brought the Gospel the same as being inhospitable to travelers? They were travelers, weren't they?

Father JP: Yes they were, but we need to be precise, BillyLu, in explaining what the Bible says. Let's not add more to it than what it actually says. If the Bible just says that the punishment will be worse for those who reject the Gospel, then that's all that it says.

Leslie: But in Genesis, the Bible doesn't tell us what the sin of Sodom was.

Father JP: OK, Leslie, let's read what Genesis says. Here we read how Lot receives into his home two visitors—angels appearing as men. Then it says:

> But before they lay down, the men of the city, the men of Sodom, both young and old, all the people to the last man, surrounded the house; and they called to Lot, "Where are the men who came to you tonight? Bring them out to us, that we may know them." Lot went out of the door to the men, shut the door after him, and said, "I beg you, my brothers, do not act so wickedly (Genesis 19:4-7).

Lot begs the men of Sodom not to do evil, that is, not to try "to know" them.

Margie: And when the Bible says, "that we may know them," it means that the people of Sodom wanted to have sex with the two visitors, correct?

Leslie: Well, that's one of the biblical meanings of the word, "to know," Margie. A much more common meaning of "to know" can also mean "to get acquainted with." That meaning is found much more frequently in the Bible than the meaning "to have sex."

However, that the men of Sodom insisted on raping the visitors doesn't quite fit the scene. This implies that the entire male population was gay and everyone of them wanted to rape these two men. Even by the highest estimates of the most "lenient" society, 10 percent is considered high for the percentage of homosexuals in a given population.

Much more likely, the whole male population of the town would want *to get acquainted* with the strangers who had entered their town. These strangers were potential spies and could do harm to the security of the city.

Father JP: And indeed they were spies, Leslie, spies for God. God sent them, "to see whether they have done altogether according to the outcry which has come to me" (Genesis 18:21).

But getting acquainted with potential spies was not their sin, Leslie, it was because they had engaged in "unnatural" promiscuous behavior, as 2 Peter 2:1-19 and Jude 17 explicitly say. This was just exemplified by what they attempted to do with the visitors.

Leslie: Wait one minute, Father JP, there are difficulties with that interpretation. If Genesis was really attempting to condemn homosexual rape, then it seems awfully strange that it would advocate the rape of Lot's virgin daughters. Look at what this Bible of yours says:

Lot went out of the door to the men, shut the door after

him, and said, "I beg you, my brothers, do not act so wick-
edly. Behold, I have two daughters who have not known
man; let me bring them out to you, and do to them as you
please; only do nothing to these men, for they have come
under the shelter of my roof" (Genesis 19:6-8).

Margie: That's horrendous, Father! Why would God encourage
or even allow that?

Father JP: Notice, Margie and Leslie, God did not allow that;
the young women are not raped. Neither Lot nor the angels allowed that to happen. Lot seems to offer his daughters to them,
but it is more as a way to express horror at the crime they pro-
pose doing — "It would be a worse crime than to rape my own
precious daughters before my eyes, God forbid." I'm sure Lot
would never permit his daughters to be mistreated.

Interesting enough, Leslie, you point to this passage where
the verb "to know" must mean sexual intercourse — not "to get
acquainted with" — only this time it refers to the heterosexual rape
of Lot's virgin daughters instead of the homosexual rape of the
visitors.

BillyLu: Then why does the Bible suggest that it is OK for Lot to
offer his daughters to be raped? Does this mean that it is OK to
rape women, but not to rape men?

Father JP: This doesn't say that rape of women is OK, but to
show how desperate Lot was. The men of Sodom would have
known how horrible it would be to Lot to rape his dear virgin
daughters before his eyes — Lot was trying to communicate in as
graphic way as possible that what they intended to do — to rape
these sacred visitors — was as horrible as anything could be to
him.

Lot knew his visitors were sent from God. They had been
with his cousin, Abraham. He considered them as men conse-

crated to God, as God's representatives. For the men of Sodom to rape such sacred personages would be to carryout the greatest sacrilege possible against God. It would be equivalent to raping God.

The Destruction of Gibeah

Leslie: But in the Book of Judges, Scripture does approve the rape of a virgin daughter.

Father JP: OK, Leslie, let's look at that passage too. Yes, in Judges 19 something similar to Sodom did happen in Gibeah, a small town near Jerusalem. A Levite priest was returning home with his rebellious wife or concubine. They were staying in Gibeah when the men of Gibeah rose up to rape the Levite man.

Margie, would you mind reading the text for us? Here, read this paragraph.

Margie: Sure, Father JP. The passage reads:
Behold, the men of the city, base fellows, beset the house round about, beating on the door; and they said to the old man, the master of the house, "Bring out the man who came into your house, that we may know him." And the man, the master of the house, went out to them and said to them, "No, my brethren, do not act so wickedly; seeing that this man has come into my house, do not do this vile thing. Behold, here are my virgin daughter and his concubine; let me bring them out now. Ravish them and do with them what seems good to you; but against this man do not do so vile a thing" (Judges 19:22-24).

Father JP: Again, it was homosexual rape against a man consecrated to God due to his Levitical priesthood. The host showed the townsmen how despicable their plan was that he considered the rape of his virgin daughter less of a crime than "raping" God by raping his sacred minister.

Margie: But this time around, the virgin daughter was raped, wasn't she?

Father JP: No. Even though the men did not listen to the host and calm their passions, he did not give his daughter to them. Instead, the men:

> Seized [the Levite's] concubine… and they knew her, and abused her all night until the morning. And as the dawn began to break, they let her go. And… the woman came and fell down at the door of the man's house where her master was, till it was light (Judges 19:25-26).

There the woman died.

Leslie: So, the Bible approves raping a woman to death as long as she is not a virgin? How do you explain that, Father JP, the Bible accepting things like raping non-virgin women? Wow, how sick! After this, homosexuality doesn't sound so bad after all!

Father JP: No, Leslie, the Bible does not approve of this hideous crime. Scripture tells us that God blamed all the twelve tribes of Israel for this crime:

> And all who saw it said, "Such a thing has never happened or been seen from the day that the people of Israel came up out of the land of Egypt until this day; consider it, take counsel, and speak" (Judges 19:30).

All Israel rose up "as one man" and utterly destroyed Gibeah for what they had done (Judges 20), just as the angels had done to Sodom. So, the Bible agrees with you that this was "sick."

Scripture Says Nothing About Homosexuality

Leslie: OK, Father… but even still… the sin of Sodom and the sin of Gibeah were huge sins because they were to be committed against persons consecrated to God, not because the sins entailed homosexual sex.

Father JP: Correct, Leslie, but they only could have carried out this sin against consecrated persons by means of homosexual acts. Even before either of these events occurred, Sodom was considered "wicked," with "great sinners against the LORD" (Genesis 13:13), whose "sin is very grave" (Genesis 18:20).

Leslie: But that says nothing about a loving, respectful, caring, life-long relationship that we see among many homosexuals today. Nowhere does the Bible refer to this kind of homosexuality. The Bible gives no specific guidance on modern forms of homosexuality.

However, Christianity does proclaim that creation is something good (even us homosexuals). God loves all that he created (yes, even homosexuals)! But no—Christian groups like Exodus International and Courage say we have to change, because God made a mistake when he made us, we are bad.

Father JP: Leslie, I agree with you that everything God creates is good. As created by God, you and I are good. To the extent that I sin, that I make selfish choices, I am not good.

Look, the Bible doesn't mention many things we consider sins. For example, the Bible does not say anything about a loving, respectful, caring, life-long incestuous relationship between a father and daughter, or between brother and sister. Nor does it say anything about a loving, respectful, caring, life-long sexual relationship between man and "man's best friend"—his dog. The Bible doesn't describe the kind of cyber-porn we see today, nor does it describe virtual child-porn that is available on the Internet. However, Bible principles are sufficient to discern that these are immoral.

In the Bible, God reveals many things about himself, about who we are, and about the relationship to which he calls us. We need to respect what he says.

Leslie: Agreed, we need to respect what he says and what he avoids saying. Jesus never says anything about homosexuality. We can only come to a legitimate conclusion about homosexuality in God's Kingdom from a proper understanding of Christ's Gospel message, which is a Gospel of God's love for us all... every single one of us, Father JP! Cultural bias in the early Church has given us the anti-gay and lesbian hate that we see among so-called Christians today.

Christ will condemn you like the angels did to Sodom, for not welcoming us gays and lesbians:

> Then he will say to those at his left hand, 'Depart from me, you cursed, into the eternal fire prepared for the devil and his angels; for I was hungry and you gave me no food... a stranger and you did not welcome me" (Matthew 25:41-43).

You're very smart and know a lot about the Bible, Father JP, but you need to learn how to live the Gospel, too.

Father JP: Leslie, I am trying to live it and to welcome you. I feel God is obliging me to speak the Gospel to you as it has been entrusted to me. If I were to water it down in any way, I would also be condemned.

The Catholic Church does welcome and respect those with homosexual inclinations. Every human being is endowed with great dignity as a child of God. So, it is serious sin to show grave disrespect or lack of compassion or insensitivity toward a gay or lesbian person (cf. CCC 2358). This teaching is faithful to Christ's Gospel. But it is also part of Christ's Gospel that sex outside of marriage—whether heterosexual or homosexual sex acts—is also a grave sin.

And I am also trying to help you understand some of those difficult passages of the Bible. I am trying to do so with charity, but in my weakness I may fail you at times. I'm sorry for my inadvertent failures.

Margie: Thank you, Father, for addressing these difficult topics. I appreciate the efforts you are clearly trying to make to be faithful to Christian teaching while remaining sensitive to those who are not living this teaching. Many Christians would have just gotten frustrated and angry. I admire your poise and charity while speaking the truth.

BillyLu: I also appreciate those efforts, Margie, but the fact is the only thing that the Bible clearly condemns is sexual abuse, rape, prostitution, and ritual sexual orgies. It doesn't say anything explicit about a modern, loving and caring homosexual relationship. So, if the Bible doesn't mention modern homosexuality then how can you use the Bible to condemn it?

Father JP: In the Bible, God reveals his plan of salvation, his plan to redeem his Bride, the Church. Let's suppose that a man proposes to marry a woman and the woman accepts. The man promises to share his vast wealth with his future bride, but under the stipulation that she must be faithful to him. In particular, the man warns her about continuing any relationship with past boyfriends and lovers. She accepts his invitation with those conditions.

Later, the man catches the woman in bed with another woman. Would it be unfair for the man to cut the woman out of any relationship with him and out of the inheritance?

BillyLu: That would be fair and reasonable. She had been unfaithful.

Father JP: But the woman may say to her ex-fiancé, "Look, you only mentioned ex-boyfriends and ex-lovers. You said nothing about a loving, caring, relationship with a woman."

Margie: She'd be gone no matter how she argued it. Fidelity means preserving one's body and the gift of oneself exclusively for one's life-long love. Having sex with a woman, a man, or a beast, or even with oneself would violate that fidelity.

Father JP: Well Scripture presents us with God's invitation to enter into a relationship with him. He tells us what offends that relationship and what things will prevent us from entering the Promised Land:

> And the LORD said to Moses, "Say to the people of Israel... You shall not do as they do in the land of Egypt, where you dwelt... You shall do my ordinances and keep my statutes and walk in them. I am the LORD your God... And you shall not lie carnally with your neighbor's wife, and defile yourself with her. You shall not give any of your children to devote them by fire to Molech, and so profane the name of your God: I am the LORD. You shall not lie with a male as with a woman; it is an abomination. And you shall not lie with any beast and defile yourself with it, neither shall any woman give herself to a beast to lie with it: it is perversion... But you shall keep my statutes and my ordinances and do none of these abominations... (for all of these abominations the men of the land did, who were before you, so that the land became defiled)... For whoever shall do any of these abominations, the persons that do them shall be cut off from among their people" (Leviticus 18:1-30).

I am trying to be true to this message and to communicate it to you as faithfully as possible. If I don't, I will have to answer to God for my error.

Leslie: But these Old Testament warnings have been superseded by Paul's promise to believers:

If you confess with your lips that Jesus is Lord and believe in your heart that God raised him from the dead, you will be saved. For man believes with his heart and so is justified, and he confesses with his lips and so is saved. The scripture says, "No one who believes in him will be put to shame." (Romans 10:9-11).

Why do you stick to some Old Testament list of sins when Paul tells us that all we need to do is believe and confess Jesus as Lord?

Father JP: Leslie, these Old Testament warnings are almost identical to Paul's:

Do you not know that the unrighteous will not inherit the kingdom of God? Do not be deceived; neither the immoral, nor idolaters, nor adulterers, nor sexual perverts — i.e., homosexuals — nor thieves, nor the greedy, nor drunkards, nor revilers, nor robbers will inherit the kingdom of God. And such were some of you. But you were washed, you were sanctified, you were justified in the name of the Lord Jesus Christ and in the Spirit of our God (1 Corinthians 6:9-11).

And again Paul says:

Now the works of the flesh are plain: fornication, impurity, licentiousness, idolatry, sorcery, enmity, strife, jealousy, anger, selfishness, dissension, party spirit, envy, drunkenness, carousing, and the like. I warn you, as I warned you before, that those who do such things shall not inherit the kingdom of God (Galatians 5:19-21).

Neither Paul nor I want to see you cut off from either the Promised Land or from your inheritance in God's heavenly kingdom. True faith means conversion of heart.

Risky Behavior is Immoral

Leslie: Father JP, I too appreciate your efforts, even though I disagree with your scriptural analysis. It is a very fundamentalist approach and a bit old-fashioned, but I respect you for your sincerity. And you do a lot less gay bashing than most.

BillyLu also told me about some of the scientific studies you cited. From what I understood, you claim that science proves that homosexuality is immoral.

Father JP: I claimed what?

Leslie: Well, that the homosexual life-style is immoral because it carries a greater risk. I guess, the argument goes that since homosexual activity is risky, and risky activity is immoral, then homosexual activity is immoral.

Margie: Well, that's true, Leslie.

Leslie: But are you so sure that it is true, Margie?

Sure, some forms of homosexual sex are risky, just as some forms of heterosexual sex are risky. For example, unprotected anal sex between gay men is riskier for transmitting the HIV virus than heterosexual sex. However, heterosexual sex is riskier for transmitting the HIV virus than lesbian sex. Therefore, your argument fails. You ought to be recommending lesbianism as a way of reducing risky and immoral behavior!

Father JP: Your logic is almost correct, Leslie, but those were not the concerns we discussed. We did not focus on the *risks* of homosexuality but on the *impact* that it may have on one's own physical and psychological health, as well as, the *impact* it may have on family, society, and other relationships.

We also discussed this in parallel to alcoholism. We focused not so much on the *risks* of alcoholism, but on the *impact* that it may have on the person, on his family, on his friends, and on society as a whole. Alcoholism may increase one's risks for certain diseases and accidents, but it also causes great harm to families and to society.

Certainly every behavior carries with it certain risks, but the risks do not make the behavior immoral. If that were the case, then a person should stay at home instead of driving a car to work—because driving a car significantly increases a person's risk of dying in an automobile accident. But usually the benefits of driving to work significantly outweigh the minor increase in risk due to driving.

BillyLu: But, getting back to Leslie's argument, it is also true that lesbian sex is less risky than heterosexual intercourse. Therefore, we shouldn't condemn it as immoral.

Father JP: Regarding transmitting the HIV virus, lesbianism may be physically less risky than sex between a man and a woman who have multiple partners, but those who "dare" to experiment with lesbianism are also more likely to engage in riskier heterosexual sex and have more overall sex partners. So, the lesbian is usually at greater risk than a heterosexual woman for contracting HIV.

In addition, recent studies at UCLA show that oral sex—"lesbian sex"—can also transmit the HIV virus and increase the risks for getting throat cancer from the HPV virus. One also can contract herpes, syphilis, and gonorrhea this way. Lesbians have a higher risk for breast cancer. In no way is it safe.

If a man and woman really do things according to God's plan and wait until marriage to have sex, their health risks become absolutely nil.

Leslie: But should people care if we increase our private risk, as long as it doesn't incur any additional public risk? Deciding to drive to work rather than walking or taking the bus increases my private risk, but that is my own business and nobody should give this any more importance than that.

Engaging in one form of sex or another is a private matter that may increase my private health risks, but that is my own business and nobody has a right to intervene or object to that.

Father JP: Should we care whether an alcoholic drinks too much, as long as it doesn't affect others and any public risk?

The problem with asking such questions, Leslie, is that it assumes that our actions have no impact on others or on public welfare. However, if someone over-drinks it usually does hurt others. It hurts his relationship with his family, especially if he or she becomes abusive. It affects his or her health, and thus will cause expenditures from insurance or public healthcare programs and cause the premiums to increase for those who do not abuse alcohol.

Now, we don't want to micromanage people's lives, but we need to realize that everything we do impacts others.

Leslie: But homosexuals are not a threat to society, not even to the family. We just want to live out our lives in peace. We too can be devoted to our families. As long as these families are full of love, empathy, and commitment—that is, family values—what is wrong with that?

There is no way that the vast majority of people are going to stop entering into heterosexual marriage. We don't want that. We don't seek that. Are you people so paranoid so as to fear that happening? It's just that some people are happier in homosexual relationships and others are happier in heterosexual relationships, and some are happier living on their own. When people are happy, that's good for them and it's good for society.

Father JP: Leslie, I don't see homosexuality so much as a threat to the family or society, but as a threat to the individual and his or her true happiness.

How often I have seen teenagers insist on pairing up and having a boyfriend or girlfriend. The two become emotionally and physically involved with each other only to become severely hurt when they breakup. One may become so hurt, that he or she thinks one cannot live—be happy—without the other, so the person commits suicide. It has even happened that the distraught teen kills his ex-boyfriend or girlfriend along with him- or herself.

So, as I present my concerns about homosexuality, it is more a concern about you and BillyLu as persons—for your true happiness, both here and hereafter—than it is about the threat to family and society.

BillyLu: Why do you have to tell me and Leslie what will make us happy? We are adults, not immature adolescents. Can't we decide that for ourselves?

Father JP: Although the analogy is not exactly the same, BillyLu, compared to God we are like adolescent teens, or even smaller. He is concerned about our true happiness and wants to help us achieve it.

Therefore, we can see by our example of the distraught teen, who would say the same thing you just did—"Being with my boyfriend or girlfriend is what will make me happy. Who are you to tell me what will make me happy? If I can't have that, then…"

True concern for distraught teens means we are trying to help them find true happiness, even when that seems impossible to them at the time.

But Homosexuality Is a Good Thing

Leslie: But homosexuality is not just tolerable, but is morally good, Father JP.

First, for us homosexuals, gay sex is very pleasurable. Pleasure is something good, because God created it. Our puritanical society tries to make us feel guilty when we seek pleasure, but it is a human good in which we should rejoice. To disvalue or disdain pleasure is itself immoral.

Father JP: I agree with you, Leslie, that God created pleasure as something good. But we also know we can pursue it selfishly. You would not approve of a man receiving intense pleasure abusing your daughter, would you?

BillyLu: No, of course not, Father JP. But that's not pleasure arising from consenting adults.

Father JP: The point is: pleasure is not an end in itself, but an accompanying motivation. When we make it an end in itself, we confuse pleasure with happiness and we excuse all sorts of abuses.

Going back to our distraught teen, he or she finds intense pleasure in the physical relationship with his girlfriend or her boyfriend. Yet that pleasure can drive him or her to despair, depression, suicide, and even murder.

Just because homosexual acts are pleasurable, does not mean they are good in themselves.

Leslie: But the pleasure found in homosexuality, Father JP, also includes another moral good: it is a means of intimate interpersonal communication. There's no denying that human interaction, including sexual interaction, is a moral good. Perhaps you favor celibacy, but that's not for everybody. If you were to force this celibacy on homosexuals like us, then you rob us of a very important form of intimacy and connection to other human beings.

Father JP: I can't force celibacy on you or on any one else. Besides, I see it as a special gift from God that enables me to achieve intimate interpersonal communion with God. I thank him for it.

The Church is the first to exalt the sexual union as a special place of interpersonal communication. Not only is it special, it is sacred, meaning that it is also a place to encounter God.

But it can also be abused. Neither forced celibacy nor forced intimacy is good. Nor is physical intimacy between people who are not meant to be intimate, as with siblings, or with a man and his mistress. The physical intimacy of these relationships runs contrary to the spiritual and emotional relationship that ought to be present.

So, Leslie, it is good that you want to have intimate interpersonal communication, but it must be with the right person, at the right time, and in the right way in order to be moral.

BillyLu: But what's wrong with it taking place between two consenting adults of the same sex? That's the question we ask.

Father JP: BillyLu, let's look at the previous example I just mentioned regarding a man and his mistress. The man and his mistress may both be consenting adults, but that doesn't mean their behavior does not or will not impact others. Certainly it does impact the man's wife, their children, and society as a whole that now has to deal with additional costs associated with a broken marriage and family.

So, it's not enough that the behavior is between consenting adults, it's about justice, charity, peace, and happiness.

I would rather you ask the question: does it bring true happiness? Momentary pleasure is different from true happiness. If this behavior does bring happiness, then why is there so much depression, suicide, and other self-destructive behavior that goes along with it?

Leslie: But our homosexuality doesn't do that. It really is a source of emotional growth. Having a romantic, sexual relationship forces us to "get outside of ourselves." It fosters empathy, patience, and generosity, and many other noble, human virtues.

Father JP: I understand what you are trying to say: it is important for all of us to get out of ourselves in order to grow spiritually and emotionally. Relationships—every relationship—help us to do that, whether it is a relationship with our mother or father, brother or sister, grandparent, friend, or co-worker. Our relationship with God is important, as is our relationship with others: God created woman for man, so that he would not be alone (Genesis 2:18), drawing him out of himself.

Each relationship helps us to get out of ourselves and find ourselves through the sincere gift of ourselves to another. Every healthy human relationship fosters virtues, even an employee-employer relationship.

Nevertheless, one doesn't need sex to "get out of ourselves." If anything, if one needs sex to be "forced to get outside of ourselves" then one wonders whether there is not some emotional co-dependency going on. We would be better to develop the positive attitude: "I am getting good grades because I am virtuous, not because my parents are bribing me with money..." or with sexual pleasure, in the case of a non-marital sexual relationship.

Leslie: But most people find happiness in being coupled to a special someone. Personal happiness promotes social stability, and stable relationships lead to people living longer, healthier lives, with greater personal satisfaction. People in a stable relationship tend to have less medical expenditures than single people, because they are physically and psychologically healthier.

Father JP: However, gay and lesbians on average have greater physical and psychological health problems, and live shorter and less satisfied lives—at least that is what the scientific studies show.

So, although you long to be healthy, happy, and emotionally stable in your lesbian relationship, and you long for that relationship to be stable and long-lasting, the general tendency found by researchers is that homosexual relationships do not bring the happiness and stability that homosexuals long for.

Leslie: That's ridiculous. Perhaps a lot of gay and lesbian couples are "less stable" than a lot of heterosexual couples — there are many good reasons for that. But I personally know a gay couple who have been together in a faithful, loving relationship for over twenty years... so how can you tell me that it's just a fantasy.

Father JP: You have a point, Leslie. We could also come up with an example or two of "happy" women in stable, long-lasting polygamous marriages in Utah or Texas. But that doesn't prove that it is good.

INTERRACIAL MARRIAGE AND SAME-SEX MARRIAGE

Leslie: Well, what about interracial marriage, Father JP?

Father JP: What about it, Leslie? I thought we were talking about homosexual relationships? What does interracial marriage have to do with that?

Leslie: I bring it up, Father JP, because it is an issue very much like homosexual relationships. Let's face it: the institution of marriage has been in flux in the U.S. for quite some time. Divorce used to be prohibited, then discouraged but allowed for very abusive situations, and now one can easily get a divorce — even a woman can file for it! — and get it granted without having to prove fault. The injustice and oppression of women in abusive marriages was finally resolved.

Interracial marriage is another issue — it was forbidden for African-Americans to marry those of European descent until the 1967 Supreme Court ruling struck down the Virginia State Racial Integrity Act of 1924; that was the case of Loving vs. Virginia.

Those arguing against interracial marriage said that such marriages are not in the best interest of children, that it goes against God's plan for marriage, and that interracial marriage would bring other kinds of moral depravity along with it.

These are the same hate-filled arguments used against homosexual marriage, Father JP.

Father JP: That is a pretty strong accusation you are making, Leslie. You seem to be saying that I am hate-filled and misogynous. What did I say to give you that impression?

Leslie: Well, you are attacking homosexual relationships with such religious fervor that you marginalize all of us.

Father JP: Religious fervor? Marginalizing you? I've been trying to have an open discussion about the issues. You brought up the Bible and I tried to show you how Catholics and traditional Christians read it. You assumed that I considered homosexuality was wrong because it is risky behavior—but I did not use that argument, rather I tried to focus on your true happiness.

Lastly, you defended homosexual behavior as a moral good; I tried to have a reasonable discussion of it by giving you a handful of counter arguments.

Now you bring up interracial marriage and accuse me of racist attitudes.

Leslie: But justice is justice. We are battling for marriage equality not on race but on gender. We are struggling like our African-American brothers to have the same rights as everyone else. Just as one doesn't choose one's race, one doesn't choose one's sexual orientation. One doesn't choose to be of Hispanic descent just as one doesn't choose to be lesbian.

Now you are saying that BillyLu and I can't marry and have a lifelong loving and sexual relationship. You keep telling us: "You lesbies must be celibate, there is no other option. If not, you don't deserve to…"

Margie: Leslie… We don't need to be disrespectful in expressing ourselves.

Father JP: Leslie, I'm not going to break up your relationship with BillyLu. The truth is, I can't. What goes on between you two is outside my control. However, I do want you to be free. I want you to be truly happy, with a happiness that goes way beyond temporary pleasure. I want you to be happy with God in heaven, and I look forward to some lively discussions with you when we get there.

You are a precious daughter of God and He has a wonderful plan for you. But God won't force this on you. In fact, he won't even try to reveal it to you until you freely decide to look for him, to open your heart to him, and be open to his plan for you.

All this being said, I cannot change God's plan for marriage:

> [Jesus] answered, "Have you not read that he who made them from the beginning made them male and female, and said, 'For this reason a man shall leave his father and mother and be joined to his wife, and the two shall become one flesh'? So they are no longer two but one flesh. What therefore God has joined together, let not man put asunder" (Matthew 19:4-6).

From the beginning, God has joined man and woman in marriage. So what God has joined let us not put asunder. I believe this. I ask you to respect people like me who do not believe exactly what you believe. If we cannot respect each other and what the other believes then "all hell will break loose." Neither of us wants that, so let's respect each other.

Leslie: But why do you consider that marriage between two people of the same sex is going to threaten society, the Church, and heterosexual marriage? Do you think that the sex BillyLu and I have is so powerful and so destructive? It seems that you think we were some kind of Islamic terrorists ready to blow up New York City and then destroy the world with the love we show each other in bed. Our sex may be powerful, but it doesn't have that kind of impact.

Father JP: Leslie, 'I don't see so-called "gay marriage" so much as a threat, but what concerns me and others is how it would impact society, the Church, and marriage. Everything each and every one of us does impacts others and impacts society. Would "gay marriage" be as disastrous as non-fault divorce in caus-ing a skyrocketing divorce rate and with more unhappy and emotionally unstable children who are more prone to drugs, pre-marital sex, suicide, and who are less successful in education and in their adult professions? I can't say, but I do know it would have a significant impact.

So You Want to Fix Me

Leslie: But the lack of gay marriage has an immediate impact on me and BillyLu. The only other option you leave us, JP, is to fix us. You don't really respect either of us. You think that we are broken and that we need some counseling to fix us, right?

Father JP: No, Leslie. I don't know you enough to find anything broken.

You are a precious soul, with obvious gifts and talents. I do want you to be happy. I sense that something is missing in your life, but I don't want to fix you, but to help you discover your true gifts. I'm just trying to get you to ask yourself some basic ques-tions: Who am I? Why did God create me? Does he love me and want a relationship with me? If I were to die today, what impact would my life have had on the world? What will Jesus say about me?

Leslie: Think about it, Father JP, how would you feel if someone were to suggest to you that you should get counseling to fix you? Perhaps if things were different in our society—that there wasn't this prejudice against gays and lesbians—they might suggest to you that you get some counseling to help you change from being heterosexual to homosexual. Just a little bit of counseling and you could change your orientation, right?

Hell no. You know that counseling wouldn't change you. So, why do you think that we homosexuals should undergo counseling to change? Can you understand how we feel when you guys make such a suggestion?

Father JP: Leslie, BillyLu will tell you that I make no such suggestions. I have given her some ideas on how to develop better relationships: with God, family, and friends. These relationships are the basis of our identity, so we can improve our identity and sense of self-worth by improving relationships. I didn't tell her she needed counseling to change.

Margie: But didn't you tell Jeremy that he should see a counselor, Father?

Father JP: I gave him that as an option, as a way to heal some of the emotions that impact how he relates to others. We had discussed some incidents from his past where he felt wounded and I wanted to offer a way to help him heal those emotions that he felt were paralyzing him.

Leslie: So, you were indeed trying to fix Jeremy, but you say you don't want to fix me. Let's be consistent, JP.

Father JP: Let me give you a more complete example of what I recommended to Jeremy. If a person has uncontrollable anger, that uncontrolled emotion could be very detrimental to his relationships. Getting counseling to learn how to control his anger and direct his emotions in a healthy manner can help him improve his relationships and thus improve his identity and sense of self-worth.

Therapy can be helpful to identify and resolve other emotional conflicts, deal with insecurities, sadness, anxiety, loneliness, compulsions, etc. By assisting us in unraveling our complex array of emotions a therapist can help us develop a strategy to resolve and redirect them and thus better engage others in relationships. Thus it is not about "fixing" a person, but helping a person develop a more complete and healthy web of relationships, the basis of our identity and sense of self-worth.

Leslie: But homosexuals know what is good and proper in a relationship. We don't need help to build up relationships. Such a suggestion assumes that homosexuals are immoral and incapable of healthy relationships. To associate incest with homosexuals, for example is blatantly wrong, because there is far more heterosexual incest than homosexual incest.

Father JP: If everything is good and right in homosexual relationships, then how do you explain, Leslie, the frequent break-ups of those relationships?

In regards to incest, there are far more heterosexual rapists than homosexual rapists, but that may simply be a numbers game, as there are more heterosexual than homosexual men. Whether it is homosexual or heterosexual, rape and incest are immoral.

Leslie: Well, how do you explain break-ups in heterosexual relationships? Why do you keep pressing the argument that homosexual sex is wrong? It's wrong because Christians have always taught that it's wrong. That's it, Father JP, that's it. Your human tradition! You make no reasoned argument to distinguish between homosexual acts and heterosexual acts. You don't prove that one is beneficial and the other is detrimental; one is moral the other immoral.

Father JP: Leslie, break-ups occur in relationships due to a lack of emotional stability and maturity, and often due to sin. That's an oversimplification but that's usually what happens.

Regarding the distinction between homosexual and heterosexual acts, you're right: I haven't made any clear distinction between the two forms of sex. That just hasn't been my argument.

No, the argument I've been using over and over again is the distinction between sex outside of marriage and sex within marriage, because that is the argument. Sex outside of marriage is immoral, whether with a man, a woman, an animal, or with oneself.

Leslie: But then you exclude homosexual sex because you exclude homosexual marriage. In doing so you deny fulfilling relationships to us gay and lesbian people without any better reason than "that's how we have always done it."

Father JP: Leslie... Leslie... you're changing the argument.

Leslie: This attitude deserves to be severely rejected, because it rejects people for the loving, compassionate, caring relationships they have. It is to reject people because they are different, that they feel called to give themselves generously to another in an intimate emotional, spiritual, and physical way that is not acceptable to you, simply because it is different.

We should reject this attitude for the same reason we should reject opposition to interracial relationships: it simply is wrongheaded and unjust.

Those who call homosexuals and homosexual sex immoral are themselves gravely immoral. It is perverted to condemn people because they love another person. It is immoral to cause such pain and anguish in others, subjecting them to threats and fear simply because they chose to love. It is a crime to keep people locked up in a closet, not allowing them to be themselves and employ their talents and gifts for the good of others.

This is the crime that you and all your kind impose upon the world. "The Moral Majority" —yeah, right! The "Immoral" majority...

Margie: Leslie, let Father JP answer you…

Leslie: Why should I, he's just going to keep attacking me and my homosexuality.

Fantasy Relationship

Father JP: Leslie, I can tell you are frustrated with me. I didn't intend to say anything to be mean and hurtful. I didn't intend to say anything that would be taken as an attack against you in any way. I really do care about you and want you to be happy. But I would not truly care if I were to ignore reality.

Leslie: You say you care, JP, but all you do is attack us. You attack us by attacking and condemning the loving and caring relationship that BillyLu and I have. That is reality, the reality that you do indeed ignore.

Father JP: But, Leslie, your desire for a loving, caring, sensitive, and secure relationship has driven you into a world of fantasy. You seem to only want to see what supports this fantasy. It's like a man or woman preparing for a wedding—they do everything possible to create the storybook perfect wedding, while they can't see that the marriage is going to be a disaster. The fantasy of the perfect wedding clouds their view of the disastrous defects in their future spouse. Such a person is happy in the fantasy of the perfect wedding, not in a true loving and caring relationship.

BillyLu: What you are saying is offensive, JP. You are saying that our desire for a loving and stable relationship is fantasy. It couldn't be more real. When we met at church that day, I just knew that nothing else could fill my life but Leslie.

Father JP: You both seem to have such strong desires to have a loving, tender, intimate relationship with someone, and it is a reasonable desire. We all long for that. But seeking to fulfill that desire with someone of the same sex causes you to see only the part of reality that fits the fantasy. When we looked at Scripture, you only saw the part that fits your fantasy in order to eliminate the condemnation of homosexual sex in the Bible — "to know" only meant sexual intercourse when it fit this fantasy.

Your fantasy seems to have limited your view of the risks of homosexual sex. You only see that lesbian sex is less dangerous than heterosexual intercourse and anal sex, but then you don't look at how lesbians are still contracting sexually transmitted diseases at a higher rate than the general population of women.

Your fantasy wants society to change its view on marriage so you can have the storybook relationship.

Margie: And your fantasy, Leslie, causes you to see Father JP as a racist bigot. You haven't acknowledged how he has tried very hard to be sensitive to you and your concerns.

Leslie: You guys think my relationship with BillyLu is a fantasy, but it's real and you can't face the fact that it is real.

Father JP: Perhaps that relationship with BillyLu really is fantasy, too. Perhaps you are just using her to try to live out a fantasy relationship that you wanted to have with your mother growing up. You couldn't have it then, so you are trying to recreate the whole world in order to have it now.

Leslie: Where are you getting this crap, Father JP? I don't need any fantasy relationship with my mother. We're fine with each other. Your f___ing psychoanalysis crap is the true fantasy.

Father JP: I'm not using any psychoanalysis, I'm just trying to point out how you have a kind of schizophrenic and disjointed way of looking at things, seeing only what you want to see.

Leslie: I love my mother and we always have had a very good and loving relationship. No matter how hard you try, you cannot make me fit into your preconceived psychoanalytic categories.

BillyLu: But wait a minute, Leslie, you do not have a good relationship with your mother. You have told me that you hate your mother, that you despise her.

You told me very clearly that she was never there for you growing up, but always spending time with a new boyfriend. You made it clear that she never showed you the kind of tender and compassion that you needed, but was always harsh and demanding instead. How often you reminded me how you longed for her gentle caress and affectionate hug; you saw her offer her boyfriends such signs of affection and resented that.

You hate her because she did not offer you any security, how her boyfriends would verbally and physically mistreat you, and how she blamed you when you told her about the sexual abuse.

Leslie: Now, everyone is ganging up on me… You all think our love is a fantasy, that our sex is a fantasy, too.

Father JP: But for many people, sex is a substitute, a fantasy, for love…

Leslie: As though you know anything about love and sex. You priests just want everyone to be "holy" and celibate like you — you sex-less holy rollers! Sex is evil for you, especially gay sex. I just can't see how what I do in bed is somehow going to destroy the world and our society.

Father JP: Sex is not evil, Leslie — sin is. And all sin fosters hate and division in the world. It causes neglect and abuse of children; it causes the breakup of families and fosters desires for revenge; it produces war and the death of many innocent people through violence.

Sex is not evil, Leslie, but there are many people in our society who fantasize that their sexual relations are love. They think that that is all there is to love. Their lives are full of sex, but have never experienced true love. The sex anesthetizes the pain, hurt, depression, loneliness, and meaninglessness of their lives, but it's pure fantasy, an escape.

There are others who have never experienced sex but whose lives are filled with love, with loving and caring relationships. I think of Mother Teresa who picked up the sick and dying off the streets of Calcutta—her life was full of love. I think of my sister who never married, but who is the beloved aunt to so many nephews and nieces; whose life is filled with many who love her, both co-workers and close friends—many of whom became religious monks, nuns, and priests; a sister who spends her time going to Mexico to help the poor, or running errands for a local monastery, or ministering to incarcerated inmates who have no friends.

Although their lives are not without difficulties, they have no need to escape into a sexual fantasy—their lives are filled with love.

Leslie: And what is love?

Leslie shrugged her shoulders. Silence fell.

Leslie pushed her chair back, threw a few bucks on the table and left. BillyLu hesitated, looked down, then got up and walked out. She made a quick, helpless glance back at Margie before going out the door.

Margie's eyes welled up in tears, but she said nothing. In that noisy pizza parlor, Father JP led Margie in prayer, asking God to forgive them for failing to understand Leslie and BillyLu fully and for failing to properly incarnate Christ's love in their witness to him. They prayed that God would make up for their mistakes and enlighten all of them to seek the truth in charity.

CHAPTER 12

Born to Love

Responding to Father JP's invitation, Jeremy arranged to see Father JP for some spiritual direction and guidance.

Jeremy: Thank you for getting together again, Father JP. I want you to know I've made a lot of changes but I still feel I have a long way to go.

Father JP: It is always good to get together with you, Jeremy. How are things going with your new approach to life?

BE YOURSELF

Jeremy: Frankly, Father JP, I sometimes—well, more than sometimes—have second thoughts about what I'm doing. There really is a big hole in my heart and I often wonder whether I'm being true to myself by leaving the gay life-style?

There is a nagging voice inside me that I keep hearing, "Jeremy, you're gay... You've always been gay... It's OK to be gay... Don't be afraid to be yourself." What can I do, Father JP, when such thoughts cross my mind like that?

Father JP: Remember, Jeremy, you are not some static being, like a rock, but a human person who can grow by giving himself to others and forming more and deeper relationships. This is where your identity really is to be found.

When those thoughts pop into your head, acknowledge their presence: "My thoughts are revolving around the idea that I am statically gay—as though I were a rock! But I am deciding to become a dynamic person whose identity is based on many profound relationships."

Jeremy: Why do I get these crazy ideas in my head at all, Father JP? I wish I could keep my focus on other things and not let these ideas in and get the better of me. I'm afraid I'm going to believe them.

Father JP: You see, Jeremy, these kinds of thoughts will pop into our heads precisely when that hole in our heart is empty. We need to fill it with good, wholesome friendships.

So ask yourself, why am I thinking in this way? Am I focusing on myself or on others? Am I doing all that I ought in giving myself to others? Have I been rejected in some way—or do I fear such rejection—so that my thoughts gravitate toward what is safer, although they isolate me from others.

Jeremy: Now that I think about it, you're right: those thoughts tend to pop into my head when I'm lonely and thinking that having close friends is next to impossible—that the ones I seem to have are really just a farce!

But am I being realistic? Can I really become normal? I mean, I know I can't become the smartest man in the world no matter how hard I try. Can I really make myself "straight"?

Father JP: Don't focus on changing or on becoming "straight," but strive to give yourself to others and to develop the talents that increase your ability to give yourself to others. Thus you will develop more and better friends. Your identity will fill itself with all these stable relationships. It will all happen in a very natural way.

It is true, you cannot make yourself the smartest man in the world, but you can become smarter than you are right now by studying, reading, and developing the talents you have. The same is true of so many other gifts and talents, including the ability of developing friendships. We all should employ the talents God has given us in the service of others. This will fill our lives.

FRIENDS

Jeremy: In the past, I've noticed that I rarely kept friends over an extended period of time. "Straight" guys I would keep at a distance even if I really wanted to be their friend. I think my sense of inferiority made me ask, why would any guy even want to be my friend? I felt I didn't have anything to offer them, or I feared that they would always treat me as "different." Consequently, I didn't return phone calls or wouldn't do anything to hang out with them.

Father JP: What about your friend Sam, Jeremy?

Jeremy: Sam wasn't really that close to me until recently. Although we did do speech and debate together in high school, we were not that close.

Father JP: I think Sam cares more about you than you think. You need to give him more credit than this.

Jeremy: You're right, Father JP. Sam has been a good friend and support. I don't deserve such a good friend.

Father JP: We don't ever deserve someone's friendship. It always is a gift. Appreciate this gift and then look for ways to give yourself to others and to offer them your friendship.

Jeremy: Recently I have befriended two other very "straight" guys. These guys came to me, and I remembered what you said about how important relationships were, so I made an effort to respond to them. And amazingly they didn't reject me. After going to a ball game with them, they invited me to go to another one with them next week. We even hung out at a normal bar and I felt like "one of the guys."

But I still get those feelings that this may evaporate and that I'll be hurt and lonely again.

Father JP: Continue along this line. Don't sabotage your friendships for fear that you may be hurt. As humans, and in order to grow, we need to risk being hurt. If we focus on ourselves and our potential hurt and loneliness, then the relationship will die.

Focus on your new friends and not on yourself. Think about what they like. If one has a keen interest in a particular team, learn about that team. If he admires a particular player, do a little research and find out more. Then you will have something to offer your friends, something to share, and a way to bring them out of themselves. This is how friendships grow, through thinking about the others and giving ourselves to them.

Jeremy: Is it possible or even healthy for me to do this with a man who is significantly older than I am? It seems a little odd, but this idea kind of attracts me.

Father JP: Sure, Jeremy, it can be very healthy. It would be good to have a good mentor, especially someone who can be a good father figure and pass on to you some of his paternity. It will be good for you to be treated as an adult-son and for you to learn how to be a father to your own son, if God grants you that gift. Even if God does not, you are called to develop a spiritual brotherhood and fatherhood by giving yourself to others in their needs—a good mentor will lead you in that direction.

Telling Your Friends

Jeremy: But I shouldn't tell him about my issues with homosexuality, should I?

Father JP: Jeremy, if you had had a very tender and loving father, would you tell him about your homosexual "issues"?

Jeremy: Sure I would. But that would be because he was my father and should love me just as I am.

Father JP: Then, if someone is going to mentor you in paternity, you'll have to give him a chance to show you how a father listens to a son and accepts you just as you are. This means, telling him about hidden aspects of your struggle and giving him a chance.

Jeremy: What about my other "straight" friends, should I tell them too?

Father JP: First, I would start by refraining from calling your friends "straight." They should be your friends because they are your friends, unconditionally.

Then, as you get to know your friends, they will share some more intimate things about their lives with you. By this they are conveying to you that it is safe to be open with them. They are thus giving you assurance that you can trust them with your secrets because they have trusted you with theirs.

In other words, don't go broadcasting your struggles with homosexuality to the world—as though this struggle defines you as a person—but don't be afraid to tell those who you can reasonably trust.

Jeremy: I don't know about that, Father JP. I'm afraid that if they learn about this they will bolt from our budding friendship. That will hurt a lot.

Father JP: If they do, Jeremy, there was no relationship nor any hope for a deep relationship.

Besides, if you pretend to be someone who never had to deal with same-sex attraction then you would be living a lie with your friend. You will never share with this friend who you really are. Thus you will not give him the opportunity to love and care for you just as you are; instead he will be dealing with someone who exists only as an "act." And when they do find out the truth—and they will—they will feel betrayed, that you lied to them for all this time.

Remember, you have Sam as a friend and he knows about your struggles. Little by little give other guys a chance too and expand your web of deep friendships.

Jeremy: This is not going to be easy, Father JP. I don't know whether I can do it. It entails quite a bit of risk and potential hurt.

Father JP: Try this, Jeremy. Tell Our Lord that you don't want to tell your friend. You can pray by telling Christ: "Lord, you know it is hard for me to tell my friend about my struggle. So if I do tell him, Lord, it would be only to please you."

If you have fears, address those fears with Our Lord: "Lord, I fear that my friend may reject or laugh at me. But you will be at my side. If he does, I will unite this sacrifice to yours, to the rejection you experienced on the Cross."

Often, this will motivate us to have the courage to do what we find hard or impossible. You can also reassure your friend of your efforts to remain chaste, and that you are getting therapy and spiritual direction to aid you in these goals.

Jeremy: But when my friends hear that I'm in therapy the will think that I'm mentally sick and not want to have anything to do with me, Father JP.

Father JP: Jeremy, don't worry. Just tell your friend that you are in therapy to help you overcome some emotional neediness that causes you to cling to him. In fact, tell him he can help you too: he can point it out to you if he notices that you are being needy or clingy with him, just as Sam did.

If you do this, you will feel so good when your friend responds to you like a real friend.

Jeremy: Oh, I know it would feel so good—no, it would feel awesome! But is it worth the risk?

I know I should try, but I can't guarantee that I will do it, Father JP.

God Loves You

Father JP: That's all I would ask of you.

Jeremy, our relationship with God is the foundation for everything else. As you come to realize how much God really does love you, you will no longer fear what man can do to you—you will not fear rejection.

Jeremy: How can I really "know" God's love for me, I mean, I want to feel it?

Father JP: Don't look for a fleeting emotional experience. Knowledge goes beyond feelings to the very core of our being.

I would encourage you to read both the Old and New Testaments, and see how God loved his people. Put yourself into their shoes and imagine God loving you as he did Adam and Eve, Cain and Able, and all the patriarchs of old. Imagine yourself in their shoes and experience God's love as they did. Also, put yourself into Lazarus' shoes, or those of the apostle John or Peter. There you will experience God's burning and passionate desire for you (Ezekiel 16:1-22). You will experience him dying on the Cross out of love for you. You will see how our heavenly Father's mercy for you is so great that he is willing to sacrifice the life of his only begotten Son to find you, the lost sheep, and bring you back to your heavenly Father (Luke 15:1-7).

God's love has the true power to heal, not just the homosexual condition, but any sinful condition.

Jeremy: I am trying to develop my relationship with God, and reading the Bible in the way you suggest will be helpful for me, trying to experience God's love by putting myself in the shoes of the different protagonists. I really want to experience a deep and intimate relationship with God the Father, and with his Son, Jesus Christ, and with the Holy Spirit too.

Father JP: Jeremy, friendship with God leads to holiness, because God is holy and calls us all to be holy (Cf. Leviticus 11:44-45; 19:2; 20:7,26; 1 Peter 1:16). The Second Vatican Council reminds us that "all Christians in whatever state or walk of life are called to the fullness of Christian life and to the perfection of charity, and this holiness is conducive to a more human way of living even in society here on earth."

Jeremy: Are you saying that God is calling me to holiness, to be a saint? Even after all that I have done? That seems impossible for someone like myself who has been so involved in the gay life-style.

Father JP: God calls us all to be saints. This call to holiness includes those persons with a homosexual inclination:

This will unavoidably involve much struggle and self-mastery, for following Jesus always means following the way of the Cross. "There is no holiness without renunciation and spiritual battle."

The Sacraments of the Eucharist and of Penance are essential sources of consolation and aid on this path. These sacraments invite every person to enter into the dying and rising of Christ, for the Paschal Mystery is at the center of Christian life.

Jeremy: You know, Father JP, I have been trying to go to Mass and Communion frequently. I'm also trying to spend time daily in a personal dialogue with Our Lord, as you suggested. What more can I do?

Father JP: If we can cultivate an awareness of God's presence throughout the day, then we refer everything to him, even our weaknesses. If we get tempted, we know God is there and we can tell him about it right away and then dismiss it.

As Catholics, we want to develop a relationship with everyone Our Lord has a relationship with, such as with his Blessed Mother, with the angels and with our brothers and sisters who have gone before us marked with the sign of faith.

Should I Become a Priest?

Jeremy: One thing that has crossed my mind since our last conversation is whether God might be calling me to the priesthood. Is this something I should explore?

Father JP: Is this your idea, Jeremy, or has someone suggested this to you?

Jeremy: It is certainly my idea, Father JP, although I know it would make my mother very happy.

Father JP: Well, since you're just coming back to your faith, it is important not to rush this conversion process. Additionally, be careful about doing things just to please your parents. It's not uncommon that a parent may push a homosexual son to become heterosexually active, or to get married, or to become a person with a celibate commitment to God as a quick fix to this uncomfortable situation. This would only resolve the problem on the surface, and end up putting other souls at risk through divorce or a potential scandal.

As you take possession over yourself—self-mastery is necessary before being able to give yourself to another—you will have a clearer idea of how God may be calling you. This means you need a deep faith life and to reach a solid sense of emotional normalcy and maturity in the area of sexual attraction, as well as self-control, before considering a vocational commitment to either marriage or celibacy.

As the *Catechism* tells us:

> *Chastity includes an apprenticeship in self-mastery which is a training in human freedom. The alternative is clear: either man governs his passions and finds peace, or he lets himself be dominated by them and becomes unhappy (Cf. Sir 1:22) (CCC 2339).*

Jeremy: But what if this is truly from God and not just an idea planted in my head by my parents; can I be ordained a priest? Will you help discern God's path for me?

Father JP: I would be misleading you, Jeremy, if I told you that it would be easy. I'm not saying it is impossible—because all things are possible with God (Mark 10:27)—but you have a lot of spiritual growth that you need to go through, which includes emotional maturing.

Jeremy: Why is that, Father JP, I'm twenty-eight years old? Am I not mature enough to make such a decision? Come on... now I feel like there are conditions on this love...

Father JP: You have experienced a lot of hurt, Jeremy. These emotionally intense experiences, especially the emotionally intense sexual experiences, have become etched into your psyche. Now, you are striving to purify yourself of all that.

As the U.S. bishops have stated:

> Chaste living overcomes disordered human desires such as lust and results in the expression of one's sexual desires in harmony with God's will. "Chastity means the successful integration of sexuality within the person and thus the inner unity of man in his bodily and spiritual being."

So, maturity means ordering our human desires in such a way that we fully integrate our sexuality and other emotion to reflect our relationship with God and others according to our state in life. For those who are married, it means ordering our desires and sexuality to reflect fidelity, unity, and unconditionality to spouse, and openness to life. For those who are not married, it means ordering our desires toward a celibate and virginal expression of love.

Jeremy: But you have said that everyone has temptations, even priests. I imagine seminarians also have temptations. So, why are my temptations so different?

Father JP: Let me use a real example that I have shared with Sam and Margie.

A young man had been living a very promiscuous heterosexual life, sleeping with many, many women. He would use them for his own selfish purposes and then discard them. Most of the women were equally using him.

One day the man met a very beautiful woman—she was even more beautiful on the inside. Being a good Christian, she refused to have sex with him or any man until she was married. Attracted to this woman of substance, he agreed to wait and even became Christian in the process. Later the two married. Years later the man confessed, "I have never been alone with my wife! Every time the two of us come together to become intimate, my past girlfriends pop into my head. Although, I don't give into them, the images of these past relationships haunt me, they keep me from really having the intimacy with my wife for which I truly long."

It would be better not to bring such "baggage" into marriage and into family life. Likewise, the Church has discerned that it is best not to bring this kind of "baggage" into seminary or into priestly ministry. This is what is meant by maturing emotionally and by "successful integration of sexuality within the person."

Jeremy: But is this really what Jesus Christ would do? I can't imagine him excluding people from ministry just because they are carrying a bit of emotional "baggage."

Father JP: Christ has given us some wonderful examples of great conversions. Remember the man who was possessed by a legion of demons (Luke 8:26-39)? After Our Lord cured him, he begged Christ to allow him to accompany him as an apostle. But God gave him another vocation, one to return to his family and to evangelize them and the ten cities from which he came. The miracle of his conversion would speak loudly of the power of the Gospel, much more than his ministry as a priest.

Likewise, the Gospel gives us the example of the sinful Samaritan woman who became a believer of Jesus Christ (John 4:4-42). Her conversion won over the whole town to Jesus Christ, but she did not have to become a nun or priest to do this.

Then Should I Marry?

Jeremy: If it is not a good idea for me to become a priest, then should I get married?

Father JP: Marriage too is a vocation, a call from God. It too requires a good degree of emotional maturity to fulfill it.

Every vocation requires the affective (emotional) maturity to make the gift of one's whole person to the Church, or to another person who represents the Church, as in marriage (Ephesians 5:21-33). A husband and father needs to be able to relate correctly to men and women as a man, especially to his wife and children—they will imitate him and follow his example. A priest also needs to be able to emotionally relate to men and women as a man—as Christ. Therefore all vocational commitments require a level of emotional maturing that gives one the ability to relate to men and women properly and to be able to make oneself a gift for another.

Jeremy: OK, Father JP, I agree that Jesus does give us examples where people who have complex backgrounds do not take leadership roles in evangelization. I also agree that emotional maturity is necessary for marriage and the priesthood. However, I know that some gay men have married women and the marriage has turned out OK. I also imagine that there have been some good gay priests.

Father JP: There have been good priests who have struggled to remain chaste and celibate while facing their own same-sex attraction. Yes, that is true. I've known some who have developed a healthy male identity by cultivating a good web of relationships, with God and with people.

However, their struggles have not been easy. It would be like a man or woman who was abused as a child, going into marriage without healing that wound. It can be done, but it would be better for the individual as well as for the spouse and children to resolve that problem before marrying. If we love the Church and love those with whom we would consider being family, we should not want them to have to deal with extra complications due to our emotional tendencies.

Moreover, if a priest considers himself "gay," then it means that his identity is rooted in his homosexual inclinations and in his particular form of temptation. This contradicts his sacramental identity as Christ. Thus, such priests—if not healed of this conflict—feel pulled emotionally in two directions. This often leads to a double life.

No one should have to endure that, so before you jump into something, work on resolving your own emotional conflicts, building up a good web of healthy relationships, and taking possession of your emotions—of the gift of yourself—so you can freely give it whole and entire.

Jeremy: Well, Father JP, that really is what I want, to give myself whole and entire and to be free of the emotional conflicts that may interfere with the giving of myself.

Father JP: What you should ask yourself is whether that desire to be whole and free of emotional conflicts is the driving force and motivation for you wanting to be a priest or for you wanting to get married.

Both marriage and the priesthood are holy vocations. Spiritual direction will help you and the Church discern where God is calling you to use your gifts in the service of the Church. As you grow emotionally, spiritual direction will help you sort out the various human motivations that may direct your decision making process so that you can freely choose what God is asking of you.

The Homosexual Witness

Jeremy: Then is there nothing for me to do in the Church until I discern a vocation to the priesthood or to marriage? I might as well just leave since I'm not good enough for either one or the other. This whole conversion process seems to be a farce.

Father JP: No, no, Jeremy, it is not a farce at all. God loves you enormously: you are worth all the blood of Jesus Christ, poured out on the Cross.

I can see that you have good desires. I just ask you to be

patient. You're growing but we must go at God's pace not at our own.

You have many gifts to offer the Church and society, even while your homosexual inclinations endure. The Church wants and encourages your full and active participation.

I can see that you have a greater sensitivity to emotional woundedness than most. This gives you an increased ability to respond to the emotional and physical needs of others. Perhaps God is calling you to use this and your creativity to help the weak and marginalized of our society.

Jeremy: Why can't I have a vocation like you, Father JP?

Father JP: But you do have a vocation like me, Jeremy, since we both have a vocation to be a saint.

It is wrong to think that one has to be a priest to be holy. God is calling all of us to holiness. He wants men and women of all walks of life, in the middle of the world, to witness to his love for mankind.

Yes I have a vocation to witness to God's love as a priest, but the world needs that witness in many other forms too. Think of how Sam and Margie have witnessed to you of God's love. Would you have entered into this wonderful dialogue we have had if Sam were a Jewish rabbi instead, or if Margie was a Catholic nun?

Jeremy: No, probably not.

Father JP: Imagine how different your life could have been if you had friends who truly witnessed to God's love.

We also need doctors and nurses who have the emotional sensitivity to truly meet the needs of those who are sick, to serve them as Christ would. We need witnesses to God's love in business, making decisions that can promote the true welfare of their employees and not *just* improve the bottom line.

The world needs politicians who witness to God's love with sensitivity toward the needs of our society, especially toward those who cannot help or defend themselves.

We need social workers, caregivers, and volunteers who can witness to God's love in serving the elderly, infirm, or handicapped.

Jeremy: I've actually begun to do that, Father JP. Sam invited me to join him and Margie in volunteering in a program that helps handicapped children. It has been so great.

Father JP: That's good, Jeremy! Those children need you to witness to them of God's great love for each one of them. I think you have the sensitivity to do a very good job of that.

Jeremy: But I want to use my creativity to serve the Church.

Father JP: But you already are, Jeremy. By your efforts to live God's call to love and to perfect holiness you are serving God and the Church. The Church appreciates your particular gifts and she wants to encourage you to use them for the good of all.

You and I will strive to discern where God is calling you to use those talents in his service. Pope John Paul II reminds us: "Every *vocation has* a profoundly *personal and prophetic meaning*," not just the vocation to the priesthood or to marriage.

At the present time, I would encourage you to orient your chastity toward purification. I would encourage you to focus on this for the time at hand. This will be a powerful witness to those still living unchaste lives that chastity is possible; that happiness is possible in chaste living.

Jeremy: I still can't see how just living chastity will impact other people's lives. Can you give me an example of how this chastity oriented toward purification might work?

Father JP: There is a wonderful example in the Bible. A sinful woman came up to Our Lord while he was dining at the home of a rich Pharisee. Obviously repentant, she bathed Our Lord's dirty feet with her tears and wiped them dry with her hair, and anointed Our Lord with her costly perfume. This both scandalized Simon, the rich Pharisee, and gave us all a witness to what God is seeking from us—Love:

> Now when the Pharisee who had invited him saw it, he said to himself, "If this man were a prophet, he would have known who and what sort of woman this is who is touching him, for she is a sinner." And Jesus answering said to him, "Simon, I have something to say to you." And he answered, "What is it, Teacher?"
>
> "A certain creditor had two debtors; one owed five hundred denarii, and the other fifty. When they could not pay, he forgave them both. Now which of them will love him more?" Simon answered, "The one, I suppose, to whom he forgave more." And he said to him, "You have judged rightly." Then turning toward the woman he said to Simon, "Do you see this woman? I entered your house, you gave me no water for my feet, but she has wet my feet with her tears and wiped them with her hair. You gave me no kiss, but from the time I came in she has not ceased to kiss my feet. You did not anoint my head with oil, but she has anointed my feet with ointment. Therefore I tell you, her sins, which are many, are forgiven, for she loved much; but he who is forgiven little, loves little." And he said to her, "Your sins are forgiven" (Luke 7:39-48).

The way you live your life from this point on will teach proud people like Simon what truly pleases God—not a perfect life, but love.

ROLE IN THE CHURCH

Jeremy: Is it possible to give that witness and still take some active share in Church activities and leadership?

Father JP: Certainly it is possible, Jeremy. There is so much you can do.

For example, once you get a little more formation, you could teach religious education to grade school children, or even to high school youth, or to adults. Perhaps you would like to sing in the parish choir or use your talents in many other ways that can serve the parish.

What I would suggest is that you begin to get involved. Don't take a leadership role yet, but find ways to help and build up some good friendships in the Church. Little by little you will find where you can be most effective.

Jeremy: Should I let people know about my past struggles with homosexuality?

Father JP: In most situations it will not be useful. If you were teaching second-graders, you can identify and stop situations where one child may be teasing another in a way that may be hurtful to the child. Certainly do stop it. You may even explain to the victim or to the perpetrator how you were hurt by such teasing at their age. Nevertheless, telling them all the details of your journey will only likely confuse them or make it worse.

Think of it this way: if you were a father, would you tell your son or daughter details of your past sexual exploits?

Jeremy: I probably would, Father JP. Why not? Shouldn't children know what their father or mother went through?

Father JP: Not always, Jeremy. For a second-grader to learn this about a father, mother, teacher, or whoever, would make it harder for that child to see God's authority behind them.

Likewise, it would be wrong for a father to tell his children that he had sex with dozens of women before he married their mother, because if it were OK with dad doing it then it must be OK for them. Or, they may think, "Well I'm not as good as my dad is, therefore, why try to follow his advice and wait until marriage."

Nor should a woman generally tell her children that she was raped or abused as a child, because it might plant all sorts of images in the child's mind that could cause fear, hate (toward the rapist), or sexual fantasies. A child shouldn't have to deal with that.

Jeremy: How can I tell whether it would be appropriate or not to tell a particular group or individual? For example, if I were dealing with a high school boy who obviously had homosexual tendencies, would it be wrong to share my story with him? I think sharing my story could possibly help him avoid a lot of the same mistakes that I made.

Father JP: You're right, Jeremy, that could be very helpful. However, I would recommend you first talk to the pastor and to one or two parents of children his age. Give them the particulars of the young person's situation and what you were thinking could help.

Since the pastor knows the context of how the parents or other people in the parish community may interpret your good intentions, they can help you make a more prudent decision and be most effective in your efforts.

Jeremy: What about with college students? Would it be appropriate for me to speak more openly with them to help them?

Father JP: Again, it may be helpful to check with the college chaplain or campus minister, first. You want him to back you up in any efforts you take.

Again, I would recommend you first become a participant, looking for ways to assist those who are already in positions of leadership. With time, more formation and experience, and your availability, God may ask you to take a leadership role.

With more spiritual direction, we will discern your interior dispositions in greater detail and you will grow in your relationship with God and others. That will help us discover God's great plan for you.

Jeremy: Thank you, Father JP, for your patience. Being a good Christian, a good Catholic, is not easy for me. I know I get a little impatient at times... and a bit rebellious.

Father JP: Don't worry, Jeremy, it's hard for all of us. Thank God that he is patient with each one of us—we don't deserve it.

Postscript

Jeremy continued his spiritual direction with Father JP and his friendship with Sam and Margie.

Although BillyLu did return to Leslie and cut off her relationship with Margie and Father JP, in less than a month's time Leslie found another relationship and left BillyLu.

BillyLu wavered in going back to her kids. She wavered in calling Margie. She was hurt. She was scared. She wanted to blame someone for this failed relationship. She started to blame God... Father JP... Margie... herself. She just needed time to figure where she was and where she wanted to go.

Acknowledgements

I want to thank the many individuals struggling with homosexual inclinations—as well as those who were trying to help friends and family members with this condition. My conversations with them have been the underlying foundation for this dialogue.

I also want to thank the Catholic students at Trinity University who motivated me to begin jotting down my ideas. Ashleen, Katherine, and John were particularly helpful and encouraging in getting this project started.

Special thanks to my many reviewers: besides giving me good suggestions to improve the content and style also they gave me the affirmation that the work I was doing was worthwhile. These include Bernie, MaryLu, Kerry, Sheila, Professor David Crockett, Ken and Janie, Melinda, Paul, John Corvino, Philip Sutton, Fr. Jim Tucker, SS, Dr. Rick Fitzgibbons, Dr. Gerard van den Aardweg, Dr. Joseph and Linda Nicolosi, Dr. Aaron and Jennifer Kheriaty.

Endnotes

INTRODUCTION

Page

vi — "A man of mission and dialogue...," JP2 (1992) 18 and 43.

vii — "a subject who decides for himself," JP2 (1988) 18.

viii — 'Man "cannot fully find himself ...",' JP2 (1988), 18.

THE SETTING OF THE DIALOGUE

Page

1 — "*Couples in Love*" — Waiss (2003).

WHAT DOES THE BIBLE SAY ABOUT HOMOSEXUALITY?

Page

15 — "the 'logic of love'," Waiss (2003) 48-74.

15 — "God's love for his people is certainly spousal, even, erotic," Benedict (2005) 9: "The Prophets, particularly Hosea and Ezekiel, described God's passion for his people using boldly erotic images. God's relationship with Israel is described using the metaphors of betrothal and marriage; idolatry is thus adultery and prostitution."

26 — "human dignity of gays and lesbians," Cf. USCCB (2006) 15.

HOMOSEXUALITY AND GOD'S PLAN

Page

39 — "checking out a hot chick...," Cf. Waiss (2003) 31-41.

42 — "It is crucially important," USCCB (2006) 6.

43 — "the positive aspects of sexual morality," eight paragraphs deal with God's plan for sexuality (CCC 2331-36 and 2392-93), twenty-seven paragraphs with chastity (CCC 2337-59, 2358-59, 2394-95), twenty-one paragraphs with marriage (CCC 2360-2378, 2397-2398), and fifteen paragraphs with purity of heart and modesty (CCC 2514-2524, 2530-33).

43 — "eleven paragraphs deal with sins against chastity," CCC 2351-2356, 2396, 2525-26,28-29.

43 — "fourteen paragraphs deal with sins against marriage," CCC 2380-91, 2399-2400.

43 — "Only two paragraphs deal with the sin of homosexual sex," CCC 2357, 2396.

43 — "divorce is condemned at much greater length," CCC 2382-2386.

45 — "not responsible for the action because it is outside his control," cf. USCCB (2006) 6.

"But God Made Me This Way"

Page

51 — "study was done in 1952 by Kallman," Kallman (1952a).

51 — "study by Bailey, Dunne, and Martin," Bailey, et al. (2000). Other twin studies show similar results: Bailey and Pillard (1991), Eckert, et al. (1986), Friedman, et al. (1976), Green (1974), Heston and Shield (1968), McConaghy and Blaszczynski (1980), Parker (1964), Rainer, et al. (1960), Zuger (1976).

53 — "research project that began in 1993 by Dr. Dean Hamer," Hamer (1993).

53 — "Rice, Anderson, Risch, and Ebers," Rice, et al. (1999) 666. A more recent genome wide study of 465 individual confirms that no genetic basis for homosexuality could be found, Mustanski (2005). Nor has there been any evidence that persons with homosexual tendencies have an excess of opposite sex hormones, Gooren (1995), Meyer-Bahlburg (1984), Byrne and Parsons (1993), Banks and Gartrell (1995).

53 — "Similar research is being conducted on alcoholism," Kendler, et al. (1992). Pickens & Svikis (1991 and 1988). Hrubec, et al. (1981). Partanen, et al. (1966).

54 — "lose that same-sex tendency by age of 25," Laumann, et al. (1994) 294-296; Dickson, et al. (2002).

55 — "frequently those striving to discover the biological basis for homosexuality," Herrn (1995) 31-56.

56 — "promiscuity is returning to those levels again," Bell & Weinberg (1978). McKusick, et al. (1985) 625, Table 1. CDC (1999) 45.

56 — "50 lifetime sex partners," Fethers, et al. (2000) 347. Price, et al. (1996). Ferris, et al. (1996) 581. Skinner, et al. (1996).

57 — "by between 8 and 20 years," Hogg, et al. (1997) 659. Since 1996, death from HIV has dropped significantly; cf. CDC (October 10, 2001) and Cameron, et al. (1994) 249.

57 — "more likely to contract HIV," CDC (December 2001).

57 — "cigarette smokers whose life expectancy is 13.5 years shorter," CDC (2002).

CIVIL RIGHTS

Page

69 — "the definition and meaning of love," Cf. Waiss (2003) 48-74.

70 — "The complementarity of man," USCCB (2006) 3.

71 — "to make us whole and fully human," Nicholas Berdyaev, *Freedom and the Spirit* (Freeport, NY: Libraries Press, 1972).

72 — " contraception," Cf. Waiss (2003) 75-97.

75 — "The Synod of Bishops confirmed the Church's practice," Benedict (2007) 29.

81 — "the Church has a right ," USCCB (2006) 17.

83 — "1.2 and 2.7 times more married couples," Popcak (2006).

84 — "decrease in family stability," Fontana, et al. (2005).

84 — "higher rates of spousal abuse," Lockhart, et al. (1994); Lie & Gentlewarrier (1991); Island & Letellier (1991) 14; Bureau of Justice Statistics (1994) 2.

85 — "more likely to be abused," Russell (1984; Wilson & Daly (1987).

THE PSYCHOLOGY OF HOMOSEXUALITY

Page

88 — "suicide rates among active gay males," Hogg, et al. (1997) 660. Bagley & Tremblay (1997); Garofalo, et al. (1998); Remafedi, et al. (1991) , Warner, et al. (2004).

88 — "suicide than his co-twin without," Herrell, et al. (1999).

88 — "major depression, anxiety disorder, substance abuse," Fergusson, et al. (1999). Non-medical drug use, Cochran, et al. (2004). Mental illness rates were higher, Warner, et al. (2004), Sandfort, et al. (2006).

88 — "borderline personality disorder," Parris, et al. (1995) and Zubenko, et al. (1987).

88 — "schizophrenia," Gonsiorek (1982) 12.

88 — "pathological narcissism," Bychowski (1954) 55 and Kaplan (1967) 358.

88 — "profound loneliness," Friedman and Stern (1980) 434, Silverstein (1972) 4, and Fitzgibbons (1999) 85 - 97.

89 — "Dutch study," Sandfort, et al. (2001).

96 — "inappropriate sexual behaviors," Beitchman, et al. (1991) 544.

96 — "men... abused as children," Doll (1992) found that 42% of 1,001 homosexual men reported childhood sexual abuse; Stephan (1973) found that 24% of homosexuals first orgasms occurred with homosexual contacts versus 2% of heterosexuals, with the average age of homosexuals first orgasms occurred much earlier than heterosexuals. Also, see Finkelhor (1984) and (1986).

96 — "women... abused as children," Gundlach and Riess (1967) reported

that lesbians were 3 times more likely than non-lesbians to report having been raped or attempted being raped before age 16. Also see Bradley and Zucker (1997, 1998 and 1995) and Engel (1982).

96—"sexually active at a very young age," Bell, et al. (1981) report that homosexuals' average age of their first homosexual sexual encounter is 9.7 years old, two full years earlier than for heterosexuals' first sexual encounter. Also, see Stephan (1973).

96—"without telling parents or anyone else," Johnson and Shrier (1985).

99—"By forgiving others you will find freedom," Fitzgibbons (1999).

IDENTITY: WHO AM I?

Page

103—"Identity: Who Am I?" Pope John Paul II's personalism is the basis for this chapter. Personalism focuses on man—*the way of the Church* (JP2 (1979) 14 and (1994) 1)—and his dignity and vocation as a human person, especially as it is fully disclosed in Christ (Vatican (1964) 22; JP2 (1994) 13 and (1988) 2). In his reflections on the Blessed Trinity (JP2 (1994) 6,8 and (1988) 7), John Paul II discovers a new definition and description of man, one that goes beyond the notion of a rational animal, that reaches the person, the human "I", as a unique subjectivity of relationships (JP2 (1994) 4 and (1988) 4). "We must… *seek a deeper understanding of the truth about the human person…* the only being in the world which God willed for its own sake. The human being is a person, a subject who decides for himself. At the same time, man 'cannot fully find himself except through a sincere gift of self'… [T]his description, indeed this definition of the person, corresponds to… the human being—man and woman—in the image and likeness of God…, an essential indication of what it means to be human, while emphasizing the value of the gift of self, the gift of the person." JP2 (1988) 18.

Pope Benedict XVI concurs with this vision of personal identity: "As a spiritual being, the human creature is defined through interpersonal relations. The more authentically he or she lives these relations, the more his or her own personal identity matures. It is not by isolation that man establishes his worth, but by placing himself in relation with others and with God. Hence these relations take on fundamental importance." Benedict (2009) 53.

109—"Identity Based on Performance," basing one's identity and self-worth falsely on performance leads one to see himself as a thing or object (JP2 (1994) 13), and to let himself be used as a means to an end, especially as a means of "pleasure" (JP2 (1994) 12,13). This is the basis of individualism, which encourages the destructive exploitation of human weaknesses by having one follow one's "real" feelings (JP2 (1994) 14).

111—"Identity Based on Relationships," Identity based on relationships requires a sincere gift of self to another and the welcoming acceptance of another's gift (JP2 (1994) 7,14,16). This establishes a relationship, a communion of persons. Thus, one truly finds himself—one's true identity—through the sincere gift of himself to others (JP2 (1994) 9,11 and (1988) 7), by existing in relationship to another "I" (JP2 (1988) 6,7). Thus one's relationships "both to God and to creatures" (JP2 (1994) 8), becomes the basis of his identity, self-worth, and dignity (JP2 (1994) 12). With the relationship-based identity where one's sense of self-worth is based on being willed by God for one's own sake (JP2 (1994) 12), independent of parental or peer acceptance, sicknesses, disabilities, etc. (JP2 (1994) 9).

113—"One forms his initial relationships in the family," (cf. JP2 (1994) 6,12). Yet the person is called to form other relationships—friends, colleagues, and his own family—which allows his identity received in the family to develop and mature (cf. JP2 (1994) 2,6).

115—"you spoke to Margie and me about this," Waiss (2003) 170-172.

125—"God wills for them the fullness of good," JP2 (1988) 9.

Supporting the Homosexual Person

Page

132—"male friends who don't view him as an object," USCCB (2006) 10-12.

137—"Without truth, we ignore his wound," we must live the truth with charity (JP2 (1994) 10,14,16).

142—"Conversion and contrition," JP2 (1984) 31.

145—"Jesus is present... as the *one who has been rejected,*" JP2 (1994) 22.

146—"Parents' Role," Parent and siblings should receive each child not as a burden but as a "gift" (JP2 (1994) 11), meaning with unconditional acceptance, affection, and love. Love conditioned on good behavior or performance where a child may feel rejected or inadequate by constant disapproval, may move him to seek his personal identity outside the family (JP2 (1994) 11). Parental "honor," acknowledging the child as a person by affirming his natural and God-given gifts as a male or female (JP2 (1994) 15,16). Authentic education in chastity and modesty appropriate to each child's age, while avoiding a new Manichaeism that puts the body and spirit in opposition (JP2 (1994) 19).

151—"By "honoring" young people," JP2 (1994) 15.

151—"The place and task of the father," JP2 (1981) 25.

155—"by far most priests are faithful," John Jay (2002) reveal that the majority of the abuse by priests was of male teenagers, perpetrated by a very small number of priests.

156—"Sadly, experts report that 10 percent of all boys," Russell and Bolen (2000) 149-50.

156—" report by Dr. Charol Shakeshaft." Shakeshaft (2004) and Hendrie (2004).

156—"[T]he truth of God's love," Benedict (2007) 85.

TAKING CONTROL OF OUR IDENTITY

Page

166—"re-orientation therapies and found them effective," Cf. Spitzer (2003). In 1973, Dr. Spitzer is a prominent psychiatrist who led the movement to delete homosexuality from the diagnostic manual—the DSM-II—of the APA. Dr. Spitzer says that, "like most psychiatrists, I thought that homosexual behavior could be resisted—but that no one could really change their sexual orientation. I now believe that's untrue—some people can and do change." His research found that 67 percent of homosexual men were successful in changing unwanted homosexual attraction. Other researchers have reached similar conclusions, Rogers, *et al.* (1976), Kronemeyer (1980), Moberly (1983), Siegle (1988), Nicolosi (1991), Satinover (1996), Throckmorton (1996), Goetze (1997), Nicolosi, et al. (1998).

166—"developing healthy life-habits that help them restrain some desires," USCCB (2006) 9.

168—"Healing Our Relationship with God," Taking responsibility for our part in sin enables us to take responsibility for our own lives and a way to recover our dignity of free subjects (JP2 (1988) 14). Then we will feel eternally loved by God and our freedom restored (JP2 (1988) 15).

172—"Deepening Our Relationship with God," USCCB (2006) 12 and Benedict (2009) 53-54.

183—"to become prisoners of our past," JP2 (1997) 3.

187—"therapist is qualified, and understands and respects your Catholic and Christian faith," USCCB (2006) 7.

189—"support groups for parents," Cf. USCCB (2006) 22.

191—"develop your relationship with God," A person finds himself through a gift of himself to God (JP2 (1994) 11). "Precisely *in and through prayer, man comes to discover in a very simple and yet profound ways his own unique subjectivity:* in prayer the human 'I' more easily perceives the depth of what it means to be a person" JP2 (1994) 4; cf. 10.

193—"Precisely in and through prayer," JP2 (1994) 4.

193—"And [human] love," JP2 (1994) 7.

FEMALE HOMOSEXUAL IDENTITY

Page

206—"One such "maternal" quality," Pope Benedict XVI (2007) 139-140.

217—"True Feminine Identity," By "mutually being 'for' the other, in interpersonal 'communion,' there develops in humanity itself, in accordance with God's will, the integration of what is *'masculine'* and what is *'feminine'"* (JP2 (1988) 7).

218—"In our own time," JP2 (1988) 30. Cf. JP2 (1995) 9 and 12.

Second Thoughts

Page

225—"Second Thoughts," Many of the arguments in this chapter have been gleaned and reformulated from articles written by Dr. John Corvino, "Homosexuality and Morality," published in Michigan's *Between the Lines*, from November 22, 2002 through February 7, 2003. Some of the arguments on the Bible were gleaned and reformulated from Rev. Kenneth W. Collins, which are posted on his website, http://www.kencollins.com.

239—"increase the risks for getting throat cancer," D'Souza, et al. (2007) and Dean, et al. (2000).

248—"non-fault divorce in causing a skyrocketing divorce rate," Cf. Friedberg (1998).

248—"more prone to drugs, premarital sex," Waite and Gallagher (2001) 124-40. Forehand, et al. (1986), Webster-Stratton (1989), Spruijt and de Goede (1997), Chase-Lansdale, et al. (1995), Cherlin, et al. (1998): 239.

250—"In regards to incest," it is important to note that exact numbers are hard or impossible to find on incestuous sexual abuse. Hypothetically, let's suppose that 55% of all incestuous child abuse was done by heterosexual males and 40% by homosexual males, and 5% by females. But since homosexuals make up between 1 and 3 percent of the population, then 97% of the male population would be responsible for 55% of all child abuse and the 3% of homosexual males would be responsible for 40%. This would mean that 11 out of 970 (1.1%) heterosexual males were child abusers and 8 out of 30 (22%) homosexual males were child abusers, which would mean that a homosexual male was 18 times more likely to be a child abuser than a heterosexual male.

Using this kind of analysis and the best available data, Russell (1984) and Wilson & Daly (1987) found that homosexual partners were 50 times more likely than married heterosexual couples to sexually abuse children incestuously.

Born to Love

Page

264—"calls us all to be holy," USCCB (2006) 12. Everyone is called to love and to perfect holiness (JP2 (1994) 14). "The dignity of every human being and the vocation corresponding to that dignity find their definitive measure in *union with God"* (JP2 (1988) 5).

264—"all Christians in whatever state or walk of life," *Lumen Gentium* 40.

264—"This will unavoidably involve much struggle and self-mastery," USCCB (2006) 13 quoting CCC 2015. See Second Vatican Council, *Sacrosanctum Concilium*, 6.

267—"Chaste living overcomes disordered human desires," USCCB (2006) 8, citing CCC 2337.

270—"Both marriage and the priesthood are holy vocations," "Every *vocation has* a profoundly *personal and prophetic meaning,*" (JP2 (1988) 16), not just the vocation to the priesthood or to marriage.

271—"full and active participation," Cf. USCCB (2006) 16-17.

271—"greater sensitivity to emotional woundedness," can give persons a greater ability to respond to the emotional and physical needs of others (JP2 (1988) 15), an increased creativity toward the weak and marginalized (JP2 (1988) 19), and a greater awareness of "suffering of consciences as a result of sin." Thus a life given over to God can be a powerful witness to those still trapped in sin (JP2 (1988) 19).

272—"Every *vocation has* a profoundly *personal and prophetic meaning,*" JP2 (1988) 16.

References

J.M. **Bailey** and Richard Pillard, "A genetic study of male sexual orientation," *Archives of General Psychiatry*, 48 (1991) 1089-1096.

J.M. **Bailey**, M.P. Dunne, N.G. Martin, "Genetic and environmental influences on sexual orientation and its correlates in an Australian twin sample." *Journal of Personality and Social Psychology* 78(3) (2000) 524-536.

C. **Bagley** and P. Tremblay, "Suicidal Behaviors in Homosexual and Bisexual Males," *Crisis* 18 (1997) 24-34.

Amy **Banks** and Nanette Gartrell, "Hormones and Sexual Orientation: A Questionable Link," in DeCecco & Parker (1995) 263.

J. **Beitchman**, K. Zucker, J. Hood, G. DaCosta, D. Akman, "A review of the short-terms effects of child sexual abuse." *Child Abuse & Neglect* 15 (1991) 544.

Alan P. **Bell** and Martin S. Weinberg, *Homosexualities: A study of Diversity Among Men and Women*, Simon and Schuster, New York (1978) 308, Table 7.

—— with S. Hammersmith, *Sexual Preference: Its Development in Men and Women*, Indiana University Press, Bloomington IN (1981).

Pope **Benedict** XVI

—— Encyclical Letter: *God is Love—Deus Caritas Est* (2005).

—— Post-Synodal Apostolic Exhortation: *Sacrament of Charity—Sacramentum Caritatis* (2007).

—— *Jesus of Nazareth* (2007) Doubleday, New York.

—— Encyclical Letter: *Charity in Truth—Caritas in Veritate* (2009).

Nicholas **Berdyaev**, *Freedom and the Spirit*, Libraries Press, Freeport NY (1972).

S. **Bradley** and K. Zucker, "Gender identity disorder: A review of the past 10 Years." *Journal of the American Academy of Child and Adolescent Psychiatry* 34(7) (1997) 872-880.

—— "Drs. Bradley and Zucker reply," Journal of the American Academy of Child and Adolescent Psychiatry 37(3) (1998) 244-245.

—— Gender Identity Disorder and Psychosexual Problems in Children and Adolescents, Guilford, New York (1995).

Bureau of Justice Statistics, "Violence Between Intimates," *Selected Findings* NCJ-149259 (November 1994) 2.

G. **Bychowski,** "The structure of homosexual acting out." *Psychoanalytic Quarterly* 23 (1954) 55.

William **Byne** and B. Parsons, "Human sexual orientation: The biologic theories reappraisal," *Archives of General Psychiatry*, 50 (1993) 229-239.

Paul **Cameron**, et al., "The Longevity of Homosexuals: Before and After the AIDS Epidemic" *Omega: Journal of Death and Dying* 29 (1994) 249.

— and K. **Cameron**, "Homosexual Parents," *Adolescence* 31 (1996) 772.

CCC=*Catechism of the Catholic Church*, 2nd ed. (revised in accordance with the official Latin text promulgated by Pope John Paul II), 1997, United States Catholic Conference, Inc. and Libreria Editrice Vaticana.

CDC=Center for Disease Control

— "Smoking costs nation $150 billion each year in health costs, lost productivity," *CDC Press Release* (April 12, 2002) www.cdc.gov/od/oc/media/pressrel/r020412.htm

— *THE HIV/AIDS Surveillance Report* (December 2001).

— "Life Expectancy Hits New High in 2000; Mortality Declines for Several Leading Causes of Death," *CDC News Release* (October 10, 2001) www.cdc.gov/nchs/releases/01news/mort2k.htm.

— "Increases in Unsafe Sex and Rectal Gonorrhea among Men Who Have Sex with Men — San Francisco, California, 1994-1997," *Mortality and Morbidity Weekly Report* 48(03) (January 29, 1999) 45-48.

P. Lindsay **Chase-Lansdale**, Andrew J. Cherlin, and Kathleen E. Kiernan, "The Long-term Effects of Parental Divorce on the Mental Health of Young Adults: A Developmental Perspective," *Child Development* 66 (1995) 1614-34.

Andrew J. **Cherlin**, P. Lindsay Chase-Lansdale, and Christine McRae, "Effects of Parental Divorce on Mental Health Throughout the Life Course," *American Sociological Review* 63 (1998) 239.

CMA=Catholic Medical Association, "Homosexuality and Hope : Statement of the Catholic Medical Association" (2005) http://www.cathmed.org/publications/homosexuality.html.

Susan D. **Cochran**, Deborah Ackerman, Vickie M. Mays, Michael W. Ross, "Prevalence of non-medical drug use and dependence among homosexually active men and women in the US population," *Addiction* 99(8) (2004) 989–998

Dr. John **Corvino**, "Homosexuality and Morality," published in Michigan's *Between the Lines*, from November 22, 2002 through February 7, 2003.

John **DeCecco** and David Parker, eds., *Sex, Cells, and Same-Sex Desire: The Biology of Sexual Preference*, Haworth Press, New York (1995).

Nigel **Dickson**, C. Paul, P. Herbison, "Same-sex attraction in a birth cohort: prevalence and persistence in early adulthood," *Social Science & Medicine* 56 (2002) 1607-1615.

L. **Doll**, D. Joy, B. Batholow, J. Harrison, G. Bolan, J. Douglas, L. Saltzman, P. Moss, W. Delgado, "Self-reported childhood and adolescent sexual abuse among adult homosexual and bisexual men." *Child Abuse & Neglect* 18 (1992) 825-864.

Gypsyamber **D'Souza**, Aimee R. Kreimer, Raphael Viscidi, Michael Pawlita, Carole Fakhry, Wayne M. Koch, William H. Westra, and Maura L. Gillison, "Case–Control Study of Human Papillomavirus and Oropharyngeal Cancer" in *The New England Journal of Medicine* 19(356) (May 10, 2007) 1944-1956.

Laura **Dean**, et al., "Lesbian, Gay, Bisexual and Transgender Health: Findings and Concerns," *Journal of the Gay and Lesbian Medical Association* 4(3) (2000) 101-151.

E. **Eckert**, *et al.*, "Homosexuality in monozygotic twins reared apart," *British Journal of Psychiatry*, 148 (1986) 421-425.

B. **Engel**, *The Right to Innocence*, Jeremy Tarcher, Los Angeles (1982).

R.D. **Enright** and R. Fitzgibbons, *Helping clients forgive: An empirical guide for resolving anger and restoring hope*, American Psychological Association, Washington (2000).

D. **Fergusson**, J. Horwood, A. Beautrais "Is sexual orientation related to mental health problems and suicidality in young people?" *Archives of General Psychiatry*. 56(10) (1999) 876-888.

Daron **Ferris**, et al., "A Neglected Lesbian Health Concern: Cervical Neoplasia," *The Journal of Family Practice* 43(6) (December 1996) 581-584.

Katherine **Fethers**, Caron Marks, et al., "Sexually transmitted infections and risk behaviours in women who have sex with women," *Sexually Transmitted Infections* 76(5) (October 2000) 345-349.

D. **Finkelhor,** *Child sexual abuse: New theory and research*, The Free Press, New York (1984).

——— et al., *A Sourcebook on Child Sexual Abuse*, Sage, Newbury Park CA (1986).

Richard **Fitzgibbons**, "The origins and therapy of same-sex attraction disorder," in C. Wolfe, *Homosexuality and American Public Life*, Spence, Dallas TX (1999) 85-97.

M. **Fontana**, P. Martínez, P. Romeu, "No Es Igual: Informe Sobre el Desarrollo Infantil en Parejas del Mismo Sexo," (May 2005). http://www.fides. org/spa/approfondire/2005/spagna_noesigual.html.

Rex **Forehand**, et al., "Divorce/Divorce Potential and Interparental Conflict: The Relationship to Early Adolescent Social and Cognitive Functioning," *Journal of Adolescent Research* 1 (1986) 389-97.

Leora **Friedberg**, "Did Unilateral Divorce Raise Divorce Rates? Evidence from Panel Data," *American Economic Review* 88 (1998) 608-27.

R. **Friedman** and L. Stern, "Juvenile aggressivity and sissiness in homosexual and heterosexual males." *Journal of the American Academy of Psychoanalysis* 8(3) (1980).

R. **Friedman**, F. Wollesen, R. Tendler, "Psychological development and blood levels of sex steroids in male identical twins of divergent sexual orientation," *The Journal of Nervous and Mental Disease.* 163(4) (1976) 282-288.

R. A. **Garofalo**, et al., "The Associations Between Health Risk Behaviors and Sexual Orientation Among a School-Based Sample of Adolescents," *Pediatrics* 101 (1998) 895-902.

R. **Goetze**, *Homosexuality and the Possibility of Change: A Review of 17 Published Studies*, New Directions for Life, Toronto, Canada (1997).

J. **Gonsiorek,** "The use of diagnostic concepts in working with gay and lesbian populations," in J. Gonsiorek, *Homosexuality and Psychotherapy* Haworth, New York (1982) 12.

Louis **Gooren**, "Biomedical concepts of Homosexuality: Folk belief in a white coat," in DeCecco & Parker (1995) 237.

Richard **Green**, *Sexual Identity Conflict in Children and Adults*, Penguin, Baltimore (1974).

R. **Gundlach** and B. **Riess**, "Birth order and sex of siblings in a sample of lesbians and non-lesbians." *Psychological Reports* 20 (1967) 62.

Dean **Hamer**, et al., "A linkage between DNA markers on the X chromosome and male sexual orientation," *Science*, 261 (1993) 321 -327.

Rainer **Herrn**, "On the history of biological theories of homosexuality," in DeCecco & Parker (1995) 31-56.

Caroline **Hendrie** (March 10, 2004) "Sexual Abuse by Educators Is Scrutinized" *Education Week*, 23(26) 1,16

R. **Herrell**, J. Goldberg, W.R. True, V. Ramakrishnan, M. Lyons, S. Eisen, M.T. Tsuang, "Sexual orientation and suicidality: a co-twin control study in adult men," *Archives of General Psychiatry* 56(10) (1999) 867-874.

L. **Heston** and J. **Shield**, "Homosexuality in twins," *Archives of General Psychiatry.* 18 (1968) 149-160.

Robert S. **Hogg**, S. A. Strathdee, et al.
— "Modeling the Impact of HIV Disease on Mortality in Gay and Bisexual Men," *International Journal of Epidemiology* 26(3) (1997) 657-661.
— "Gay life expectancy revisited," *International Journal of Epidemiology* 30(6) (**2001**) 1499

Z. **Hrubec** & G.S. Omenn, "Evidence of genetic predisposition to alcoholic cirrhosis and psychosis: Twin concordances for alcoholism and its biological endpoints by zygosity among male veterans." *Alcoholism: Clinical and Experimental Research* 5 (1981) 207-212.

D. **Island** and P. Letellier, *Men Who Beat the Men Who Love Them: Battered Gay Men and Domestic Violence*, Haworth Press, New York (1991).

John Jay College of Criminal Justice, "The Nature and Scope of the Problem of Sexual Abuse of Minors by Catholic Priests and Deacons in the United States" (2002). http://www.usccb.org/nrb/johnjaystudy/

JP2=Pope John Paul II
— *Encyclical Letter: The Redeemer of Man—Redemptor Hominis* (1979).
— *Post-Synodal Apostolic Exhortation: Reconciliation and Penance* (1984).
— *Apostolic Letter: On the Dignity and Vocation of Women—Mulieris Dignitatem* (1988).
— *Post-Synodal Apostolic Exhortation: I Will Give You Shepherds— Pastores Dabo Vobis* (1992).
— *Letter to Families* (1994).
— *Letter to Women* (1995).
— *Message for the Celebration of the XXX World Day of Peace: Offer Forgiveness and Receive Peace* (1997).

R. **Johnson** and D. Shrier, "Sexual victimization of boys: Experience at an adolescent medicine clinic." *Journal of Adolescent Health Care* 6 (1985) 372-376.

E. **Kaplan**, "Homosexuality: A search for the ego-ideal." *Archives of General Psychology* 16 (1967) 358.

K.S. **Kendler**, A.C. Heath, M.C. Neale, R.C. Kessler, & L.J. Eaves, "A population-based twin study of alcoholism in women." *Journal of the American Medical Association* 268(14) (1992) 1877-1882.

Alfred **Kinsey**, et al., *Sexual Behavior in the Human Male*, Philadelphia (1948 and 1953).

Franz **Kallman**, "Comparative twin study on the genetic aspects of male homosexuality, *Journal of Nervous and Mental Disease*, 15(4) (1952a) 283-298.

— "Twin and sibship study of overt male homosexuality," *American Journal of Human Genetics*, 4(2) (1952b) 136-146.

R. **Kronemeyer**, *Overcoming Homosexuality*, Macmillian, New York (1980).

E. O. **Laumann**, et al, *The Social Organization of Sexuality: Sexual Practices in the United States*, University of Chicago Press, Chicago (1994) 294-296.

Simon **LeVay**, "A difference in hypothalamic structure between heterosexual and homosexual men," *Science* 258 (1991) 1034-1037.

Gwat Yong **Lie** and Sabrina Gentlewarrier, "Intimate Violence in Lesbian Relationships: Discussion of Survey Findings and Practice Implications," *Journal of Social Service Research* 15 (1991) 41-59.

Lettie L. **Lockhart**, et al., "Letting out the Secret: Violence in Lesbian Relationships," *Journal of Interpersonal Violence* 9 (1994) 469-492.

N. **McConaghy** and A. Blaszczynski, "A pair of monozygotic twins discordant for homosexuality: Sex-dimorphic behavior and penile volume responses," *Archives of Sexual Behavior*, 9 (1980) 123-131.

Leon **McKusick**, et al., "Reported Changes in the Sexual Behavior of Men at Risk for AIDS, San Francisco, 1982-84 — the AIDS Behavioral Research Project," *Public Health Reports* 100(6) (November-December 1985) 622-629.

H. **Meyer-Bahlburg**, "Psychoendrocrine research on sexual orientation: Current status and future options," *Progress in Brain Research*, 61 (1984) 375-399.

Elizabeth **Moberly**, *Homosexuality: A New Christian Ethic*, James Clarke, Cambridge, England (1983).

B.S. **Mustanski**, et al., "A genome wide scan of male sexual orientation," *Human Genetics*, 116(4) (2005) 272-278.

Joseph **Nicolosi**, *Reparative Therapy of Male Homosexuality*, Aronson, Northvale NJ (1991).

Joseph **Nicolosi**, Dean Byrd, R. Potts, *Towards the Ethical and Effective Treatment of Homosexuality*, NARTH, Encino CA (1998).

David **Nimmons**, "Sex and the Brain," *Discover* (March 1, 1994) 64-71.

N. **Parker**, "Homosexuality in twins: A report on three discordant pairs," *British Journal of Psychiatry*, 110 (1964) 489-492.

J. **Parris**, H. Zweig-Frank, J. Guzder, "Psychological factors associated with homosexuality in males with borderline personality disorders." *Journal of Personality Disorders*. 9(11) (1995) 56-61

J. **Partanen**, K. Bruun, & T. Markkanen, "Inheritance of Drinking Behavior." Helsinki: *Finnish Foundation for Alcohol Studies* (October 2000).

R.W. **Pickens** & D.S. Svikis, "Genetic influences in human substance abuse" *Journal of Addictive Diseases* 10 (1991) 205-214

—— "The twin method in the study of vulnerability to drug abuse" in National Institute on Drug Abuse Research, *Biological Vulnerability to Drug Abuse. Monograph Series* No. 89. DHHS Pub. No. (ADM) 88-1590, Supt. of Docs., U.S. Govt. Print. Office, Washington DC (1988) 41-51, http://www.drugabuse.gov/pdf/monographs/download89. html.

Gregory C. **Popcak**, "Misplacing Children," *First Things* (June/July, 2006).

Pontifical Council for the Family

— *Lexicon: Ambiguous and debatable terms regarding family life and ethical questions*, topics "Homosexuality and Homophobia" and "Homosexual 'Marriage,'" Human Life International, Front Royal VA (2006) 425-459.

James **Price**, et al., "Perceptions of cervical cancer and pap smear screening behavior by Women's Sexual Orientation," *Journal of Community Health* 21(2) (1996) 89-105.

J. **Rainer**, et al., "Homosexuality and heterosexuality in identical twins," *Psychosomatic Medicine*. 22 (1960) 251-259.

Gary **Remafedi**, et al., "Risk factors for attempted suicide in gay and bisexual youth," *Pediatrics* 87(6) (1991) 869-875.

George **Rice**, Anderson, Risch, and Ebers, "Male homosexuality: Absence of linkage to microsatellite markers at Xq28," *Science* (April 1999) 665-667.

Carl **Rogers,** *et al.*, "Group psychotherapy with homosexuals: A review," *International Journal of Group Psychotherapy*, 31(3) (1976).

Diana E. H. **Russell**, "The Prevalence and Seriousness of Incestuous Abuse: Stepfathers vs. Biological Fathers," *Child Abuse and Neglect* 8 (1984) 15-22.

— with R.M. Bolen, *The Epidemic of Rape and Child Sexual Abuse in the United States*, Sage Publications, Thousand Oaks CA (2000).

Sacred Congregation for Catholic Education
— *Instruction Concerning the Criteria for the Discernment of Vocations with regard to Persons with Homosexual Tendencies in view of their Admission to the Seminary and to Holy Orders* (2005).

Sacred Congregation for the Doctrine of the Faith
— *Persona humana: Declaration on Certain Questions Concerning Sexual Ethics* (1975)
— *Letter To The Bishops of the Catholic Church : On the Pastoral Care of Homosexual Persons* (1986).

Theo **Sandfort**, Ron de Graaf, et al., "Same-sex Sexual Behavior and Psychiatric Disorders: Findings from the Netherlands Mental Health Survey and Incidence Study (NEMESIS)," *Archives of General Psychiatry* 58(1) (2001) 85-91.

Theo **Sandfort**, Floor Bakker, François G. Schellevis, Ine Vanwesenbeeck, "Sexual Orientation and Mental and Physical Health Status: Findings From a Dutch Population Survey," *American Journal of Public Health*, 96(6) (2006) 1119-1125.

Jeffrey **Satinover**, *Homosexuality and the Politics of Truth*, Baker, Grand Rapids MI (1996).

Jeffrey **Schwartz** and Sharon Begley, *The Mind and the Brain: Neuroplasticity and the Power of Mental Force*, Regan Books, NY (2002).

Dr. Charol **Shakeshaft**, "Educator Sexual Misconduct: A Synthesis of Existing Literature," prepared for Planning and Evaluation Service Office of the Undersecretary US Department of Education, Hofstra University and Interactive, Inc. (2004).

Elaine **Siegle**, *Female Homosexuality: Choice without Volition*, Analytic Press, Hillsdale NJ (1988).

C. **Silverstein** "Behavior Modification and the Gay community." Paper presented at the annual convention of the Association for Advancement of Behavior Therapy, New York (October 1972).

C. **Skinner**, J. Stokes, et al., "A Case-Controlled Study of the Sexual Health Needs of Lesbians," *Sexually Transmitted Infections* 72(4) (1996) 277-280.

Dr. Robert L. **Spitzer**, "Can some gay men and lesbians change their sexual orientation? 200 participants reporting a change from homosexual to heterosexual orientation," *Archives of Sexual Behavior* 32(5) (October 2003) 403-417 summarized at www.narth.com/docs/evidencefound.html

Ed **Spruijt** and Martijn de Goede, "Transition in Family Structure and Adolescent Well-being," *Adolescence* 32 winter (1997) 897-911.

W. **Stephan**, "Parental relationships and early social experiences of activist male homosexuals and male heterosexuals," *Journal of Abnormal Psychology* 82(3) (1973).

W. **Throckmorton (1996)** "Efforts to modify sexual orientation: A review of outcome literature and ethical issues," *Journal of Mental Health and Counseling*, 20(4) 283-305.

USCCB=United States Conference of Catholic Bishops
——*Ministry to Persons with a Homosexual Inclination: Guidelines for Pastoral Care* (November, 2006).

Vatican Council II: The Conciliar and Post Conciliar Documents, new revised edition, ed. Austin Flannery, OP, Northport NY, Costello Publishing (1996).
—— *Constitution on the Sacred Liturgy, Sacrosanctum Concilium* (December 1963).
—— *Dogmatic Constitution on the Church, Lumen Gentium* (November 1964).

John R. **Waiss**, *Couples in Love: Straight Talk on Dating, Respect, Commitment, Marriage, and Sexuality*, The Crossroad Publishing Company, New York (2003).

Linda **Waite** and Maggie Gallagher, *The Case for Marriage* Doubleday, New York (2001).

James **Warner**, Eamonn McKeown, Mark Griffin, Katherine Johnson, Angus Ramsay, Clive Cort, and Michael King, "Rates and predictors of mental illness in gay men, lesbians and bisexual men and women," *The British Journal of Psychiatry*, 185 (2004) 479-485

Carolyn **Webster-Stratton**, "The Relationship of Marital Support, Conflict and Divorce to Parent Perceptions, Behaviors and Childhood Conduct Problems," *Journal of Marriage and the Family* 51 (1989) 417-30.

M. **Wilson** and M. **Daly**, "Risk of Maltreatment of Children Living with Stepparents," in *Child Abuse and Neglect: Biosocial Dimensions*, ed. Gelles and Lancaster, Aldine de Gruyer, New York (1987).

G. **Zubenko**, A. George, P. Soloff, P. Schulz, "Sexual practices among patients with borderline personality disorder." *American Journal Psychiatry* 144(6) (1987) 748 - 752.

B. **Zuger**, "Monozygotic twins discordant for homosexuality: Report of a pair and significance of the phenomenon," *Comprehensive Psychiatry*, 17 (1976) 661-669.

Books and Resources for Parents, Pastors and Educators:

General Books on Homosexuality

Gerard van den Aardweg, *Homosexuality and Hope a Psychologist Talks About Treatment and Change*, Servant Books, Ann Arbor MI (1985). Spanish edition, EUNSA (1997).
— *The Battle for Normality*, San Francisco, Ignatius Press (1997).

Richard A. Cohen (Laura Schlessinger, Foreword), *Coming Out Straight : Understanding and Healing Homosexuality*, OakHill Press, Winchester VA (2001).

John F. Harvey, *The Homosexual Person: New Thinking in Pastoral Care*, San Francisco, Ignatius Press (1987).
— (ed) with Gerard V. Bradley (ed.), *Same-Sex Attraction: A Parents' Guide*, South Bend IN, St.Augustine's Press (2003).

Jeff Konrad, *You Don't Have to Be Gay: Hope and Freedom for Males Struggling With Homosexuality or for Those Who Know of Someone Who Is*, Pacific Publishing House, Newport Beach CA (2001).

Peter J. Liuzzi, O.Carm., *With Listening Hearts : Understanding the Voices of Lesbian and Gay Catholics*, Paulist Press, New York (2000).

Joseph Nicolosi, Ph.D. and Linda Ames Nicolosi,
— *A Parent's Guide to Preventing Homosexuality*, InterVarsity Press (2002).
— *Reparative Therapy of Male Homo-sexuality: A New Clinical Approach*, Jason Aronson, New Jersey (1997).

Claudio Risè,
— *Il mestiere di padre*, Edizioni San Paolo, Cinisello Balsamo, Italy (2004).
— *Il padre l'assente inaccettabile*, Edizioni San Paolo, Cinisello Balsamo, Italy (2005).

Peter Sprigg (ed.), Timothy Dailey (ed.) *Getting it Straight: What the Research Shows about Homosexuality*, Family Research Council (2004) www.FRC.org.

Stefano Teisa, *Le strade dell'amore. Omosessualità e vita cristiana*, Città Nuova Editrice, Roma (2002).

Neil E. Whitehead, Briar Whitehead, *My Genes Made Me Do It! : A Scientific Look at Sexual Orientation*, Huntington House Publishers, Lafayette LA (1999).

WEBSITES DEALING WITH HOMOSEXUALITY

—Information on "gay marriage:" www.catholic.com/library/gay_marriage.asp

—Information on homosexuality: www.catholiceducation.org

—www.drthrockmorton.com

—Studies of healing SSA: www.newdirection.ca

—Dr. Spitzer Report. Influence of peer rejection. Gender Identity Disorder, health risks, adoption, child's need for both a mother and a father: www.narth.com

—*Homosexuality and Hope* (2000) www.Cathmed.org [Spanish translation: www.vidahumana.org/vidafam/homosex/informe.html].

—health risks: www.corporateresourcecouncil.org/white_papers/Health_Risks.pdf

—Theology of the Body and SSA: www.christendom-awake.org

—Vatican statement on civil and same sex unions: www.catholiceducation.org/articles/homosexuality/ho0067.html

—Online support groups: www.peoplecanchange.com

—Teens: www.inqueery.com

—Courage (Catholic): www.Couragerc.net

—Exodus International (Protestant): www.exodus-international.org/

—JONAH (Jewish): www.jonahweb.org

—Evergreen International (Mormons): www.evergreeninternational.org

—Homosexuals Anonymous (Non-religious): www.ha-fs.org

—"I Do Exist," DVD: www.idoexist.com

For the Rest of the Story, Read...

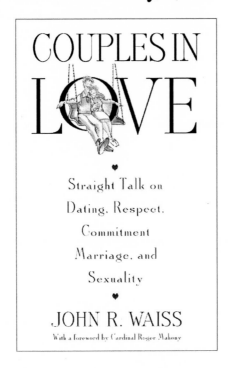

COUPLES IN LOVE

Straight Talk on
Dating, Respect,
Commitment
Marriage, and
Sexuality

JOHN R. WAISS

With a foreword by Cardinal Roger Mahony

A great book for all young couples, parents and teachers.

A solid, clear presentation of Catholic teaching on sexuality and related topics. Fr. Waiss grounds his presentation in John Paul II's personalist philosophy, focusing on the intrinsic meaning of sexuality as created by God, which is much more helpful than enumerating lists of "dos and don'ts."

The dialogue format gives the book an engaging, easy-going feel, and yet Waiss is completely faithful to what the church has taught "always, everywhere, and by all". Waiss' great strength is to present Church teaching positively. He calls on the reader's love of God, and emphasizes the abundant life to be had by living in correspondence to God's design for human sexuality. As I read the book, I was inspired...

This is a solid book, and I highly recommend it for teens or twenty-somethings dating and/or thinking of marriage, their parents and youth ministers, and to anyone who wants to clearly and faithfully understand what the Church teaches us about our sexuality.

Craig K. Galer (Michigan)

Waiss makes controversial statementsóstatements that will make you say, ìHow could he believe that?î And then he goes on to show why, and by the end, you say, ìWhy didn't I believe that before?î

James F. Kane (Washington, D. C.)

Breinigsville, PA USA
10 September 2009
223816BV00001B/3/P